SCIENCE and CREATION

SCIENCE and CREATION
Geological, Theological,
and Educational Perspectives

Robert W. Hanson
EDITOR

Issues in Science and Technology Series
American Association for the Advancement of Science

MACMILLAN PUBLISHING COMPANY
NEW YORK

Collier Macmillan Publishers
LONDON

AAV 1954

Macmillan Publishing Company
866 Third Avenue, New York, NY 10022

Collier Macmillan Canada, Inc.

Printed in the United States of America

Printing: 2 3 4 5 6 7 8   Year: 7 8 9 0 1 2 3 4 5 6

Library of Congress Cataloging in Publication Data

Main entry under title:

Science and creation.

(AAAS series on issues in science and technology)
"Based on symposia presented at the Annual Meeting of
the American Association for the Advancement of Science
held in Washington, D.C., in January 1982"—Pref.
Includes index.
1. Science—Philosophy—Congresses. 2. Science—
Study and teaching—United States—Congresses.
3. Creation—Study and teaching—United States—Congresses. 4. Evolution—Study and teaching—United States
—Congresses. I. Hanson, Robert W. II. AAAS National
Meeting (1982 : Washington, D.C.) III. Series.

Q174.S23 1985   501   83-50822
ISBN 0-02-949870-8

This book is dedicated to

KIRTLEY F. MATHER
(1888–1978)

Teacher, scholar, scientist, leader of organizations,
lecturer, defender of academic freedom,
and mediator between science and religion.

Contents

Preface

The present volume is based on symposia presented at the annual meeting of the American Association for the Advancement of Science held in Washington, DC, in January 1982. The sessions were very well received, so much so that the speakers were asked to prepare formal papers to present their perspectives on the geological, theological, and educational aspects of the creation/evolution controversy to a wider audience. I hope that this volume will preserve the points made at the Washington sessions. What is missing, of course, is the sense of the meeting itself: the interested audience that packed the room all day to listen in thoughtful silence to the speakers, which then broke up slowly into questions and discussions. The symposia arrangers, Rolf Sinclair of the National Science Foundation, Joseph Dasbach of AAAS, and myself, are grateful to that audience and to the speakers who gave so much time and effort to their presentations and to the preparation of chapters for this volume. We thank AAAS for recognizing the topic as one proper for its annual meeting, and Allan Bromley (then president of AAAS) for the original suggestion that such sessions be organized. And I gratefully acknowledge the editorial assistance provided by Rolf Sinclair, Joseph Dasbach, Kathryn Wolff, Arthur Herschman, and several of the authors, especially Langdon Gilkey, James Skehan, and Stephen Brush.

Robert W. Hanson

About the Authors

Stephen G. Brush, a historian of science at the University of Maryland, specializes in the historical approach to teaching physics and the nineteenth and twentieth century history of geophysics and astrophysics. He has written on the evidences for the antiquity of the solar system.

William E. Ellis is a historian at Eastern Kentucky University. His interest in the history of Christian fundamentalism led him to investigate the attitudes of Kentucky biology teachers toward the teaching of evolution.

Langdon Gilkey, an educator and theologian at the Divinity School, University of Chicago, authored the book *Religion and the Scientific Future* in 1970 and was a key witness in the Arkansas trial that led to Judge Overton's landmark statement defining "creation science" as a movement to promote a particular religious viewpoint.

Robert W. Hanson retired in May 1985 from the University of Northern Iowa where he was professor of chemistry and science education for 22 years. From 1967 to 1983 he was the executive director of the Iowa Academy of Science.

Wayne Moyer was executive director of the National Association of Biology Teachers at the time he wrote his chapter for this book. He is now the executive officer of People for the American Way. In recent years he has been an active writer in the evolution-creation controversy.

Dorothy Nelkin is a sociologist and educator at Cornell University and has authored books on the political aspects of the creation-evolution equal time movement, among many other societal issues that involve technology and sociology.

Craig E. Nelson, a biologist at Indiana University, has studied the wide spectrum of views that integrate evolution with creation, using an approach in teaching that considers the "consequences" of the various points of view.

Kenneth Saladin of Georgia College is active in the American Humanist Society and has written much about the political aspects of movements in Georgia to legislate equal time for "creation science".

James W. Skehan, S.J., is director of the Weston Observatory near Boston and an active professional geologist, having founded the department of geology and geophysics at Boston College.

William M. Thwaites, with his colleague Frank Awbrey, originated a course at San Diego State University that allowed equal time for "scientific creationists" to present their views alongside their own presentation of the evidences for evolution. These experiences have led to many public debates and writings about the equal-time movement.

Stanley Weinberg was a high school biology teacher in the state of New York before retiring to Iowa. He is the author of a widely used high school biology textbook and has been instrumental in setting up the Committees of Correspondence to counter grass-roots movements to adopt equal time legislation for "scientific creationism."

SCIENCE and CREATION

Introduction:
Science or Belief,
A False Dichotomy

Robert W. Hanson
University of Northern Iowa

The literal interpretation of the Genesis account of creation is immensely appealing to a great many people. It is such an easy-to-understand story that an accomplished Fundamentalist preacher can give the elements of a recent seven-day creation to an audience in less than an hour. Many people relish this sort of simplicity and, in fact, demand it. On the other hand, the study of the sciences whose findings establish an extremely long and complex history of the earth requires much time and a mental discipline of a high order. Those creationists who believe in a literal seven-day creation do not accept scientific concepts that counter the notion of fiat creation and a young earth. Nevertheless, "scientific creationists" attempt to support an essentially religious idea with selected and sometimes outdated scientific data, and they foster the erroneous notion that the creation/evolution controversy is a simple dichotomy. They attempt to force a choice between two ideas that are not mutually exclusive, as though evidence that does not support one idea (evolution) thereby proves the other (creation). This is a false dichotomy, and the fundamental problem that is addressed in this book.

During the past few years the scientific community at large and the education community in particular have awakened to the public's concern about restoring traditional values in American society. The theory of evolution is seen by many Fundamentalists as responsible for the destruction of

1

these values. Thus, in an attempt to restore this value system, a substantial part of the public has supported the movement to teach "creation science," which purports to show that a literal interpretation of the Genesis account of origins, including the notion that the universe is only a few thousand years old, can be supported scientifically.

Many scientists and their scientific societies have expressed concern about equating "creation science" with science. The interest of the American Association for the Advancement of Science (AAAS) in this continuing controversy is to do justice to science while acknowledging the validity of deeply held religious beliefs. The AAAS sponsored a symposium at its 1981 (Toronto) Annual Meeting entitled "Views of the Universe: Science versus Tradition," and attendance and interest were high.[1] At its 1982 Annual Meeting in Washington, D.C., two sessions, "Science and Belief: The Interface" and "Science and Belief: Problems for Science Education" were held.[2] These symposia also attracted a large and interested audience. At the the the symposia, science and creation were discussed together by scientists, theologians, educators, and historians in the context and format of a scientific meeting rather than as a debate between opposing groups. This book draws substantially on the formal presentations at the Washington symposia.

One way to assure that "creation science" would be taught in school would be to make it a legal requirement. However, legislative attention to the creation/evolution controversy quieted down considerably following the decision in the trial which struck down the "Balanced Treatment for Creation-Science and Evolution-Science Act" of the Arkansas legislature (see Appendixes A and B) and the decision in Louisiana in a later trial of a similar law.[3] However, the alternative approach of getting creationism into the schools through action at the local school board level rather than by legislation continues, and in the absence of state laws, may be expected to intensify.

In the end, the success of the "creation-science" movement will depend not so much on legislated course content that includes equal time for "creation science" and evolutionary concepts as on the readiness of school boards and the public they serve to accept the arguments of the "scientific creationists." It seems clear that public understanding of what science is and is not has *not* emerged from all the past efforts to improve the science curriculum. That, coupled with low enrollments in science courses, the dubious competence of some teachers, and few opportunities for adults to learn more about science, has produced a citizenry—including some teachers—that is easily influenced by the equal time, fair play, and academic freedom arguments which are being used to foster the teaching of "creation science." (It is important to note also that an understanding of the nature of religion has long been a neglected topic in the American school curriculum.)

A typical argument offered by a supporter of "creation science" is contained in a guest editorial in the journal *American Laboratory*.[4] The writer, D. G. Calbreath, was responding to a published letter from Wayne

Moyer,[5] then executive director of the National Association of Biology Teachers and one of the contributors to this volume. The letter dealt with the evolution/creation controversy along the usual lines of evolutionist argument. Calbreath, describing himself as a "committed Christian" with respectable scientific credentials, took issue with "Dr. Moyer's attempt to portray the battleground as being between scientists who support evolution and believers in creationism who are nonscientists," adding that "much of the opposition to evolution comes from scientists . . . who reject evolution on the basis of their scientific knowledge." But he also said that, "On the basis of both my religious convictions and my scientific background, I cannot accept evolution as the explanation for the origin of man."

By claiming to speak as a scientist and then introducing his world view into the argument, Calbreath illustrates an important point that is often overlooked or deemphasized in the creation/evolution controversy. And when scientists, whether they be "scientific creationists" or not, introduce their world views into the creation/evolution controversy, they demonstrate the lack of understanding of the nature of science and of religion which is pervasive on both sides of this controversy.

On the other hand, an impression is frequently created by the nature of the exchanges between "evolutionists" and "creationists" that creationism is an expression of more than just Fundamentalist Christianity. Christian Fundamentalism is identified with Christianity as a whole, with "commitment," with religion, and with all churches. Then the way is prepared to view the controversy as one more battle in the long "war" between the "benighted" forces of religion and the "enlightened" forces of science. Theologian Langdon Gilkey contends that this identification has itself been instrumental in creating the controversy. But he points out that in the Arkansas trial churches and ministers were arrayed largely *against* the creationists.[6] The witnesses for the defense had scientific credentials, and all but one had no training in theological or Biblical studies. As Gilkey points out in Chapter 11, both religion and science appear on both sides of this controversy, with "elite" religion and science on the one side against "popular" religion and science on the other, and our language must learn to encompass alike these different sorts of religion *and* science. Part of that language requirement is that a careful distinction be made between "creation" and "creationism."

The fact is, as in the Arkansas trial, the major churches and synagogues resist *creationism* and at the same time state unequivocally that they believe in and publicly affirm *creation*. What they disagree with is not "creation" but a literal account of it, and they object to the Arkansas law and similar laws mandating the curriculum to be taught in the public schools. Gilkey goes on to say that much of the scientific community, except for those scientists who are actively religious, assumes that a literal interpretation of Genesis is what *all* churches hold. So the scientific community must learn to speak clearly of the *creationist* view of creation and not to use "creation" and "creationist" synonymously. There is a nonliteralistic view of creation which almost everyone connected with the mainline churches, synagogues, and seminaries holds.

Secular Humanism as Religion

Calbreath made reference in his editorial to another argument used regularly by proponents of the teaching of "scientific creationism":

> Concern is expressed about teaching religious doctrine in the public schools. Presumably, the opposition is to the teaching of traditional Biblical concepts, such as creation. However, the secular humanism prevalent both in the classroom and in teacher training programs must be considered just as much a religion. Both the Judeo-Christian teaching and humanism offer a concept of the individual, both offer a world view and a moral code, both make statements concerning man's origins and man's destiny, and both speak regarding the existence of deity and the possibility of supernatural events. Since both deal in some realms that cannot be dealt with completely by scientific experimentation, a certain element of faith is necessary for the acceptance of the tenets of the system. The question then becomes one of determining which religion will be allowed to be taught in our public schools. It is true that statements affirming the existence of God are religious statements; however, a statement that there is no God is just as much a religious proposition as a statement that God exists. If religious doctrine is not to be taught, then all religion must be banned, not just the Judeo-Christian concepts.[7]

Whether secular humanism is a religion is debatable. The historical reality of an intellectual movement by this name is, however, undeniable. Nevertheless, this phrase has been appropriated by Fundamentalists and provides a rallying point for those who are sincerely concerned about the apparent deterioration of moral values in society. It is also appealing to a sizable fraction of the population which prefers to look for simple causes and simple solutions to problems. As noted earlier, many who hold this reductionist view point to the teaching of evolution as the core of the materialistic, atheistic world view that is supposedly responsible for the deterioration of moral values in American society.

What is needed, we believe, is to engender a better understanding of the limitations of science and of the nature of religion wherever either is taught. And the scientific community should recognize that some well-known spokesmen for science have extended their naturalistic world view beyond the proper limits of science, as though religion were an anachronistic, prescience area of human concern. Furthermore, some attention must be given to the Fundamentalists' contention that secular humanism is a "religion" being deliberately advanced in the public schools to replace traditional religious beliefs, as well as their use of the term to polarize the population.

Some of the authors of this volume have focused on the essential difference between "knowing" through the processes of science and "knowing" through the exercise of one's faith in revealed truth. They identify a misunderstanding of this difference as basic to the current controversy. Gilkey (Chapter 11) makes the point that "scientific creationists" typically and erroneously say that since evolutionary science explains origins without reference to God, it is therefore naturalistic, atheistic, and humanistic, when in fact there is nothing intrinsically atheistic about a scientific hypothesis that doesn't mention God—unless the scientist goes on to state a naturalistic philosophy or religious view of the universe as a whole. Such extensions go beyond the proper realm of science, and some well-known scientists have been guilty of making this mistake, leaving the false impression that scientists in general and evolutionists in particular believe traditional religious belief in God can be directly discredited by scientific discovery. The actual fact is that science is silent on religious matters.

That the "creation-science" movement has been clearly identified with Christian Fundamentalism is pointed out by several of the authors. The attempts in this movement to identify and base belief in fiat creation and a young earth on scientific evidence *alone* show how confused the issues are. Experiences with shared-time instruction in evolution and "creation science" (see Chapters 7 and 8) show clearly that such religious beliefs generally suffer as a result of this dichotomous approach. Skehan (Chapter 2) and Gilkey both point out the need to harmonize the findings of science with revealed truth (as it is understood) rather than confronting students (and scientists) with a choice of one or the other. The "scientific creationists" are demonstrably guilty of placing students in this either/or situation when they campaign for equal time and the presentation of a "two-model" course and by fostering the erroneous notion that acceptance of the theory of evolution is synonymous with atheism. The age of the earth and of mankind is central to the arguments of both sides of this controversy. Skehan discusses the evidence for the earth's antiquity and argues that the Genesis account is not inconsistent with that evidence.

Nelkin (Chapter 3) points out some fallacies in the actions taken by scientists in supporting position statements put out by their societies. These statements all emphasize the neutral character of science and its distinction from personal beliefs. They appeal to rationality, assuming that others see science from the same perspective as do scientists. Nelkin maintains that scientific argument has failed to stem the influence of "scientific creationists" simply because several fallacies actually contribute to the persistence of the creation/evolution controversy: arguing scientific neutrality given the political realities of science education; drawing rigid distinctions between scientific rationality and religious belief; failing to recognize the strength of creationist beliefs in light of the political and ideological ascendency of the New Right. There is a ubiquitous tendency in our society to translate value issues into technical terms, and "scientific creationists" have made an extraordinary parody of this tendency. In Nelkin's view, with the political ideology that prevails, their influence is likely to persist.

The problems for science education that hinge on the science/creation or creation/evolution controversy are the concern of the authors of Chapters 4–9. They accept the reality of religious commitment among students, teachers, school board members, legislators, and scientists and attempt to deal with this reality rather than polarizing the controversy through dogmatism and stubborn adherence to naturalism or empiricism as the only means of knowing.

In Chapter 4, Moyer examines the "truth" claims of both science and creationism, and then considers "scientific creationism" as a political force. He concludes with a summary of approaches that teachers can use without offending the belief systems of their students. (This chapter contains a detailed statement of Christian Fundamentalist belief.)

The emergence of "creation science" as a way of getting away from constitutional objections to creationism's religious roots is examined by Weinberg in Chapter 5. He then describes strategies used successfully in Iowa and elsewhere to counteract the influence of proponents of "scientific creationism" on teachers and school boards, citing particularly the Committees of Correspondence, now active in forty-nine states, which had their beginning in Iowa.

Taking a look at the assumptions made by creationists and scientists, Ellis in Chapter 6 describes the results of an informal survey of biology teachers in Kentucky and elsewhere. He found that evolution seems to receive less emphasis than "conservatives" believe to be the case but that, in these instances at least, it is stressed more than "liberals" assume. Ellis found that most of the Kentucky biology teachers he surveyed have some religious commitment and have worked out an accommodation between their responsibility to science education and the religious mores of their constituents without submitting to any mandate to include "scientific creationism."

In Chapter 7, Thwaites describes a two-model course at San Diego State University that deals with the creation/evolution controversy and gives equal time to "scientific creationist" speakers. They are invited to present the best possible case for recent fiat creation while the course instructors (1) define the original and modified postulates of Darwinian evolution and point out how each has been repeatedly tested, (2) define various types of creationist beliefs and point out the apparent relationship of these to the Genesis accounts of creation, and (3) show how creationist tenets taken as scientific hypotheses can be refuted easily with existing observations. He concludes that the presentation of misinterpretations of science by "scientific creationists" provides valuable insight into logical and emotional pitfalls into which even the most diligent of scientists might fall.

Saladin (Chapter 8) relates his experience in teaching a seminar and other courses in which "creation-science" claims are examined, although he does not undertake a systematic exposé of "creationist pseudoscience," as does the course by Thwaites (see Chapter 7). He concludes that the claim of "scientific creationists" that "two-model teaching" can be a thought-provoking classroom format is valid but that it has the effect of backing creationists into a corner where they declare that belief in the creation stands or falls on scientific evidence alone, and they surrender the usual exemption of their religious faith from scientific scrutiny. He points out that the educational efforts he describes are not a mere crusade or reverse evangelism for "evolutionism," but rather an argument for informed faith as opposed to blind faith, and that they may perhaps instill in a few graduates the habit of open-mindedness.

Nelson indicates in Chapter 9 that there is another way out for science teachers caught in the controversy over the false creation/evolution dichotomy. The approach he describes allows the teacher to discuss both scientific and religious values without demeaning the religious choices of others and without imposing the teacher's own value choices on the students. The strategy is to present not just the two extremes of the dispute—evolution without creation or creation without evolution—but the whole range of possible combinations. Focusing on the value assumptions made by each side, students may understand the values taken for granted by supporters of each position and then may be better able to make their own judgments in the matter.

In Chapter 10, Brush presents the view of an historian of science as he examines the role of skepticism in both science and religion, calling it a "wild card, a weapon that can be used by either side." In this sense, there is merit in examining skepticism in the perennial contest between science and belief, and one concludes that extreme dogmatism in either area is untenable.

Gilkey, in Chapter 11, looks at the creation/evolution issue as a theologian. He discusses the complex relation of scientific thought to religious thought in a technological society, pointing out that religion, as a pervasive aspect of corporate and individual life, has grown in importance because of the anxieties, frustrations, and dilemmas of an advanced technological age. In a scientific age every form of religion tends to become "scientific," but some religious forms are demonic, uncreative, ideological, and dogmatic. According to Gilkey, science and religion will be related to one another in any case, and that can be extremely dangerous to both science and religion if the relationship is not rational and sane, on the one hand, and responsible and humane, on the other. Are there possibilities for a more creative union between science and religion than is offered to us in "creation science"?

Both the religious and the scientific communities bear real responsibility for the crisis represented by the "creation science" movement, says Gilkey, and in a comment to the editor during the assembling of this book, he wrote:

> That creation science is clearly identified with Fundamentalism is certainly correct. . . . I have debated creationists often; each time it has been against a person with an earned doctorate degree in one of the sciences from a good university. Surely, it is not only informative because true, but also *honest* to admit that connection with "science" as well as the other connection with fundamentalism. We who are involved with the churches *have* to take responsibility for our "demonic fringes" and "wild fellow communicants." In an age when science is turning up so many unsavory elements (because it is so powerful, fashionable, and offers so much wealth, prestige, and certainty), it is very important that the scientific community *itself* recognizes and interprets these new elements within its own body as a part, if an unwelcome part, of that body. . . . To say they do not represent "*real* science" is to avoid the issue— neither were the persecutors *real* Christians, though they misguidedly thought they were. It is, I think, time that an established social force like science . . . recognize *its own deviant forms*, take some responsibility for them, and seek to deal with them as problems within its own body. And only by recognizing *its own* active part in the genesis of this controversy—instead always of viewing itself as the *victim*—will the scientific community begin to change its graduate educational programs so as to include the philosophy and history of science! For it is an almost total lack of those disciplines in scientific training that has caused the unfortunate *misunderstanding* of science itself and of religion that has helped to breed this controversy.[8]

As we move on with science into the future, it is well to acknowledge that none of man's earlier experiences prepared him for what we would discover with the invention of science. None of these discoveries was expected or matched earlier preconceptions. Consider how man's conception of the universe has changed in the past few hundred years. In a succession of leaps we have extended our senses and experiences in space and time. We have gone from the naked-eye limit of a millimeter to 10^{-23} millimeters in the study of elementary particles; our idea of the size of the universe has gone from a few thousand kilometers to multiples of 10^{22} kilometers; our measurement of time has been extended a millionfold from the historical record to our determination of the age of the universe in its present state of expansion (15 billion years or so). New evidence will be forthcoming as time goes on, and belief has to stay in equilibrium with this constant flow of new knowledge and use it, not avoid it.

Groups that have actively promoted the teaching of "creation science" as a legitimate alternative to evolution use all the techniques of public persuasion, while opponents of this movement have been slow to recognize the political nature of the controversy. The drawing power of debates between "scientific creationists" and evolutionists testifies to the reality of the concern of both scientists and the public about the relationship between science and belief. Clearly, we need both science and belief. They have served as two awesome driving forces, interweaving to lead us to where and what we are today. But if they are to coexist, each must respect and learn from the other. It is in that spirit that we offer this book.

Notes

1. "Views of the Universe: Science versus Tradition," arranged by Rolf Sinclair. Symposium presented at AAAS Annual Meeting, Toronto, Ontario, 6 January 1981.
2. "Science and Belief: I. The Interface," arranged by Rolf Sinclair and Joseph Dasbach, and "Science and Belief: II. Problems for Science Education," arranged by Robert W. Hanson.
3. Louisiana's creationism law, passed by the state legislature in July 1981, was struck from the statute book by federal judge Adrian Duplantier on 22 November 1982. He declared that the law violated the state constitution, which does not allow the state legislature to establish curricula. The decision is under appeal. Meanwhile, there is now no law in the land that mandates the teaching of the Genesis account of creation as science.
4. D. G. Calbreath, guest editorial, *American Laboratory*, November 1980.
5. Wayne Moyer, letter to the editor, *American Laboratory*, August 1980.
6. Langdon Gilkey, letter to the editor, 10 February 1983.
7. Calbreath, guest editorial, *American Laboratory*.
8. Gilkey, letter to the author, 10 February 1983.

CHAPTER 2

The Age of the Earth, of Life, and of Mankind: Geology and Biblical Theology versus Creationism

Rev. James W. Skehan, S.J.
Boston College

Recently, laws have been proposed and/or passed requiring that equal time be given in public school science classes for "creation science," so-called, comparable to that given to the theory of evolution. The basic position of "creation science" is set forth in the preface to *The Remarkable Birth of Planet Earth* by Henry M. Morris, director of the Institute for Creation Research in San Diego:

> The origin and early history of the earth and man is a marvelous and fascinating story . . . given by revelation in the Bible and now strikingly confirmed by modern science. The theory of evolution has dominated our society, especially the schools, for almost a hundred years, and its influence is largely responsible for our present-day social, political, and moral problems. Many people today, including scientists, . . . find that evolution is merely an unreasonable theory, containing many scientific fallacies. Creation, on the other hand, is a scientific theory which does fit all the facts of true science, as well as God's revelation in the Holy Scriptures.[1]

In this chapter I present a summary of a modern scientific perspective on the age of the Earth and of its life forms, including mankind. Additionally, I present a modern theological perspective on the great body of religious and theological literature, but especially the Book of Genesis and the Babylonian creation story, both of which deal with the creation of the Earth and the origin of mankind. I maintain that the age and origin of the Earth, and of life, including man, are the proper subject of scientific research, and that as a result of such studies it is proper to maintain that the Earth is some 4.6 billion years old. Moreover, the earliest life forms yet discovered are about 3.5 billion years old, and the record in the rocks indicates that mankind is at least 2 million years old. Among Biblical theologians there is wide agreement that the story of the creation of the Earth and of mankind, in the first chapters of Genesis, is presented to recount the beginning of the religious history of the people of Israel, and is not a scientific analysis to establish either the age or mode of origin of the Earth.

My position on this subject is fundamentally different from that taken by those who interpret the Book of Genesis literally as regards the creation story, or who hold that the age of the Earth is approximately 6000 to 10,000 years based erroneously on Biblically derived computations of time (Table 2–1). Such computations were based on the assumption that the time interval between the creation of the Earth and the birth of Christ can be derived from computations based on Biblical genealogies and extrapolated intervals of time between "events" in the Old Testament in general, and those in Genesis in particular. The latter point of view has itself evolved from a literal reading of the Old Testament on creation and other topics to an elaborately developed program, now referred to by its proponents as "scientific creationism" or "creation science."[2]

A clear distinction must be drawn between what science and Genesis can or cannot tell us about this subject matter. On the basis of modern creation theology and Biblical archeology, I maintain that the Genesis narrative and the conclusions of science belong to two completely separate realms of existence and knowledge. Research on the age and origin of the Earth, of life, and of mankind is within the domain of science, and Genesis in no sense is a scientific treatment of those topics. On the other hand, Genesis is a primitive religious history of the people of Israel, and as such is one of the noblest and most remarkable documents of our civilization.

Age of the Earth

The question of the age of the Earth has fascinated mankind for hundreds of years, but it has been of pressing interest to the general public mainly since the time that Darwin published his theory of evolution. However, keys to unlocking these secrets have been found only slowly and relatively recently.

Xenophanes of Colophon (570–470 B.C.) is the first philosopher recorded as focusing on the problem. He recognized the significance of fossils as remnants of former life. He correctly inferred that sedimentary rocks

originated as tiny particles of rock deposited on the sea bottom and concluded that they must be of great antiquity. This primitive natural history
study took place, we may note, only about a century after the final synthesis of the Genesis manuscripts into the translated and printed forms in
which we know it. Both types of writings, the scientific and religious, recorded within a thousand miles of each other and at approximately the same
time, were concerned with origins and past history, but from greatly different points of view.

Herodotus, the well-known Greek historian, about 450 B.C. observed
the thin annual layers of sediment deposited by the Nile and concluded that
it would take at least many thousands of years for the Nile to build up its
delta from the series of floods that would be required to lay down such
deposits.

Aristotle and other Greek and Roman philosopher-naturalists
strengthened and expanded this type of scholarly method of observation combined with deduction. They left a legacy of exploration of natural history
to early Christian scholars, including St. Augustine who, in all essentials,
continued this tradition. But the thread of that kind of deductive thinking
modified by results of investigation was temporarily broken in the late
medieval excesses of Christian scholasticism and theological idealism. Certain members of this school of thought turned to the literal interpretation
of the Book of Genesis for a solution to the problem of the antiquity of the
Earth. In the sixteenth and seventeenth centuries, and most especially in
modern times, including the present, there has developed an all too
widespread reaction to the perceived religious implications of scientific
explorations.[3]

A number of computations were made based on investigations of
Biblical genealogies and interpretations of intervals between recorded events.
Table 2-1 sets out several intervals of time extrapolated between events and/or
persons and gives the corresponding Biblical source important in such computations. Computations based on the Hebrew text give a total of 4163 years
from the creation to the birth of Christ. According to the Greek text the
total comes to about 5500; and the Roman martyrology for December 25
yields 5199 years from the creation of the world.[4] Analysis of these texts in
a literal fashion reached a high degree of precision when, in 1642, John
Lightfoot, a Biblical scholar, published his *Observations on Genesis*. This
account put the time of creation at 3928 B.C. and implies that man was
created on September 17 at nine o'clock in the morning.[5] In like manner,
Archbishop James Ussher of Ireland in 1650 suggested that the time of Earth's
creation was in the evening of October 22, 4004 B.C. He based his commonly
cited conclusion on both astronomical cycles and the timing of events in
the Old Testament.

When modern geology began to gather momentum there was a return

Table 2–1. Key biblical "events," persons, and textual citations from the Hebrew text of the Old Testament used in computations of time intervals to arrive at the supposed age of the Earth.

From	To	Interval in years
Adam	Flood	1656 (Gen. 5)
Flood	Abraham	290 (Gen. 11:10–26)
Abraham	Departure into Egypt	290 (Gen. 21:5; 25:26; 47:9)
Sojourn in Egypt		430 (Exod. 12:40; Gal. 3:17)
Exodus from Egypt	Foundation of the temple	480 (1 Kings 6:1)
Foundation of the temple	Departure into Babylon	430 ⎫
		⎬ 480 (1 & 2 Kings)
Sojourn in Babylon (587/6–538/7)		50 ⎭
Return from Babylon	Birth of Christ	537
Adam	Birth of Christ	4163

SOURCE: Henricus Renckens, S. J., *Israel's Concept of the Beginning: The Theology of Genesis 1–3* (Herder and Herder, New York, 1964), p. 37.

to the Greek perspective. This included the concept that a long time was necessary for present-day Earth processes to have operated in order to have uplifted mountains, to have carved valleys deeply into them, and to have deposited immense amounts of sediment. By looking at the time scale of processes and using the concept of uniformitarianism, as first set forth by James Hutton in 1785, geologists came to recognize that rocks had to be very old and the Earth much older still.

A number of physicists made a variety of calculations based on the ideas of Galileo, Newton, and others and came up with values ranging from 75,000 years to 40 million years for the age of the Earth. In 1897 Lord Kelvin gave an important address to the Annual Meeting of the American Association for the Advancement of Science, in which he reiterated his faith in his heat-loss calculations and in the physical constraints that they imposed, indicating that the age of the Earth was 20 to 40 million years. Kelvin's address on the age of the Earth was reprinted in *Science* that same year. T.C. Chamberlain, a geologist of the then-infant University of Chicago and mentor of Kirtley F. Mather, offered a critique of Kelvin's paper in 1899 in *Science*. He speculated that new sources of energy might yet be discovered within the particles of matter that would eliminate burning and gravitational contraction as the sole possible sources of the Sun's luminosity. This debate took place shortly after the momentous discovery by Henri Becquerel of radioactivity in uranium salts in 1896. This was about the same time that Wilhelm Roentgen discovered x-rays and Marie Curie discovered and isolated radium, a radioactive element.[6]

It was not, however, until 1905 that Ernest Rutherford, who had been studying radioactive processes, suggested that radioactive minerals could be used to date rocks. He dated a uranium mineral in his laboratory at McGill University in Montreal the next year. Bertram Boltwood of Yale discovered "ionium" (which turned out to be an isotope of thorium), the first isotope to be isolated. Both Rutherford and Boltwood published ages of dated minerals, but it was not until 1913, when Frederick Soddy clarified the nature of isotopes, that the methods could be refined and made more accurate. When the full series of decay products of radioactive disintegration was firmly established, it became clear that the Earth had to be not millions, but billions of years old.

The pioneers of nuclear physics, at the turn of the century, discovered that atoms of radioactive elements spontaneously disintegrate to form atoms of a different element, liberating energy in the process. The reason why radioactive decay offers a dependable means of measuring time is that the average rate of disintegration is fixed and does not vary with any of the typical changes in chemical or physical conditions that affect most chemical or physical processes.[7]

Once isotopes were discovered and instruments invented that could make the chemical analysis for the ratios of parent to daughter isotopes, modern dating of rocks began. The amounts of parent isotopes and daughter products present in a rock sample are a measure of the time interval between the present and the time the rock crystallized. Thus, measurements based on the decay of uranium, rubidium, potassium, and samarium all give dates of crystallization of the rocks in which these minerals are found, and by geologic inference, any other rocks that bear a definite age relation to the rock analyzed. For example, when we date the crystallization of a granite, we know, also from geology, that the absolute age of the surrounding sedimentary rocks, into which the granite was intruded when it crystallized, can be no younger than the granite. If the geologic ages of these sedimentary rocks are known by fossils and these strata in turn overlie, and are thus younger than other radioactively dated rocks, we can thus establish an absolute age range, if not a precise age date, for the sedimentary rocks, even though they may contain no dateable minerals.[8]

Age of Meteorites: The Age of the Earth

Age-dating of meteorites has revealed that they are all somewhere in the vicinity of 4.5 billion years old, regardless of their composition. That there are no meteorites of any other age, regardless of when they fell to Earth, suggests strongly that they originated in other bodies of the solar system that formed at the same time that the Earth did. If so, then the meteorites give the age of the Earth, too. That this is the case is convincingly shown by the lead isochron diagram for meteorites (Fig. 2–1) which gives an age of 4635 million years. Present-day Earth lead falls on this isochron, indicating that it came from the same primordial source as meteorite lead and at the same time. Since there were greater quantities of uranium-235 and uranium-238 progressively backward in time, there were smaller quantities of lead-207 and lead-206. On the basis of computations of decreasing quantities of lead-207, the Earth's supply must have been zero at 5.6 billion years ago, and therefore the Earth can be no older than 5.6 billion years and no younger than 4.5+ billion years.[9]

Age of Rocks on Earth

Geologists studying fossiliferous sediments have developed a "clock," so to speak, which is sufficiently fine-tuned that they can distinguish the relative ages of rock units that are only a few meters thick and which may represent periods of time of less than a million years in duration. A million years, we should note, is only about 1/5000th of the Earth's history. The entire rock record of the Earth's fossiliferous sediments has been mapped and subdivided into the scheme of eras, epochs, and ages (Fig. 2–2). The major absolute time boundaries are shown at 570, 225, and 65 million years ago (Ma). The Pleistocene deposits, extending to about 2 Ma, contain the earliest remains of man yet recognized.

Once isotopic age dating was discovered, geologists welcomed it as a key that would unlock the secret of just how old each of the major geologic time intervals might be. As a result of the application of this absolute method of age-dating to the fossiliferous sedimentary rocks, the boundaries between the major eras of Earth history, and thus the time of the appearance of major and even of most minor life groups was established. Figure 2–2 shows the divisions and the vastly uneven duration of the major eras of the geological time scale.

Figures 2–2 and 2–3, showing geologic time divisions from the present to over 4.6 billion years ago, note a few milestones such as the appearance of shelled organisms of great variety by the beginning of Cambrian time at 570 Ma; the oldest fossils yet discovered at approximately 3.4 billion years, found in West Australia;[10] the oldest rock on Earth yet dated at 3.9 billion years from Greenland; the youngest and oldest moon rocks, dated about 3.2 to over 4.4 billion years, respectively; and at the center, the inferred age of the Earth at between 4.6 and 4.7 billion years. At the other end of the time clock, we note the recent appearance of man, approximately coincident with the Pleistocene ice ages, about 2 million years before the present.[11]

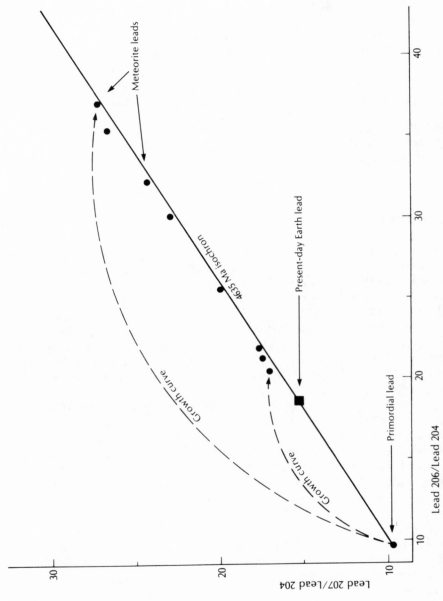

Figure 2.1 Lead isochron for meteorites gives an age of 4635 million years (Ma). Present-day Earth lead falls on the isochron, indicating that it came from the same primordial source as meteorite lead and at the same time. Source: After Tilton, 1973, in D. L. Eicher, *Geologic Time*, Foundations of Earth Science Series (Englewood Cliffs, NJ: Prentice-Hall, 1976), p. 140.

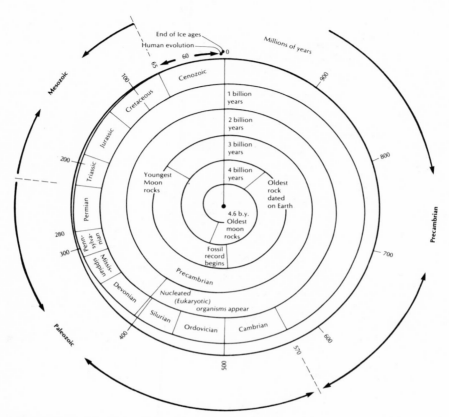

Figure 2.2 Spiral diagram showing major divisions of geologic time; numbers indicate the approximate position in time of divisions between eras and epochs in millions of years; numbers between arrows indicate the vastly unequal duration of each era; milestones in geologic history, noted in the text, are shown. Modified from Frank Press and Raymond Siever, *Earth* (San Francisco, W. H. Freeman, 1978), p. 48; and J. W. Schopf and D. Z. Ohler, ''How Old Are the Eukaryotes?'' *Science*, 193 (1976): 47–49.

The Geological Record of Life

It is clear from the fossil record that, over the eons (Fig. 2–3), life forms have changed dramatically and in great variety from the simple single-cell organisms of about 3.5 billion years ago, into animals as complex as man. The knowledge of this past life and the manner in which it has changed is well known and is based on a study of the fossil remains of many thousands of species of animals and plants which no longer exist. In the museums of the world there are estimated to be more than 100 million fossils that have

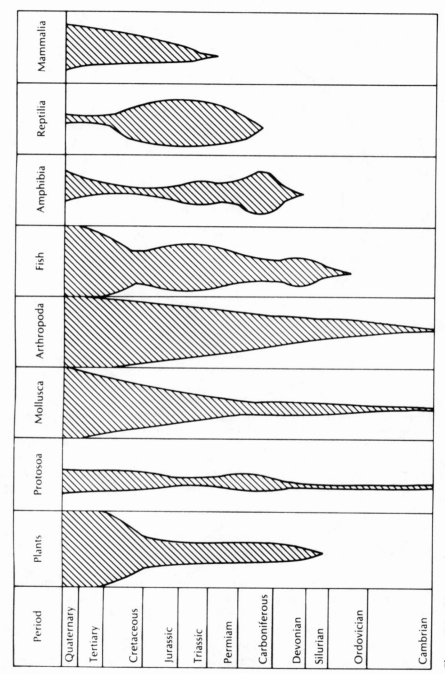

Figure 2.3 Diagram showing evolutionary development of major groups of life forms throughout geological time.

been identified and age-dated by many thousands of paleontologists. From their studies, and those of tens of thousands of other kinds of geologists and geophysicists, much has been learned about the origin and history of the Earth and its varied life forms.[12]

The fossil record dates back approximately 3.5 billion years. During the first 2.5 billion years, life forms lacked hard parts, such as skeletons, so that the fossil record is much more sketchy than the interval from 570 million years ago to the present. By that time many animals had developed hard parts, and for that reason have been more perfectly preserved as fossils.

The spiral of Figure 2-2 shows the major divisions of time, and Figure 2-3 indicates the time of first appearance, relative abundance, and duration in time of the major life forms that characterized the major divisions of Earth history. For example, trilobites first appeared and became important in the Cambrian period; fishes in the Ordovician; trees and land plants in the Silurian and Devonian; dinosaurs in the Triassic through Cretaceous; and mammals in the Triassic. Man came on the scene in the Pleistocene epoch.[13]

Apparent Conflict of Scientific Data with Genesis

Over the past several centuries, problems in reconciling inferences from scientific discovery with the literal interpretation of the Old Testament arose and became a source of great dissension between religious people and scientists. There were misunderstandings of the methods and motives on both sides. But in the course of history a number of scientists and other scholars, who were also concerned about religion and theology, have addressed themselves to these vexing questions. Among such concerned scientists, the Reverend Thomas Burnet was the author of the most popular geologic work of the seventeenth century, *The Sacred Theory of the Earth*. Among the books on scriptural geology, Burnet's *Sacred Theory* is surely the most famous, the most maligned, and the most misunderstood.[14] In it he tried to provide a geologic rationale for all Biblical events, an account that thoroughly pleased neither scientists nor theologians.

But as we have once again seen in recent years, the relationship between religion and science is very complex. Often religious leaders have actively encouraged science; at other times religious persons have felt their faith threatened by the results of science. An examination of Burnet's case, in a time and situation which in most respects we regard as very different from our own, is instructive, and its lessons are remarkably up to date. The case provides a broader understanding of the persistent forces arrayed against both science and theology on the one hand, and the practice of religion on the other. From all this conflict of the past and present, we learn that if there is any consistent enemy of science or theology, it is irrationalism, even the irrationalism of religious men and women. Burnet believed that reason and revelation are two infallible guides to truth, but in 1681 he was already urging caution. Said he:

> 'tis a dangerous thing to ingage the authority of Scripture in disputes about the Natural World in opposition to Reason; lest Time, which brings all things to light, should discover that to be evidently false which we had made Scripture to assert.[15]

Although Burnet prospered for a time as the Clerk of the Closet (Chaplain) at the court of William III and was considered as a possible successor to the Archbishop of Canterbury, he caused his own demise when, in 1692, he published a work advocating the allegorical interpretation of the seven days of Genesis. He promptly lost his job despite his profuse apologies for any unintended offense.[16]

By 1837, Charles Darwin, as a result of his five-year study aboard the Beagle, had lost his faith in the fixity of species. In 1838 he developed a theory to explain its mechanism; however, he delayed publishing it for twenty-one years, probably because of the climate of the times and the profound philosophical implications that he knew would flow from the publication of his full theory. Stephen Jay Gould of Harvard University is of the opinion that Darwin was not as much worried by his written statements showing that he espoused evolution as he was with what he reasoned was its logical conclusion, namely philosophical materialism. This is the postulate that matter is the stuff of all existence and that all mental and spiritual phenomena are its by-products. He realized that no idea could be more upsetting to the deepest traditions of Western thought, and to Biblical interpretations, than the statement that mind, however complex and powerful, is a product of brain. He published the full implications of his theory only in 1871 in the *Descent of Man* and in 1872 in *The Expression of the Emotions in Man and Animals*. It may come as a surprise to those who consider Darwin a heretic, bent on destroying God and man's self-esteem, to realize that Darwin came from a deeply religious background. There is much evidence for this, including his statement while aboard the Beagle, "I often conjecture what will become of me; my wishes certainly would make me a country clergyman."[17]

Theological Perspectives on Genesis 1:1–2:3

Most of the problems that have confronted theologians and religious people over the centuries arise from interpretations of scientific data that appear to be in conflict with the literal interpretation of the Book of Genesis. This is especially the case as regards the creation stories, which deal not only with the creation of the Earth but also with the special creation of Adam and Eve.

In an effort to resolve the question of whether Genesis should be interpreted literally, we must ask three relevant questions:

1. What are the source materials of which Genesis is composed?
2. What kind of literature is it?
3. Did the authors of the Old Testament in general, and of Genesis in particular, intend to write a history in any sense of the word, and if so what kind?

Basically, these are the questions that modern Biblical archeologists and Biblical theologians are asking. Answers to these questions can go a long way toward providing a useful theological perspective for those who are interested in solving the alleged dichotomy between conclusions derived from science and those derived from an analysis of Genesis. What follows will address the above questions briefly.

Source Materials

The Book of Genesis provides an introduction to the story of the people of Israel by describing the beginning of their religious history. Conceptually, the contents of Genesis, which narrates the story of individuals such as Abraham and reaches back to the middle of the second millenium B.C. were interpreted only by what happened in the later period. The interpretation involved two principal blocks of scriptural material (Table 2-2), namely the patriarchal narratives and the primitive history of Israel. This primitive history preceded and explained for Israel the divine intervention at the time of Abraham and later. The primitive history, so important to the topic of this chapter, was thus a general introduction to the whole of the Old Testament.

One factor to keep in mind is that the Israelites, whose homeland was at the eastern end of the Mediterranean Sea, more or less in the land of present-day Israel, had been taken into captivity in the pagan nations of Babylonia and Egypt for a prolonged period. As a result the people of Israel longed to return to the Promised Land to worship "the one true God, Yahweh."

The primitive history makes up Chapters 1–11 and includes the creation stories, the flood, and the Tower of Babel among others. The Patriarchal history (Ch. 12:1–50:26) is divided into three sections: (a) the Patriarch Abraham (Ch. 12:1–25:18); (b) the Patriarchs Isaac and Jacob (Ch. 25:19–36:43; and (c) the history of Joseph (Ch. 37:1–50:26).

The weight of evidence has led most Scripture scholars of the past two hundred years to interpret the Book of Genesis, in its original manuscript form, as a composite product of several authors or traditions (Fig. 2–4), as they are called. The most significant for our purposes are referred to as J, E, P, D, and R, a shorthand that will become clear as we proceed. In this interpretation of the resulting manuscript, the main authorship of the bulk

Table 2-2. Divisions of the Book of Genesis.

PRIMITIVE HISTORY (1–11)	THE PATRIARCH ABRAHAM (12:1–25:18)	THE PATRIARCHS ISAAC AND JACOB (25:19–36:43)	THE HISTORY OF JOSEPH (37:1–50:26)
(A) Creation of world and man (1:1–2–4a) (P)	(A) The call of Abram (12:1–9) (J, P)	(A) The birth of Esau and Jacob (25:19–34) (J, P)	(A) Joseph sold into Egypt (37:1–36) (J, E)
(B) Creation of man and woman (2:4B–25) (J)	(B) Abram and Sarai in Egypt (12:10–20) (J)	(B) Isaac in Gerat and Beer-Sheba (26:1–35) (J, P)	(B) Judah and Tamar (38:1–30) (J)
(C) The Fall (3:1–24) (J)	(C) The separation of Abram and Lot (13:1–18) (J, P)	(C) Isaac's blessing of Jacob (27:1–45) (J)	(C) Joseph's temptations (39:1–23) (J)
(D) Cain and Abel (4:1–16) (J)	(D) Abram and the four kings (14:1–24) (?)	(D) Jacob's departure for Paddan-Aram (27:46–28:9) (P)	(D) Joseph interprets the prisoners' dreams (40:1–23) (E)
(E) Genealogy of Cain (4:17–26) (J)	(E) Promises renewed (15:1–20) (J, E?)	(E) Vision at Bethel (28:10–22) (J, E)	(E) Joseph interprets pharaoh's dreams (41:1–57) (E, J)
(F) Genealogy of Adam to Noah (5:1–32) (P)	(F) Hagar's flight (16:1–16) (J, P)	(F) Jacob's marriages (29:1–30) (J, E?)	(F) First encounter of Joseph with his brothers (42:1–38) (E, J)
(G) Prologue to the flood (6:1–22) (J and P)	(G) The covenant of circumcision (17:1–27) (P)	(G) Jacob's children (29:31–30:24) (J, E)	(G) Second journey to Egypt (43:1–34) (J, E)
(H) The flood (7:1–8–22) (J, P)			

(I) The covenant with Noah (9:1–17) (P)

(J) The sons of Noah (9:18–27) (J)

(K) The peopling of the earth (10:1–32) (P, J)

(L) The Tower of Babel (11:1–9) (J)

(M) Concluding Genealogies (11:10–32) (P, J)

(H) Promise of a son, Sodom and Gomorrah (18:1–19:38) (J)

(I) Abraham and Sarah in Gerar (20:1–18) (E)

(J) Isaac and Ishmael (21:1–21) (J, P)

(K) Abraham and Abimelech (21:22–34) (E)

(L) The sacrifice of Isaac (22:1–24) (E, J)

(M) The purchase of the cave of Machpelah (23:1–20) (P)

(N) The wife of Isaac (24:1–67) (J)

(O) Abraham's descendants (25:1–18) (P, J)

(H) Jacob outwits Laban (30:25–43) (J, E)

(I) Jacob's departure (31:1–21) (E, J)

(J) Laban's pursuit (31:22–42) (E, J)

(K) The contract between Jacob and Laban (31:43–32:3) (J, E)

(L) Preparation for the meeting with Esau (32:4–22) (J, E)

(M) Jacob's struggle with God (32:23–33) (J)

(N) Jacob's meeting with God (33:1–20) (J, E?)

(O) The rape of Dinah (34:1–31) (J, E)

(P) Jacob at Bethel (35:1–29) (E, P)

(Q) The descendants of Esau (36:1–43) (P?)

(H) Judah's plea for Benjamin (44:1–34) (J)

(I) The recognition of Joseph (45:1–28) (J, E)

(J) Jacob's journey to Egypt (46:1–34) (J, E, P)

(K) The Hebrews in Egypt (47:1–31) (J, P)

(L) Jacob adopts Joseph's sons (48:1–22) (J, E, P)

(M) Jacob's blessings (49:1–33) (J)

(N) The burial of Jacob and the final acts of Joseph (50:1–26) (J, E, P)

SOURCE: E. H. Maly, "Genesis," in *The Jerome Biblical Commentary*, ed. Raymond E. Brown et al. (New York: Prentice-Hall, 1968), pp. 9–10.

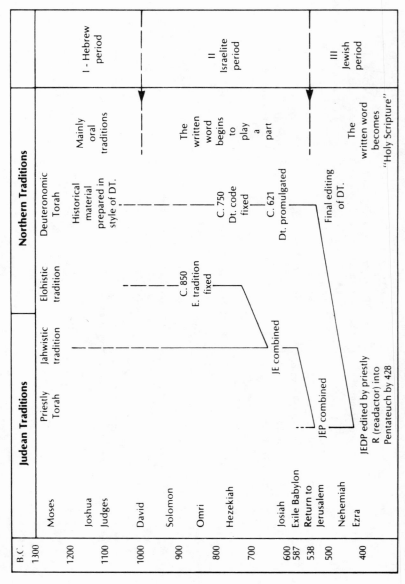

Figure 2.4 Time scale in years before Christ (B.C.), showing inferred development of several Old Testament pentateuchal traditions (J, E, P, D, and R) relative to major Old Testament personages. Modified from L. H. Grollenberg, *The Penguin Shorter Atlas of the Bible,* translated by M. F. Hedlund. (New York, Penguin Books, 1959), p. 83; and W. J. Harrington, O. P., *Key to the Bible,* vol. 2, The Old Testament (New York, Alba House, 1974), p. 6.

of the content is attributed to a Judean writer of the ninth century B.C., who provided the narrative framework. The author of this earliest discernible tradition, called the Yahwist because of the anachronistic use of the word Yahweh, the divine name, is regarded as the Father of Israelite historiography. This tradition is labeled J from the German form of the word, Jahweh. Scholars consider that he produced his work during the period when the united kingdom of David and Solomon emerged into nationhood in the period 1000 to 922 B.C. The history that he produced owes as much to the non-Israelite world of his times as it does to the uniquely Israelite experience which sharply divided Israel from that world.[18]

The Elohist tradition, E, is so named because of its author's preference for a generic title for God, Elohim, a name whose radical meaning appears to designate power. This component of Genesis may originally have been a separate redaction of the Book of Genesis but probably was added to the J manuscript largely as a supplement and modification. E displays certain theological nuances that are lacking in J.

The legislative nucleus of the Book of Deuteronomy (Ch. 12–26) was the D document. It had formed the basis of an attempted radical religious reformation in Judah under Josiah in the year 621 B.C.

The fourth document, P or Priestly tradition, with its obvious concern for liturgy, imposed the order and system on Genesis and is attributed to the priests of Jerusalem. Its style is evident throughout the Pentateuch, the first five books of the Old Testament commonly referred to as the Torah or the Law. This document probably dates from the exilic period (587–538 B.C.) and was later incorporated into the other pentateuchal material. The P narrative in Genesis is sparse, with notable exceptions being the creation and flood stories. The priestly concerns that are in question are those of the exilic and post-exilic circles and communities which codified and updated Israel's ancient cultic and moral traditions. These were attached firmly to the restored temple liturgy which was then ideally construed as having been the one divinely intended for Israel from the beginning.

Israel's faith, it is useful to remember, was under seige during the exile, and this crisis provided the background for P's history. To inculcate the prescriptions, P has presented the history of Israel with strong liturgical overtones, characterized by the exhortation, "As Yahweh is holy, so must Israel remain holy," that is, separated from and uncontaminated by any man-made morality or cult. The creation story (Gen. 1:1–2:4) has ritual and liturgical allusions and applications. The whole of Israel's history is marked by a special covenant of God with mankind and of God's revelation of himself to mankind.[19]

The fifth author is called R or Redactor of Genesis. This is the editor, so to speak, who put Genesis in its final form. The ideas proposed by Genesis are mainly those of J and P, and occasionally of E.[20]

Thus, in summary, it is generally agreed that J and E, written about 1000 B.C., preceded D written in 621 B.C.; P is post-exile or fifth century, and R, the Pentateuch as we know it, is last of all.

What Kind of Literature Is Genesis?

Much light has been shed on the Babylonian creation myths and their relation to Genesis by the archeological discoveries of tablets recording these stories. These tablets record the *Enuma elish, When On High,* the Babylonian creation story. The left column of Table 2–3 outlines the story of the origin of the pagan gods as presented in the *Enuma elish.* Marduk was the creator of the Earth in this account, a story repudiated by the author of Genesis, who offered a new theology of creation by the One God of Israel.[21] The well-known topics and sequence of Genesis are presented in the column on the right. Thus the priestly author of Genesis has followed the topics of the Babylonian story in a number of instances but rejected those which offer a contrary theology and perspective.[22]

Israel's historians made use of material of all kinds, often modified from those of her pagan neighbors or captors. These include ancient creation stories, genealogical lists, songs, proverbs, legends, customs, institutions, and idioms. The early chapters of Genesis (Table 2–2) are composed of fragments of myth, legend, and folklore, whereas the patriarchal stories are largely in the form of sagas. All contributed to the priestly author's purposes.[23]

By myth, in the technical sense, we mean a truth or opinion cast in symbolic language and passed on from one generation to the next. In the case of the creation story of Genesis, the authors modified the familiar, much older, pagan Babylonian creation myth, *Enuma elish,* as a symbolic vehicle to teach Israel the important religious truths of Genesis. The authors of Genesis used the basic Babylonian creation story only as a vehicle to oppose the pagan polytheistic teaching and to transmit truths about the benevolent one God, who had placed man over the creation that He had produced by His effortless word.[24]

Did the Authors of the Old Testament and of Genesis Intend to Write a History?

Clearly, the authors of Genesis intended to write a history. No modern scholar, however, would hold that Genesis presents history in the modern sense of that word. The authors' conception of history, as a linear movement of events determined by divine interventions and directed toward a divinely conceived goal, precludes its being considered as history in any modern sense. A preliminary

Table 2-3. A comparison of the content outlines and sequence of topics in *Enuma elish, When on High,* the Babylonian creation myth, with that of the Book of Genesis 1:1-2:3.

Enuma elish	Genesis
An account of the birth of the gods and various conflicts between them.	
Divine spirit and cosmic matter are coexistent and coeternal	Divine spirit creates cosmic matter and exists independently of it
Primeval chaos; Ti' amat enveloped in darkness	The earth a desolate waste, with darkness covering the deep (tehom)
Light emanating from the gods	The creation of light and the separation of light and darkness
Markduk's work of creation (a) The creation of the firmament	The creation of the firmament and the dividing of waters
(b) The creation of dry land	The creation of dry land, the sea, and plant life
(c) The creation of the luminaries	The creation of the luminaries; the creation of the creatures of the sea, and the fowl of the air
(d) The creation of man The building and dedication of Esagila, the temple complex	The creation of land animals and of man; God gives man a charge and blesses him
The gods rest and celebrate; the hymn to the creator, Marduk	God rests from all his work and sanctifies the seventh day
Epilogue	

SOURCE: Alexander Heidel, *The Babylonian Genesis, the Story of Creation* (Chicago: University of Chicago Press, 1951), pp. 128-129.

look at the patriarchal literature, however, will assist us in evaluating the creation stories. There is every reason for the modern historian to accept the basic "facts" of patriarchal history, although primitively recorded and preserved in popular form. Family incidents were dressed up to serve as material for ballads and sagas, sung or recounted for entertainment and the edification of the local inhabitants. Some events could be given a framework based on local cult legends or cultic practices to illustrate their religious significance. Near Easter history, and especially archaeology, strongly suggests that the underlying social, juridicial, political, geographical, and religious conditions in Genesis are those of the second millenium B.C., and therefore may not have been invented by an author living at a much later period.[25].

Primitive History

What can be said of the religious nature of the patriarchal history can also be said of the primitive history of Genesis. However, in the latter case the groundwork for the religious history is quite different. Here the events are of a cosmic order that affected universal man. They are unique, such as the creation or the flood.[26]

The authors of the creation story and generations of those who heard and read it most likely accepted this story in a general way, because Genesis had been written out of an historical experience that was independent of the materials of which it fashioned its history. They found in the materials of Genesis resonances and insights that corresponded with experience.[27] Genesis, written much later than the books of the Old Testament which succeed it (Fig. 2-4), did not present creation as an historical fact because it had human witnesses or conventional historical sources. Rather, the creation narrative was devised in its present form because of Israel's experience of a God who had revealed himself in ways that were readily recognizable in the creation story.

It was this historical experience that dictated the choice of materials, a choice that was made so wisely and so well that Genesis stands apart from the rest of Near Eastern myth and folklore to which it is otherwise so evidently related. The historical experience of the people of Israel, and their interpretation of God's direct intervention and guidance of their affairs, has in a unique way imposed its character upon materials of the primitive history that were not, of themselves or in content, originally historical.[28]

The God of Israel was seen, in the light of events narrated in Genesis chapters 1-11 and in the patriarchal sagas, as the God of all nature and of all history. Consequently, this primeval history is the theological interpretation of those events significant for the later development of Israel's own story.[29]

The primitive cosmology of the authors' time is used to teach the creation of all things by God whose absolute power as transcendent God is emphasized. Whereas the earlier pagan Babylonian creation epic *Enuma elish, When on High* (Table 2-3), which dates from at least 2000 B.C.,[30] depicted creation as the result of a struggle between the gods and the forces of chaos, the Biblical account stresses the effortless activity of the one God. The imagery borrowed from these and other accounts is employed for the authors' polemic against the Babylonian myths.[31] This table shows the points in both narratives highlighting the sequence of treatment as well as the contrasts in religious points of view. Within these topics there are profoundly different religious perspectives.

Conclusions

The Genesis narrative and the conclusions of science as to the age and origin of the Earth and of life, including that of mankind, belong to two entirely different spheres of human understanding. Genesis, however, has nothing to say about the age and mode of origin of the Earth, and of life. This is a proper subject matter only for geological and other scientific research.

The primitive history of the creation of the Earth, of man, and of other life forms narrated in Genesis is, on the other hand, an anthropomorphic reconstruction encompassed within six working days and one "sabbath" day for rest. Its purpose is not to convince the people of Israel, let alone modern man, that this was how it was actually accomplished. The Israelites were, perhaps, better aware than most of us today that the basic creation story was modeled on the well-known Babylonian myth of creation which the authors of Genesis followed meticulously topic by topic. However, the Genesis story emphasized those religious aspects of creation that distinguished Israel from her pagan neighbors, especially those among whom she lived while in exile in Babylon and in Egypt. The story of creation is a prelude to the story of Adam and Eve's fall and the consequent story of human estrangement from God. All of these are introductory to the patriarchal narratives, and ultimately to the saving acts of Exodus. Therefore, the story of creation is the beginning of salvation history and not a scientific treatment either of the age or origin of the Earth, of life, or of mankind.

It is important to recall that ultimately there can be no irresolvable issues between science and religion, for they both deal with truth, although each is concerned with a different sphere of human activity. We would do a great disservice to religion if we were to interpret the Bible as a scientific presentation rather than as a theological document of Judeo-Christian religious history. We would do a great disservice to science if we were to claim that science can provide answers to questions that lie beyond its purview, such as the human search for religious meaning of life including the relationship between God and mankind.

If we become fearful that scientific research will bring forth results that are opposed to the Bible and theological truth, we thereby forget that God, as the author of all truth, cannot contradict Himself. If, on the other hand, we can rely on the results of science to shed light on the origin and history of the Earth, and of life, we may be sure that these well-documented and well-evaluated scientific results will not truly contradict theological experience. We would do a great disservice both to science and to religion if

we were to hold to dogmas that would constrain God to perform His creation within the space of a few thousand years and in such a fasion that scientists could not find reliable answers to legitimate questions within their
disciplines.

The phenomenon of "creation science" is the potential source of some
of the most dangerous societal, educational, and religious problems of our
age. Where the distinction between religious history and science becomes
confused in the minds of the average citizen, student, or legislator, there
is danger to the quality of education generally, and to that of science,
philosophy, and theology specifically. A nation whose high school and college science is mediocre can hardly hope to be a world leader in science
and engineering research. A nation whose understanding of theology is so
meager that it cannot draw a clear distinction between science and religion
is educationally impoverished. Moreover, the confusion on the part of
religious fundamentalists and politicians, as has been demonstrated in certain parts of the United States, bodes ill not only for the quality of science
education but also for the good name of religion among thinking people.
Many scientists and theologians regard this phenomenon as the tip of the
iceberg of a fundamentalist religious movement, heralding a possibly well-
intentioned but simplistic, anti-intellectual, and potentially dangerous attempted retreat from the complex problems of the twentieth century.

Acknowledgments

I am grateful to both the scientists and theologians who read and commented
on earlier versions of this paper, but the responsibility is mine for any deficiencies in the final manuscript. These reviewers include Stephen G. Brush,
Richard T. Cleary, S.J., James Hennessey, S.J., J. Christopher Hepburn,
William J. Leonard, S.J., James P. McCaffrey, S.J. David C. Roy, Paul Smith,
and Patrick A. Sullivan, S.J. I am indebted to Philip J. King and David
Neiman in a special way for their guidance to certain sources of modern
research in Biblical theology and archaeology. Marylou Coyle drafted the il-
lustrations; Patricia C. Tassia, James P. McCaffrey, S.J., Mary L. Gannon,
and Janet L. Titsworth assisted in the preparation of the manuscript.

Notes

1. Henry M. Morris, *The Remarkable Birth of Planet Earth* (Minneapolis: Dimen-
    sion Books, Bethany Fellowship, 1972), p. iv.
2. Henry M. Morris, *The Genesis Record: A Scientific and Devotional Commentary
    on the Book of Beginnings* (Grand Rapids, Mich.: Baker Book House, 1976), pp.
    42–46.

3. Material in this section is based on Frank Press and Raymond Siever, *Earth* (San Francisco: W. H. Freeman, 1978), p. 40.

4. Henricus Renckens, S.J., *Israel's Concept of the Beginning: The Theology of Genesis 1-3* (Herder and Herder, Milwaukee, Wisc., 1964), p. 37.

5. W. R. Brice, "Bishop Ussher, John Lightfoot, and the Age of Creation," *Journal of Geological Education* 30, no. 1 (1982): 18-19.

6. Press and Siever, *Earth*, pp. 40-41.

7. Ibid., p. 42.

8. Ibid., p. 45.

9. D. L. Eicher, *Geologic Time*, Foundations of Earth Science Series (New York: Prentice-Hall, 1976), p. 138; Press and Siever, *Earth*, p. 46.

10. A. H. Knoll and E. S. Barghoorn, "Archean Microfossils Showing Cell Division from the Swaziland System of South Africa," *Science* 198 (1977): 396-98.

11. A. L. McAlester, *The History of Life*, Foundations of Earth Science Series (New York: Prentice-Hall, 1968), pp. 3-26; Eicher, *Geologic Time*, pp. 139-40; Press and Siever, *Earth*, p. 46.

12. P. M. Kier, "Evolution: A Fact," paper presented at the annual meeting of the American Association for the Advancement of Science, Toronto, January 1981.

13. McAlester, *History of Life*, pp. 3-27.

14. Stephen J. Gould, *Ever Since Darwin* (New York: W. W. Norton, 1977).

15. Ibid., p. 144.

16. Ibid., pp. 141-45.

17. Ibid., pp. 24-33.

18. E. H. Maly, "Introduction to the Pentateuch," in *The Jerome Biblical Commentary*, ed. Raymond E. Brown et al. (New York: Prentice-Hall, 1968).

19. Ibid., pp. 3-4.

20. Bruce Vawter, *On Genesis: A New Reading* (New York: Doubleday, 1977), pp. 15-24.

21. John L. McKenzie, S.J., *Myths and Realities: Studies in Biblical Theology* (The Bruce Publishing Co., Milwaukee, Wisc., 1963), p. 195; David Neiman, "The Polemic Language of the Genesis Cosmology," in *The Heritage of the Early Church: Orientalia Christiana Analecta 195*, David Neiman and Margaret Schatkin, eds. (Rome: Pontifical Institute of Oriental Studies, 1973), p. 47.

22. Alexander Heidel, *The Babylonian Genesis: The Story of Creation* (Chicago: University of Chicago Press, 1951), pp. 82-140.

23. E. H. Maly, "Genesis," in *The Jerome Biblical Commentary*, Raymond E. Brown et al., eds. (New York: Prentice-Hall, 1968), p. 7; Vawter, *On Genesis*, pp. 24-30.

24. McKenzie, *Myths and Realities*, pp. 182-200; T. H. Gaster, *Myth, Legend, and Custom in the Old Testament: A Comparative Study with Chapters from Sir James G. Frazer's "Folklore in the Old Testament"*, vol. 1 (New York: Harper and Row, 1969), pp. xxv-xxvi; Vawter, *On Genesis*, pp. 27, 37-43.

25. Maly, "Genesis," pp. 7-8; Vawter, *On Genesis*, pp. 30-33.

26. Maly, "Genesis," p. 8.

27. Vawter, *On Genesis*, p. 31.

28. Ibid., pp. 30–33.

29. Maly, "Genesis," p. 10.

30. Renckens, *Israel's Concept of the Beginning*, p. 80.

31. McKenzie, *Myths and Realities*, p. 195; David Neiman, "The Polemic Language of the Genesis Cosmology," in *The Heritage of the Early Church*, D. Neiman and M. Schatkin, eds. (Rome, Italy, Orientalia Christiana Analecta 195, 1973), pp. 47–63.

CHAPTER 3

Science, Rationality, and the Creation/Evolution Dispute*

Dorothy Nelkin
Cornell University

Of the many challenges to science in recent years, the effort of the "scientific creationists" to present creation theory as a scientific alternative to evolution theory is perhaps the most remarkable. However, it is remarkable only in the sense that science, perceived as neutral and associated with material progress, has been relatively protected from public scrutiny as compared to other social institutions. The Scopes trial in 1925 was often thought to be the last vestige of the great struggle between religion and science. Subsequently, there have been relatively few attacks on science teaching, so that scientists have assumed that religious beliefs no longer have significant bearing on science or on science education policy.

Clearly things have changed. Defying distinctions between religion and science, today's creationists argue that Genesis presents a viable theory of origins and should be given equal time in biology textbooks. In fact, they claim to be scientists and work out of educational and research centers to document the scientific validity of their beliefs. And, with some success, they use sophisticated organizational and political tools to influence the teaching of science in the public school system.

*Much of the material in this paper has been drawn from Dorothy Nelkin, *The Creation Controversy: Science or Scripture in the Schools* (New York: W. W. Norton, 1982).

In the summer of 1981, only thirteen years after the Supreme Court ruled unconstitutional the last law (in Arkansas) forbidding the teaching of evolution in public schools, the state legislatures of Arkansas and Louisiana approved the teaching of creation theory. Indeed, the creationists appear to be an increasingly effective political force. (In December 1981, the Arkansas law was found to be unconstitutional in a landmark decision by Judge William Overton; see Appendix A and B.)

Scientists often dismiss challenges to science as struggles between the forces of rationality and irrationality, between scientific rationality and religious belief. Such polarization, however, has not helped to resolve the creation/evolution controversy or to stem the growing influence of the creationists on science education. This chapter suggests that the scientists' response is unrealistic in light of the political context of science education and the ideological factors that enter the public acceptance of science. After reviewing creationist demands, I will argue that claims of neutrality and rationality as a basis for accepting the teaching of evolution are less than convincing in the present context of public concern about religious and moral values, and about order and certainty.

The Controversy

The Creationists' Demands

During the 1960s, a group of scientifically trained Fundamentalists began to reevaluate fossil evidence from the perspective of special creation as described in the Biblical record. These "scientific creationists" believe that "all basic types of living things, including man, were made by direct creative act of God during the creation week described in Genesis."[1] Literalists in their interpretation of the Bible, they choose to reinterpret organic evolution according to Biblical authority. The catalog of Christian Heritage College, the home of the most active creationist institute, describes the creationists' doctrinal position:

> We believe in the absolute integrity of Holy Scripture and its plenary verbal inspiration by the Holy Spirit as originally written by men prepared by God for this purpose. The scriptures, both Old and New Testament, are inerrant in relation to any subject with which they deal, and are to be accepted in their natural and intended sense. . . . The creationist account is accepted as factual, historical and perspicuous and is thus fundamental in the understanding of every fact and phenomenon in the created universe.[2]

The creationists are mostly solid, middle-class citizens, and many of their leaders are technically trained people working in high-technology professions in centers of science-based industry. Their broad base of support comes from Fundamentalist sects and from the most conservative wings of the Lutheran,

Baptist, and Seventh Day Adventist churches. Yet the creationists work out of organizations with such names as the Institute for Creation Research, the Creation Research Society, and the Creation Science Research Center.[3] Creationists argue that Genesis is not religious dogma but an alternative scientific hypothesis capable of evaluation by scientific procedures. They present themselves as scientists, engaged in a scholarly debate about the methodological validity of two scientific theories. And typically the active creationists have scientific credentials and sometimes academic appointments in accredited colleges and universities.

The creationists differ from evolutionists in their explanations of the origin of life, the transmission of characteristics, the nature of variation and complexity, and the character of the fossil record. Their world view rejects the theory that animals and plants have descended from a single line of ancestors, evolving over billions of years through random mutation.[4] Creationists cannot accept the idea that natural selection is opportunistic and undirected, that selection pressures act to cause genetic change only because of immediate reproductive advantage. According to creation theory, biological life began only five to six thousand years ago, when all things were created by God's design into permanent basic forms. Subsequent evolution has been a directed and purposeful process. Change would not modify the original design, for nature is static, secure, and predictable, with each species containing its full potential.

Faced with a formidable amount of evidence that supports the theory of evolution, the creationists try to demonstrate that such evidence is biased and incomplete, or that it can be reinterpreted to fit whatever conceptual system is convenient. For example, their theoreticians argue that the fossil record is far from conclusive, failing to provide the transitional forms or linkages between diverse living groups that would suggest evolution from a common ancestor. They deny the evidence from radioisotope dating, arguing that such techniques are based on unproved assumptions about the constant rate of radioactive decay.

Ultimately, when pressed by contradictory evidence, creationists argue that design in nature simply exists because of the will of the Creator. And when criticized for introducing supernatural explanations into science, they contend that evolution is but today's creation myth; that, hardly amenable to testing, it is entirely based on faith; that if one simply accepts a different set of assumptions, creation theory becomes fully as workable and fruitful a scientific hypothesis as evolution.

Creationist Influence

The creationists try to press these ideas on local school boards, state curriculum committees, and state legislatures throughout the country. They have introduced bills proposing the teaching of creationism in biology classes in the legislatures of fifteen states and in many more state textbook commissions. They won their first major success in California in 1969, where, in response to political pressure, the guidelines for a state educational system that serves one million children included a formal recommendation to teach creation theory. The guidelines provoked a deluge of letters, petitions, and resolutions from people representing all sides of the issue, and in December 1972 the state curriculum committee announced that it had found a way to ensure the neutrality of science textbooks. The committee proposed to eliminate all scientific dogmatism, to avoid any discussion of ultimate causes, and to indicate the conditional nature of evolution theory. The state board of education then published a revised science framework that avoided the question of "equal time," only to be challenged again by a creationist lawsuit in 1981.

While a number of local school boards throughout the country have approved the teaching of creation theory as a legitimate alternative to evolution theory, in fact the political and legal effort of the creationists won them few formal victories until after the 1980 presidential election and the unambiguous political ascendance of the Right. In 1981 the state legislatures of Arkansas and Louisiana each voted to approve a "Balanced Treatment for Creation Science and Evolution Science Act." But even where there is no possibility of favorable legislation, creationists attract public support and gain legitimacy by using the courts and engaging scientists in debate. Their actions are organized to gain maximum media attention. Take, for example, the 1981 lawsuit against the State of California for violating the religious beliefs of Fundamentalist Christians. This case was touted as a "rerun of the Scopes Trial," "the trial of the century," a "test of religious freedom." The State Attorney General, preparing for a major challenge, gathered together twenty eminent scientists as expert witnesses to vouch for the validity of evolution theory, but the creationists then reduced the case to an administrative detail concerning the wording of the state guidelines. For them, the event served as a major victory of public relations and helped to legitimatize their cause. Like many other protest movements, creationists have learned to use such tactics as a means to mobilize public support.

There is no doubt these days that creationists have a constituency that is receptive to their social and religious goals. Thus, they have been able to exercise considerable influence on science education in secondary schools even where there is no facilitating legislation or formal set of guidelines. First, textbook publishers, dominated by the economics of potential markets in the large and conservative Sunbelt states, have been quite ready to accommodate creationist pressures by adding qualifications to statements about evolution theory or by avoiding sensitive issues. One publisher proposed replacing a section about Leakey's archaeological discoveries of primitive man with a reproduction of Michelangelo's painting of the creation from the Sistine Chapel. Some textbooks have avoided the word evolution altogether by substituting "change." A new edition of one textbook reduced the discussion of the origin of life from 2023 to 322 words and the Darwinian view of nature from 2750 to 296 words. Another introduced a study of geology with the statement that "present ideas about the Earth's history include many speculations about the meaning of the relatively few facts that have been discovered."[5] For publishers, the economic stakes are high. Competition, especially in the nineteen states with commissions that determine textbook adoptions, is fierce. These states, including Texas (allocating more than $50 million each year for textbooks) have stringent selection procedures and are subject to heavy influence by textbook critics. If a publisher can accommodate and win acceptance, sales are virtually assured.[6]

Second, and perhaps a more important source of influence, is that many teachers are intimidated by disputes and afraid of the growing willingness of parents and local citizen groups to challenge their authority. Some have therefore chosen to avoid the subject in their classroom rather than risk confrontation. (See Chapter 5 for discussion of some cases of this type in Iowa.)

Scientists have been incredulous about the creationists' growing success. That such groups could exert influence on the definitions and boundaries of science as taught in the schools "just does not make sense in this day and age." Incredulity first led to amused disdain. A Stanford biochemist placed the creationists' arguments "in the same arena as those advanced by the Flat Earth Society." Facetious remarks were abundant. It was proposed that the Bible publishers insert a sentence in Genesis to indicate that "scientific method rejects the supernatural approach to explaining the universe." A biologist and member of the California State Advisory Committee inquired if a scientific course on reproduction should mention the stork theory.

As creationists persisted in their efforts to influence textbook selection, the biologists' amusement gave way to defense. They mobilized the most prestigious organizations in the scientific community to document the validity of evolution theory and the mass of evidence that supports evolutionary hypotheses. The National Academy of Sciences, the American Association of University Professors, the American Association for the Advancement of Science, and groups of Nobel laureates have all issued strongly worded resolutions distinguishing science from religion, emphasizing the rationality and neutrality of science and trying to discredit creationist views.

Analysis

When faced with external political pressures, scientists often take refuge in reasserting the neutral character of their work and the irrelevance of political, social, or religious considerations. Scientific societies petitioning against the teaching of creation theory all emphasize the neutral character of science and its distinction from religious or personal beliefs. They appeal to rationality, assuming that others see science from the same perspective as the scientists themselves. However, when they try to transfer their professional expectations about science to the diffusion of scientific knowledge and to their quest for credibility in the public domain, they face frustration. Several factors contribute to the persistence of the creation/evolution controversy and the failure of scientific argument to stem the growing influence of the creationists:

1. The fallacies of arguing scientific neutrality given the political realities of science education.
2. The fallacies of drawing rigid distinctions between scientific rationality and religious belief.
3. The strength of the creationist beliefs in light of the political and ideological ascendancy of the New Right.

Fallacies of Misplaced Neutrality

In their defense of teaching evolution theory, scientists emphasize the apolitical, neutral, and detached nature of science in contrast to the political and religious character of creationism. These arguments have had little influence.

First, arguments based on the neutrality of science fail to address an issue of central concern to creationists, the professional control of public education. Creationists define the debate as a political struggle over the education and values of their children. During the Scopes trial, William Jennings Bryan asked, "What right have the evolutionists—a relatively small percentage of the population—to teach at public expense a so-called scientific interpretation of the Bible, when orthodox Christians are not permitted to teach an orthodox interpretation of the Bible?"[7] Scientists responded with a different view about populist control of science curriculum: "What is to be taught as science would be determined not by a consensus of the best scientific opinion, but by the votes of shopgirls and farmhands, ignorant alike of science and the foundation principles of our civil society."[8]

Similarly, evolutionists today fight the influence of lay opinion. To biologists, one of the more irritating aspects of the controversy is that creationists, claiming to be scientists, ignore the constraints of the scientific community by seeking external political judgments of the validity of their arguments: "The State Board's repudiation of its own committee in favor of a lay opinion from the audience should ultimately become a classic example in textbooks on school administration of how not to proceed with the development of standards."[9] "Why are comments related to science made by high-priced technicians such as medical doctors and by persons in related fields of technology more readily acceptable as statements of science than those made by scientists themselves?"[10] In its testimony to the Louisiana State Legislature on a bill to require the teaching of creation science, the American Association of University Professors strongly argued that members of faculties "should be able to teach what they understand to be the truth in accord with professional standards."[11]

In the 1920s, the scientists' efforts to control the educational agenda had little effect. Publishers, depending on market prospects, continued to ignore evolutionary biology, and as late as 1959 religious views still dominated public school biology teaching. In the current social climate evolutionists may once again lose control over the content of textbooks. Economic factors still prevail, and publishers, more competitive than ever, must avoid controversy to capture the local textbook markets.

Second, arguments based on the neutrality of science are simply not convincing on historical grounds. Invariably, creationists have picked up a mode of analysis long associated with the progressive left, emphasizing (as have many of us) the values inherent in science and technology itself. While they have turned this argument inside out, it is especially salient when the issue is the diffusion of scientific ideas. While scientists may assure relative neutrality in day-to-day laboratory work by relying on impersonal procedures of verification, neutral, apolitical criteria have little meaning in the context of science education. The very origin of the new biology curriculum after 1959 was political—a part of the post-Sputnik effort to modernize science education in order to foster American technological supremacy in the cold war. And while scientists argue that academic integrity must rest on neutrality with respect to values, the congruence between scientific knowledge and values has long been explicit. Just recall the much-discussed remark by philosopher Mario Bunge: "All of nature and all of culture can be made to fall under the domain of science."[12]

This indeed has been an important thrust in the history of science. Nineteenth-century biologists had perceived their studies as a means to prove the existence of God through evidence of design and purpose in nature. In fact, the most active resistance to Darwinian evolution came from scientists themselves. Later scientists described evolution theory as a "naturalist religion" and as "a secure basis for ethics."[13] More recently a tendency to relate scientific knowledge to values is evident in efforts to extend the concepts of biology and ecology to generalizations about man and society.[14] Indeed, scientific knowledge in fields such as ecology, population studies, or socio-biology is expected to have a profound influence on values and behavior.

The difficulty of separating science from its value content is evident in the statements of scientists as they try to repudiate creationism. The scientific discourse in the dispute assumes that peculiar mix of epistemology and values that seems to characterize all debates in which science becomes a vehicle to support competing political claims. Scientists as well as creationists bemoan the moral, political, and legal implications of the alternative ideology and bring their own social concerns to the discussion of science curriculum. The influence of scientific assumptions on religious equality, as well as on educational practice, concerns both groups. Each claims that the other bases its "scientific" beliefs on faith and each group argues with passion for its own dispassionate objectivity. As each side defends its position and criticizes the other, their arguments are strikingly similar. Indeed, the debate often sounds like a battle between two dogmatic groups as the antidogmatic norms of science fade with the effort to convey the validity of a scientific theory. At times in the course of the dispute it becomes difficult to distinguish science from politics and ideology, a fact which only reinforces creationist claims.

Fallacies of Misplaced Rationality

As scientists struggle against the creationists' influence, they emphasize the many facts that contradict the creationists' beliefs. When factual arguments and direct criticism fail to turn the creationists away, scientists respond by emphasizing the rationality of science and the weight of evidence that supports their authority. Their arguments assume a kind of literalism and realism when dealing with religious claims, often ignoring that science itself is approximate and metaphoric. As psychologist Donald Campbell has observed, "Scientists hold up for religious discourse the requirement for a direct realism, a literal veridicality, even though they may recognize that this is impossible for science itself."[15] This literalism on the part of scientists when confronting opposition nearly matches the attitudes of Fundamentalists and hinders both scientific and political communication.

Convinced of the rationality and merit of their methods, scientists are constantly dismayed by the popularity of nonscientific approaches to nature, and by the proliferation of cults, sects, and pop cosmologies based on supernatural explanations of nature.[16] In 1975, hundreds of scientists signed a statement criticizing astrologers. They were puzzled that "so many people are prone to swallow beliefs without sufficient evidence" and concerned that "generations of students are coming out without any idea that you have to have evidence for your beliefs."[17] The persistence of creationism is a reminder that beliefs need no evidence and that people are most reluctant to surrender their personal convictions to a scientific world view.

For those whose personal beliefs are threatened by science, the social and moral implications that can be drawn from a scientific theory and its threats to the idea of absolute ethical values may assume far greater importance than any details of scientific verification. Increased technical information is unlikely to change well-rooted beliefs because selective factors operate to guide the interpretation of evidence, especially when the nature of such evidence is poorly understood. Creationists, as do others, avoid, debunk, or disregard information that would repudiate their preconceptions, preferring to deny evidence rather than to discard their beliefs.[18] A great deal of social reinforcement helps them to maintain their views in the face of repeated frustration. Opposition only augments the strength of their religious convictions and their desire to see these convictions represented in the educational system.

Scientists respond to the demands of creationists by denying the existence of conflict between science and religious values and by insisting that the two are simply separate and independent realms that must remain distinct. Yet, the recurrence of textbook disputes suggests that the treaty between science and religion based on the assumption that they deal with separate domains may be but another convenient yet unrealistic myth. Religion as well as science purports to be a picture of reality, a means through which people render their lives and the world around them intelligible. People seek in their beliefs about nature the values that will guide their behavior. The heart of the religious perspective, argues Clifford Geertz, is "not the theory that beyond the visible world there lies an invisible one; . . . not even the more diffident opinion that there are things in heaven and earth undreamt of in our philosophies. Rather it is the conviction that the values one holds are grounded in an inherent structure of reality."[19] For many people, religion may be more likely than science to provide a satisfactory explanation of reality on which to base their values. Indeed, except for a recent and very brief period following World War II, religion has been the major source of moral initiative and emotional fervor in American society. Today, and not for the first time, the Christian Right has monopolized the "moral vision." With strong public support, they have introduced this vision into the presidency, Congress, and—not surprisingly—into the public schools.

Creationism and the New Right

Scientists supporting evolution theory inevitably fail to convince creationists or those predisposed to share creationist beliefs, for these beliefs are motivated not only by religious but also by political and social goals of increasingly powerful Fundamentalist groups. Creationists today are a part of a religious social movement that has developed in resistance to the secularization brought about by science and that sees science as a threat to the legitimacy of religious explanations of reality.[20] Scientists may find it difficult to believe, but creationist ideas are entirely plausible for many people, for faith in the inerrancy of the Bible is widespread. According to a recent Gallup poll, some 38 percent of the American population believe that "the Bible is the actual word of God and is to be taken literally, word for word."[21] The creationists want to foster this belief as the framework for their moral and political values.

Given the respect for scientific achievements in our society, claims of scientific validity are a means to achieve extra-scientific ends. Creationists present themselves as scientists to gain legitimacy for their beliefs, and, in fact, scientific creationism has become an extraordinary example of the ubiquitous tendency in our society to translate value issues into technical terms. Nevertheless, regardless of their scientific discourse, creationists are explicit about their religious goals: "A revival of solid belief in special creation, especially among young people, could easily spark the greatest movement of true evangelism and Christian conservatism of modern times."[22] These goals are buttressed by social and political values that are powerful in the context of the current extremely conservative trends. Indeed, creationists are addressing a constituency that is receptive to both their religious message and their view of science as a moral and political force.

In the 1920s, creationists opposed the teaching of evolution because of its perceived moral consequences;[23] social problems were attributed to the weakening of the church and to the materialism fed by science. Today, also, creationists' scientific assertions quickly spill over into a mix of moral and political rhetoric characteristic of the New Right. Creationists talk about evolution theory in the same breath as abortion, pornography, sex, socialism, communism, and centralized bureaucratic government. They believe that it is "morally dangerous" to emphasize the genetic similarities between animals and man, that this encourages "animal-like behavior" with disastrous social implications. In the words of the preface to a creationist textbook,

> The theory of evolution is the philosophical foundation for all secular thought today, from education to biology and from psychology through the social sciences. It is the platform from which socialism, communism, humanism, determinism, and one-worldism have been launched. Accepting man as animal, its advocates endorse animalistic behaviour such as free love, situation ethics, drugs, divorce, abortion and a host of other ideas that contribute to man's present futility and despair . . . It has wrought havoc in the home, devastated morals, destroyed man's hope for a better world and contributed to the political enslavement of a billion or more people.[24]

For the creationists, order is a fundamental value; they are distressed by the flux, uncertainty, and doubt inherent in science and basic to the theory of evolution. In contrast, creationism provides a model of order, a distinct and coherent logical system that fully and unequivocally explains an uncertain world. This is a major source of its appeal, not only to the public, but also to some scientists. A biologist at the Institute for Creation Research explains his conversion from evolution theory: "Science can't be trusted but God can . . . . Scientific data is so permanently incomplete that it is hardly a good place to sink an anchor for anything to do with eternity."[25]

The resemblance of these ideas to those of the Moral Majority is obvious, and creationism is in essence an ideological expression of the New

Right. It is an important part of the grass-roots movement against "secular humanism" or "amoral secularism," terms loosely used to describe a secular world view that emphasizes the ability to achieve self-realization through the use of reason and scientific method and that minimizes the importance of a spiritual or moral order as a basis of ethical standards. Convinced that humans are inherently sinful, creationists seek to purify education, cleanse the libraries, introduce religion and moral values into the educational system, and take the schools out of the hands of "the elite group of professional academics and their government friends."[26] Modern biology is an especially vulnerable target for textbook watchers who blame the erosion of religious and moral values on the denial of transcendental purpose.

Creationists have links to various other organizations that are seeking to mobilize religious instincts for political causes. They have been assisted by prominent members of the Moral Majority such as the Reverend Jerry Falwell. The Heritage Foundation, a conservative political group now a policy arm of the Reagan administration, played a significant role in textbook disputes of the early 1970s when the "scientific creationists" first emerged as an influential political force.

The political ascendance of the sunbelt states has given increased political salience to Fundamentalist views, of which creationism is one expression. Those who try to refute these views simply in terms of evidence only help to legitimize the creationists' cause, as the latter are quick to observe:

> We are making considerable impact: I think this is reflected in the alarm that is being felt by evolutionists: . . . they are feeling a necessity to go out and meet our challenge. Articles have appeared in *Science, Nature, Bioscience* and *American Biology*. They are afraid of us and the power of our evidence.[27]

In the end, rationality and neutrality have little to do with public acceptance of science. For most people, it is efficacy more than evidence that guides their beliefs, and faith in science persists only when it satisfies a social need. Well before the creationist dispute, the French biologist Jacques Monod described the relationship between science and the public:

> Science wrote an end to the ancient animist covenant between man and nature, leaving nothing in place of that precious bond but an anxious quest in a frozen universe of solitude. With nothing to recommend it but a certain puritan arrogance, how could such an idea win acceptance? It did not, it still has not. It has, however, commanded recognition; but that is because, solely because, of its prodigious power of performance.[28]

While science has threatened the plausibility of nonrational beliefs, it has not removed the uncertainties that seem to call for such beliefs. Rather, the cognitive obscurity and social isolation of science has left the public dazed, resentful of professional expertise, and therefore receptive to reactionary influence. In today's social context, creationism appears to fill a void. It uses representations that are well adapted to the twentieth century; it claims scientific respectability while arguing that science is as value-laden as other explanations; and it offers intellectual plausibility as well as salvation, and the authority of science as well as the certainty of scripture. It reflects the prevailing political ideology, and its influence is likely to persist.

Notes

1. Brochure published by the Creation Research Society, San Diego, n.d.
2. Christian Heritage College Catalog, San Diego, 1974.
3. For a description of these groups and the history of the debate, see Dorothy Nelkin, *Science Textbook Controversies and the Politics of Equal Time* (Cambridge, Mass.: MIT Press, 1977).
4. Creationists' ideas are disseminated through creationist textbooks such as Duane Gish, *Evolution? The Fossils Say No!* (San Diego: Creation Science Research Center, 1972); John N. Moore and H. Slusher, *Biology: A Search for Order in Complexity* (Grand Rapids: Zondervan Publishers, 1970); Henry Morris et al., *Science and Creation* (San Diego: Creation Science Research Center, 1971). They also appear in creationist periodicals such as *Science and Scripture* and *Acts and Facts.*
5. See report of textbook changes in *Time*, 16 March 1981, pp. 80–81.
6. Robert Dahlin, "A Tough Time for Textbooks," *Publishers Weekly*, 7 August 1981, pp. 28–32.
7. Gail Kennedy, ed., *Evolution and Religion* (New York: Heath, 1957), p. 36.
8. S. J. Holmes, "Report," *Bulletin of the American Association of University Professors* 13 (8 December 1927).
9. William Mayer, "The Nineteenth Century Revisited," *BSCS Newsletter*, November 1972.
10. David Ost, "Statement," *American Biology Teacher* 34 (October 1972): 413–414.
11. American Association of University Professors, testimony to Louisiana State Legislature, 18 May 1981.
12. M. Bunge, *Scientific Research* (New York: Springer, 1967), 32. For a discussion of the value assumptions of scientists, see I. Grabner and W. Reiter, "Guardians at the Frontier of Science," in *Countermovements in the Sciences*, H. Nowotny and H. Rose, eds. (Dordrecht: Reidel, 1979), 67.
13. Julian Huxley, *Evolution in Action* (New York: Harper, 1953) and C. H. Waddington, *The Scientific Attitude* (London: Penguin Books, 1941).
14. See, for example, E. O. Wilson, *Sociobiology: The New Synthesis* (Cambridge: Harvard University Press, 1975). R. M. Young, in "Evolutionary Biology and Ideology: Then and Now," *Science Studies* 1 (1971): 177–206, discusses these tendencies to extend biology.

15. Donald T. Campbell, "On the Conflicts Between Biological and Social Evolution and Between Psychology and Moral Tradition," *American Psychologist* 30 (12 December 1975): 1120.

16. Christopher Evans, in *Cults of Unreason* (New York: Farrar, Straus and Giroux, 1973) discusses some of these cults and their relationship to science. The pop cosmologies of Velikovsky and Von Daniken have had enormous appeal—*The Chariots of the Gods* sold over 20 million copies—especially to people seeking scientific explanations that leave room for supernatural intervention.

17. Statement by Paul Kurtz, editor of *The Humanist*, in justifying the statement by 186 scientists calling astrologers charlatans who have no rational basis for their beliefs. See *The Humanist*, October/November 1975.

18. Leon Festinger, *A Theory of Cognitive Dissonance* (Evanston: Row Peterson, 1957).

19. See discussion in Clifford Geertz, *Islam Observed* (New Haven: Yale University Press, 1968) and *Interpretation of Culture* (New York: Basic Books, 1973).

20. For an extended analysis of the religious motivation of the creationists, see Vernon Lee Bates, "Christian Fundamentalism and the Theory of Evolution: A Study of the Creation Science Movement" (Ph.D. Thesis, University of California, Davis, 1976), Ch. 6.

21. Cited in Dean Fowler, "Biology Texts Under Fire" (Mimeo, Marquette University, 1980).

22. *Acts and Facts*, 20 January 1973.

23. See selection from the Scopes trial in Kennedy, *Evolution and Religion*.

24. Henry Morris, *The Troubled Waters of Evolution* (San Diego: Creation-Life Publishers, 1974), p. 5.

25. Gary Parker, "Evolution, My Religion," *Today's Student* 15 (November 1978).

26. See John Conland, "The MACOS Controversy," *Social Education* 39 (October 1975): 391. The same themes pervaded the MACOS dispute.

27. Bates, "Christian Fundamentalism," p. 174.

28. Jacques Monod, *Chance and Necessity*, (New York: Random House, 1972).

Science versus Revealed Truth: Meeting the Challenge of Creationism in the Classroom

Wayne A. Moyer
People for the American Way

Creationism is like an onion. The outer layer is scientific: Are species fixed or do they evolve? What is a transitional form? How good is the evidence that the universe is ancient? Peel that layer back, and one finds a political layer: Who should determine curricula, state legislatures or professional staff? Who controls the public schools? Peel that layer back and one finds a religious layer: Is the state establishing a religion of secular humanism by default? Is evolution theory science or religion? Is the First Amendment violated when only evolution theory is presented in science classes? Yet this layer, too, can be peeled back to reveal the core question: How do we know what is true?

In this chapter the truth claims of both creationism and science will be examined. Creationism will then be considered as a political force, and the chapter will conclude with some ways in which the challenge of creationism can be met in the classroom.

The Truth Claims of Creationism

Despite all disclaimers, the touchstone of truth for creationists is the Bible. There seems to be no doubt that creationists are first of all Christian Fundamentalists. The Institute for Creation Research (ICR), for example, identifies itself as the research division of Christian Heritage College. Dr. Henry Morris, ICR Director, was co-founder of Christian Heritage College with the Reverend Tim LaHaye, pastor of Scott Memorial Baptist Church and the Reverend Art Paters, associate pastor, in 1970. Earlier, Morris had worked with the Creation Science Research Center (CSRC), which published his textbook series. The CSRC works closely with the Bible Science Association. Moral Majority, Inc., was founded by the Reverends Jerry Falwell and LaHaye, and Falwell has followed LaHaye's lead in developing a strong television outreach and establishing Liberty Baptist College. The doctrinal orientation of all these activities is Christian Fundamentalism.

Fundamentalism had its origin among Protestants at the turn of the century who were alarmed by the liberal theology coming into vogue. Orthodox truth seemed threatened by accommodation to science and higher criticism of the Bible. By 1909, five elements, or fundamentals, of Christian faith had been identified; these are part of the doctrinal statement printed in the Christian Heritage College Bulletin (1977–78) from which the following has been extracted:

- *The absolute integrity of Holy Scripture* and its plenary verbal inspiration, by the Holy Spirit, as originally written through men prepared of God for this purpose.
- *The tri-une God—Father, Son, and Holy Spirit.* There is only one God, who is the source of all being and meaning, who is structured in three persons, each of whom is eternal, omnipotent, personal and perfect in holiness.
- *The pervasive influence of sin and the Curse.* When man first sinned, he brought himself and all his descendants, as well as his entire dominion (the universe), under God's Curse.
- *The redemptive work of Jesus Christ* . . . the great Curse finally reached its climax when the Creator Himself accepted and endured its ultimate and greatest intensity.
- *The imminent return of Christ.* Although the price has been paid, and the victory is assured, the final consummation is to be realized only when Jesus Christ, now in Heaven at the right hand of the Father, returns personally to the earth to destroy all rebellion and to establish the perfect and eternal reign.[1]

This statement of Christian belief opened the fundamentalist-modernist debate which forced Harry Emerson Fosdick out of his pulpit at First Presbyterian Church of New York because he was considered too liberal. In July 1925, the debate climaxed in its first media event: the Scopes trial in Dayton, Tennessee. Radio, just beginning on-the-scene broadcasts, gave daily reports of the trial to listeners throughout the country. Ultimately, fundamentalists withdrew from mainline denominations to form independent churches and affiliations.

Some of this history colors the preface to Henry Morris's book, *The Twilight of Evolution*, written in 1963. He wrote:

> The tale could be told a thousand times, of a Christian church, a school or mission society or some other organizations, founded by men of strong Biblical faith and with an uncompromising witness, slowly but steadily drifting off its foundation and gradually sinking into the sands of modernism and secularism. This tragedy, repeated times without number, almost always begins with a questioning of Biblical creationism.[2]

He went on to present the domino argument: accommodation of any kind leads to loss of faith and a humanistic society.

This unfailing belief in Biblical inerrancy is the key to understanding the zeal of creationism proponents. They are absolutely sure they possess a true and accurate account of cosmic and human origins. In his 1974 book, *Scientific Creationism*, Henry Morris expressed his conviction this way:

> There is not the slightest possibility that the facts of science can contradict the Bible, and, therefore, there is no need to fear that truly scientific comparisons of any aspect of the two models of origin (creation and evolution) can ever yield a verdict in favor of evolution.[3]

What, then, is this model of creation which Morris and others would like to see become part of the curricula in astronomy, chemistry, geology, biology, and social studies? Briefly stated, it is the belief that the universe, earth, energy, and life were created suddenly, from nothing, in a fully functioning form about 10,000 years ago. Sometime later there was a cataclysmic world-wide flood that destroyed virtually all life and created the earth's geology as we know it today. By implication, modern life forms, including humans, are descendants of survivors aboard one large boat. A corollary is that all plant and animal forms were created once and at the same time. Neo-creationists have added the concept of "horizontal variation" within the genetic potential of original kinds. Perhaps original kinds, according to Morris, are equivalent to the taxonomic level of family.

These points should make it clear that the creationist claim to truth is based entirely on revealed knowledge. The Overton decision in the Arkansas trial makes this point very clear (see Appendix B).

The Truth Claims of Science

What about science and its truth claims? Science is a human endeavor to draw blueprints of the universe. Each generation adds new sections, tinkers with older sections, and thinks about what to work on next. Science is thus characterized by gradual change, a sense of continuity with the past and future, and awareness of what is not known in addition to what is known. But how do we know that these blueprints of the universe are indeed true? We compare them with the real world through patient observation, using only our five senses or extensions of our senses through instrumentation. Inaccurate versions are eliminated, leaving a collection of statements accepted as true only because they work.

Consider the old problem of fixity of species—the result of one-time creation—versus changing species, or evolution, the result, perhaps, of natural selection. While we cannot go back in time to observe the original actors, we can examine casts of their skeletons and bodies in sedimentary rocks. If species are fixed, we should find the same species, closely related to modern forms, represented in sedimentary rock of all ages. Above all, we should not find species or even entire taxonomic families appearing only in younger rocks. But if species evolve we should find a discontinuous fossil record. Modern forms should appear only in younger rocks, and species should come and go in the geologic column. Many observations over many years confirm the prediction derived from the hypothesis of changing species and falsify the prediction from fixed species. Note that both hypotheses are falsifiable, but only the hypothesis of fixed species is falsified. (See Chapter 10 for a discussion of falsifiability.)

In science, if a blueprint or explanation works when compared with the real world, it is accepted as tentatively true and will be so held until someone makes an observation proving it false. Thus scientists approach truth admitting freely that absolute truth and complete, positive proof are impossible. The creationist blueprint, however, requires no comparison with observed reality because Scripture is assumed to be the ultimate source of all truth. Under this assumption falsification is impossible.

Fundamentalist Christians clearly reject all belief systems that challenge their elements of faith—not only science but all ethics and theology that are not Bible-centered. In the black-and-white world of Fundamentalists, creationism represents God-centered Christian morality, while evolution represents atheistic human-centered morality. Duane Gish, in his initial presentation during the Doolittle-Gish Debate held in Lynchburg in October 1981, characterized evolution as "a mechanistic, atheistic theory, . . . a basic dogma of agnosticism, humanism, and atheism in general."[4] Just moments before, Jerry Falwell had introduced the debate with this statement: "Anyone who knows about me is aware of my belief that the issue of special creation versus evolution is the foundational premise for all truth." Fundamentalists thus propose a dichotomy—either revealed truth *or* empirical truth—rather than modern acceptance of both revealed truth and empirical truth, each within its own realm.

Teaching both "models" sounds like fair play, letting the students make up their own minds about special creation versus evolution. It also challenges the elitism of science: everyone can look at a fossil footprint and decide who or what made it. (There is a strong populist element in Fundamentalism, just as there was in 1925 when William Jennings Bryan, the Great Commoner, represented the State of Tennessee in the Scopes trial.) Special creation looks simple—an idea whose time is come, an idea long suppressed by established science. It offers *certainty* over the changing uncertainty of science. But most of all, it is a symbol for the deep concerns people have about their children: fear that the good life is about over; that society has become self-indulgent and immoral; that science is going too far, forcing wrenching decisions on people unprepared to make them.

Creationism as a Political Force

Creationism is a grass-roots political movement. It aims to install Bible-centered education in the schools. If ever given the force of law, creationism would eventually dominate the curriculum of every subject to which it could lay claim. Consider the laws passed in Arkansas and Louisiana: in both cases the state was placed in the position of defining truth in science without reference to observed reality. A private voluntary association like a church, or the Institute for Creation Research, may certainly make such a truth claim, but it is an entirely different matter when the state does it. As Galileo, Joseph Priestley, and Andrei Sakharov remind us, the price of opposing the state version of truth can be very high.

The pressure exerted by creationists to achieve their goals through political means shows no signs of abating, but the emphasis is shifting from enactment of balanced treatment laws to quiet implementation of administrative rules. In 1974, for example, the Texas State Board of Education, acting in response to a complaint by Mel and Norma Gabler, wrote an anti-evolution textbook content rule that has markedly changed the treatment of evolution in science textbooks used throughout the nation. The operative paragraph of the rule reads: "Textbooks that treat the theory of evolution shall identify it as only one of several explanations of the origins of humankind and avoid limiting young people in their search for meanings of their human existence." An additional paragraph requires publishers to print a caveat at the beginning of their books stating that any materials on evolution is presented as theory rather than fact. This rule is given enormous leverage by the size of the Texas textbook market, the selection process which narrows the field of adopted books in any subject to just five, and the power of the Board of Education to require rewriting of textbooks to accommodate specific objections under threat of removal from the adoption list. Publishers cannot afford to produce a Texas-only edition and end up offering the made-for-Texas edition throughout the country. The result has been reduction of coverage— both in quality and number of words—of the topic of evolution, as has been documented by Gerald Skoog of Texas Tech University. (The Texas State

Board of Education repealed the anti-evolution rule in April, 1984, in response
to the Texas Attorney General's opinion that the rule was unconstitutional
and threat of litigation.)

The potential of television will continue to be exploited by creationism
proponents to achieve their goals. Creationism is tailor-made for the "news
as entertainment" television producers: it combines morality, an aura of David
attacking the Goliath of big science, and the possibility of outrageous
statements on both sides. There will undoubtedly continue to be pressure on
boards of education to adopt equal-time policies, either by issuing directives
to teach both, or by giving permission to do so. The Watchtower Society of
Johovah's Witnesses, for example, distributed the September 1981 issue of
Awake magazine to school board members in many areas. Printed across an
appealing picture of a small child in hat and bathing suit looking at a star
fish are the words: "Accidents of evolution? Or Acts of Creation?" In the spring
of 1981, San Jose school board candidates were screened by FAMPAC, a "pro-
family political committee working through candidates for positive Biblical
solutions to today's problems." Candidates were asked to respond to such questions as "Would you favor permitting the teaching of creation in the science
classroom?" and "Would you permit voluntary prayer on school grounds?"
Ultimately, three candidates received endorsement.

Also in California, "Christian monitors" of science texts and teachers
ensure that nothing is being taught that is offensive to Christian children.
This is an activity of the Christian Creed Committee, with funding provided
by Christian Voice, a neo-conservative lobby. Education kits, films on creationism, and instruction pieces on how to spot "violations" are being produced, as are radio and television ads on the Christian religious network to
present their version of the ruling in *Segraves* vs. *State of California*.[6] Parents
are being urged to initiate suits against teachers and boards that fail to comply.

Meeting the Challenge

Those opposing the teaching of a specific religious creed in the public schools
are meeting the challenge of the creationists in a variety of ways. At the school
district level, spontaneous coalitions of scientists, religious leaders, teachers,
and parents have stopped creationist initiatives. In Livermore, California, for
example, a group headed by a Presbyterian minister and a parent convinced
the local school board that the creationist textbooks purchased from Creation Life Press and used in a sixth-grade science class were religious in nature,
in violation of board policy on text selection. The texts were withdrawn and
evolution as a science unit was moved to the senior high school level.

In Lexington, Kentucky, a group headed by a rabbi and an an-
thropologist, Eugenie Scott, and a physicist, Jeff Weil (both of the University
of Kentucky), developed a well-researched response to a sixty-page curriculum

proposal from a creationist group supported by Henry Morris, who came to Lexington to conduct lectures on the subject. The school board subsequently voted three to two against providing science instruction in creation.

The Lexington group is one of over forty Committees of Correspondence formed throughout the country to provide a voice for integrity in science teaching. The committees are not an organization, but a network of autonomous groups united by telephone and the mails. Stanley Weinberg (see Chapter 5) answers inquiries and places people in touch with other people. It is a small operation but extremely effective.

At the national level, another network helps organizations in the areas of science, education, religion, and civil rights respond to the challenge posed by the fundamentalist right. The hub is People For the American Way, a First Amendment rights association founded by Norman Lear and others in 1980. Among their activities, this group:

- Maintains a Texas office to monitor the Texas textbook adoption process and seek its improvement
- Has published a "Consumer's Guide to Biology Textbooks, 1985" critically reviewing 18 high school biology textbooks
- Works with other associations to support the freedom to learn.

The National Association of Biology Teachers continues its life-long support of unfettered teaching of evolutionary theory through the J. T. Scopes Fund For Freedom. Originally established to support litigation challenging laws mandating equal time for creationism—Biblical or otherwise—the fund is also available to support individual teachers or science departments whose freedom to teach is threatened.[9]

Two periodicals also deal with the challenge:

- *Creation/Evolution* is a quarterly journal "that answers the arguments raised by creationists"[10]
- *Scientific Integrity* is a bimonthly newsletter reporting on activities around the country dealing with creationism and providing access to court findings, opinions, and so forth.[11]

Ultimately, however, creationism must be dealt with in the classroom, and it can be dealt with effectively by sensitive, informed teachers. Indeed, John Horn, a California biology teacher, received commendation from the presiding judge in *Segraves* vs. *State of California* for Horn's professional approach in handling the concerns of Fundamentalist Christian children. Teachers across the country are quietly addressing the problem by taking the following approach:

1. Science is carefully defined. It can tell us *how* the universe works but not *why*.

2. Scientific knowledge is stressed as a blueprint of reality, *not reality itself*. Not just the blueprints, but *how* they were drawn, are taught.
3. Critical thinking is encouraged by repeatedly asking, "But how do we know this is true?" (See, for example, Chapter 10.)
4. Students' understanding, but *not* belief, in evolution theory is required. Evolution is understood as a statement within the realm of science, and belief is not required to answer test questions.
5. When creationism is offered by students as an explanation, it is accepted as a statement in the realm of revealed knowedge, but as an inappropriate explanation in the empirical realm.
6. Students are encouraged to think about the moral decisions implied by scientific knowledge, and to seek help from their parents and clergy. Good teachers accept that it is not enough to teach science in the abstract; they know they *must* encourage students to develop a moral center from which they can make worthy decisions.
7. Finally, teachers remind students and parents—and board members and legislators—that there is nothing about science, or evolution theory, which precludes a deep and abiding belief in a creator God. Science practice and religious belief are compatible. (See also Chapters 2, 6, 9, and 11.)

Science can meet the challenge of creationism, but the goal should not be its defeat. Rather, science must understand the underlying message of concern of parents for their children in modern society and its response should be based on that understanding.

Notes

1. *General Catalog of Christian Heritage College, 1977–78*, pp. 17–20. Available from Christian Heritage College, 2100 Greenfield Drive, El Cajon, CA 92021.
2. H. M. Morris, *The Twilight of Evolution* (Grand Rapids, Mich.: Baker Book House, 1963), Preface.
3. H. M. Morris, *Scientific Creationism* (San Diego: Creation-Life Publishers, 1974), p. 15.
4. Transcript of a debate between Russell Doolittle and Duane Gish held on 13 October 1981, available on request from Jerry Falwell, Lynchburg, VA 24514.
5. G. Skoog, "The Coverage of Evolution in High School Biology Textbooks Published in the 1980s," *Science Education* 68, no. 2 (1984): 117.
6. On 6 March 1981, Judge Irving Perluss ruled that the remedy Segraves sought—right to free exercise of his religious beliefs—was already con-

tained in existing board of education policy. He therefore ruled that this policy should be disseminated to all publishers, institutions, schools, and persons regularly receiving the Science Framework for California Public Schools. The policy reads (Science Framework Addendum, 1984, p. 106):

That, . . . on the subject of discussing origins of life and earth in public schools:
1. Dogmatism be changed to conditional statements where speculation is offered as explanation for origins.
2. Science should emphasize "how" and not "ultimate cause" for origins.

7. The Committees of Correspondence are a project of the National Center for Science Education, Inc., Jack Friedman, President, Syosset High School, Syosset, NY 11791.

8. The guide is available from People For the American Way, 1424 16th Street, N.W., Suite 601, Washington, DC 20036, $5.00, postpaid.

9. Inquiries about the J. T. Scopes Fund for Freedom should be directed to Ms. Patricia McWethy, Executive Director, The National Association of Biology Teachers, 11250 Roger Bacon Drive, #19, Reston, VA 22090.

10. *Creation/Evolution* is edited by Fred Edwords and is available from Box 5, Amherst Branch, Buffalo, NY 14266.

11. *Scientific Integrity* is published by the National Association of Biology Teachers at the address above (see note 9).

CHAPTER 5

Creationism in Iowa:
Two Defense Strategies

Stanley L. Weinberg
Textbook Author

The creation/evolution controversy has been with us for a long time—some 200 years according to Darlington[1]—and it gives promise of being with us for a long time to come. In the United States during the twentieth century, there have been two long episodes of acute controversy. The first began in 1919 when the World Christian Fundamentals Association and several allied evangelistic organizations undertook to drive evolution out of the schools and to replace it with the Genesis story.[2] Among the groups involved in this campaign were the Supreme Kingdom, an offshoot of the Ku Klux Klan, and the Research Science Bureau, somewhat similar to today's Creation Research Society. The Research Science Bureau undertook to mount an expedition to Africa to do parallel dissections of a human and a gorilla, thereby gathering evidence to show that man and the great apes could not possibly be related. Unfortunately, this interesting enterprise never came to fruition. Also involved were the Bible Crusaders of America, the Defenders of the Christian Faith, and other frankly religious and fundamentalist groups, all committed to getting the Bible into public school science classes and getting evolution out.

Promoted by the congeries of fundamentalist zealots, the anti-evolution campaign spread across the country, lasting about forty years in one form or another, and arousing the bemused interest of other countries around the globe. The creationist drive climaxed early, with the Scopes case in 1925,[3] and although the "monkey trial" itself was inconclusive, the case, and the fundamentalist campaign as a whole, had three substantial consequences. First, in the 1920s there were forty-five creationist initiatives in state legislatures, resulting in the passage of six anti-evolution bills.[4] Overriding the apparently meager legislative results was a second and more serious consequence: the effect on teachers, schools, and school boards. In large numbers they hastily dropped evolution from their curricula. In one of the few studies undertaken of this subject, Oscar Riddle found in 1936 that half of the high schools in the nation did not teach evolution—although, of course, the other half did teach it to some degree.[5]

The third consequence of the fundamentalist-creationist drive was the effect on textbooks. As a dramatic example of this effect, in 1925 John Scopes's high school in Dayton, Tennessee, used George W. Hunter's *Civic Biology*, which had five and a half pages of frank discussion of evolution.[6] In 1926, immediately after the Scopes trial, the publishers, American Book Company, brought out a new edition under the name *New Civic Biology*.[7] It had one and a half pages on the topic, and the word "evolution" was replaced by the euphemism "development of plants and animals." The American Book Company was not alone. Publishers generally were intimidated by creationist pressures, and for many years after 1925 the leading high school biology texts either treated evolution briefly, obscurely, and hesitantly, or did not treat the topic at all.[8]

There was an interlude in the 1960s when the Biological Sciences Curriculum Study (BSCS) briefly changed the picture. The BSCS books were thoroughly evolutionary and very successful, and most commercial publishers followed their lead. Thus, for some ten years there was no widely used biology textbook in the United States that did not have a respectable treatment of evolution. But those halcyon days have ended and we are drifting back to the conditions of the 1930s. Now textbooks are coming out that deal briefly or not at all with evolution. Some secondary schools are avoiding trouble by cutting back on the topic. One county school superintendent in Georgia, for example, reports that one-half of one period of one day is devoted to evolution.[9] Scopes's old high school in Dayton stopped teaching evolution when he left, and reportedly the school does not teach it today.[10]

The period of creationist success was brought to an end in the late 1960s by a series of lawsuits, of which *Epperson* vs. *Arkansas* was the leading case.[11] The final decision in this case, handed down by the United States Supreme Court in 1968, declared the Arkansas anti-evolution law unconstitutional. The three remaining state anti-evolution laws—in Arkansas, Mississippi, and Tennessee—were wiped off the books, and there is now no law anywhere in the country that forbids the teaching of evolution.

The Emergence of "Creation Science"

The Epperson decision diverted but did not inhibit the progress of creationism. The creationists regrouped and invented "creation science." This "science"—

so called when convenient, as in pressing for legislation; otherwise generally termed a "model"—is held to be equivalent and alternative to evolution. It is said to be no less scientific than evolution, and no more religious.[12] Both the scientific community and the courts have uniformly rejected the creationists' "creation model, equal time" thesis. Thus in the case of *McLean* vs. *Arkansas Board of Education*, in which the recent Arkansas "equal time" law was challenged, the law was ruled unconstitutional. The presiding judge characterized creationism as religious doctrine, not science, and therefore not appropriate for public school science classes.[13] The courts have held similarly in several other cases.[14]

Despite these legal setbacks, the creationist drive to influence teachers, schools, and school boards continues unabated. To win their battles the creationists do not need legislative successes or favorable court decisions. These can be helpful, and they provide good publicity, but they are almost irrelevant to the decisive confrontations in the arena of public opinion in local communities. And public opinion is the basis of political control as well as of informal community pressure.

Creationism in Iowa

For reasons that are obscure, Iowa has been a major target of the current creationist drive.[15] In six years, nine creationist bills have been introduced in the Iowa legislature. None has passed, but Iowa's pro-evolutionists do not regard these legislative successes as decisive, any more than were the Epperson or McLean decisions.

It is instructive to see how simple and effective community pressure can be. In one school district, for example, the president of the school board calls in each new biology teacher and says something to this effect: "You have every right to teach evolution if you wish—but not in this district if you want to keep your job." The last teacher who was told this immediately started looking for another job and left at the end of the year. The present teacher, who was told the same thing, still works in the district, unhappily not teaching evolution.[16] In how many hundreds of school districts across the nation do similar situations prevail?

Another example: In March 1981, *Time* magazine ran an article on the creation/evolution situation. In researching the article, Time's Chicago correspondent, Madeleine Nash, approached Iowa pro-evolutionists because the controversy in Iowa had been receiving considerable national attention. She wanted to interview a teacher who was forbidden to teach evolution. Two Iowa science consultants, Jack A. Gerlovich, a science consultant for the Iowa Department of Public Instruction, and George Magrane, consultant for the Area Educational Agency 15 of Iowa, sounded out several biology teachers known to them to be in this position. None would consent to be interviewed. Further, none would even talk off the record with the *Time* researcher, for

in a small town there is no such thing as "off the record." Nash took her in-
quiry to Minnesota, where she met much the same response. In the end the
Time article, instead of quoting some harried classroom teacher, quoted
Magrane, who said:

> Teachers in Iowa are being intimidated by the controversy. Rather than teach
> both creationism and evolution, they teach neither one. It's almost a regres-
> sion in history.[17]

Creationist and Evolutionist Strategies

Why are the creationists' drives so successful, especially compared to the
hapless defenses often mounted by the scientific community and its supporters?
I think the answer lies in the nature of the controversy and in the differing
approaches to it by the opposing groups. The creation/evolution controversy
is neither a scientific nor a religious dispute. It is essentially a political battle
over public policy, with each side striving to gain the support of public opinion. In the American federal system, with its great number of autonomous
local jurisdictions, a state or national political campaign is a summation of
many local campaigns. Every political organization, every effective special
interest group, knows this truism and acts on it. In Iowa, the 1976 presidential campaign provided a vivid demonstration of this fact of political life as
one aspirant metamorphosed, in hundreds of Iowa farmhouses, motels, and
courthouse squares, from "Jimmy Who" into the eventual "President Jimmy
Carter."

The creationists understand the nature of American politics and
capitalize on it. They use the standard tactics of our public life. They hold
meetings at the local level. They distribute literature—profusely. They write
letters to the papers and call in to radio talk shows. They buy radio and television time. They buttonhole people. They lobby legislators and school board
members. And these tactics pay off.

Scientists have been less successful in their defense of evolution and in
their opposition to creationism. Certainly the scientific community has been
aware of the controversy for a long time, but the response has typically taken
the form of discussions at meetings of national scientific societies, strongly
worded resolutions by these same societies, and correspondence in *Science*
and other journals. More active involvement has generally consisted of lobbying state legislatures when creationist bills have been under active consideration or participating in lawsuits that challenged creationism. Such activities
are helpful and necessary; they define the position of the scientific community
and alert individuals to the problem; but they are not sufficient.[18]

Creationists can achieve their objectives without passing legislation or
winning lawsuits. Such successes are helpful and make good propaganda, but

of far greater importance are the creationists' persuasiveness in winning over local public opinion and the zeal with which they throw themselves into this work. Scientists, on the other hand, have been naive in seeing the national stage as the only important one and ignoring the grass roots. Also, for a variety of reasons, scientists have been reluctant to get personally involved: they have failed to take creationism seriously, treating it as an absurd joke; or they have been wary of getting into politics and have felt inept and threatened in this area; they have resented taking time from their professional work; or quite simply, they just haven't wanted to be bothered.

There are in excess of a million and a half scientists in this country, 400,000 of whom are life scientists of one kind or another, and another 80,000 of whom are earth scientists.[19] Through scores of resolutions passed by their learned societies, scientists in these disciplines have demonstrated their overwhelming acceptance of evolution. Creationists with comparable professional credentials appear to number approximately 700.[20] This tiny band carries the weight that it does because it is an activist group. If at every school board hearing, curriculum meeting, or textbook adoption proceeding with creationists present, an equal number of pro-evolution scientists were also in attendance, the creationists would not routinely carry the day as they now so often do.

Slowly, in the past several years, scientists and other pro-evolutionists have begun to learn this lesson. What has activated them? Perhaps it is the creationists' increasing visibility and aggressiveness, and their obvious successes. Or the critical factor may be the progression of major creationist targets from public schools to universities, research laboratories, museums, and scientific insitutitions in general. Particularly startling to scientists has been the lobbying in Congress for the proposed Dannemeyer bill, which calls for equal federal funding for "evolution science" and "creation science." In any event, there has been a growing activist reaction to creationism from the scientific community. The actions of Iowa scientists epitomize this development.

The Iowa Academy of Science Panel on Controversial Issues

Iowa scientists were not content with their series of legislative successes. To penetrate the creationists' solid position, creationism had to be countered at the grass roots, and two mechanisms were developed for doing this. One was a committee of the Iowa Academy of Science (IAS) called the Panel on Controversial Issues.[21] The panel consisted of about thirty-five scientists and science teachers who made their services available to help local communities resolve controversial issues arising in science teaching. The panel's membership was shared largely with a second evolution defense group, the Committee of Correspondence (C/C), a part of a nationwide network of pro-evolution groups.[22]

Members of the Panel on Controversial Issues were prepared to deal with a variety of issues, although their major attention was given to creation/evolution. To a community in difficulty, they presented, in a temperate way, the sense of the scientific community on the issue in question. Panelists came to a community or school district only on invitation. They did not seek confrontations; rather, they aimed to resolve them. When a situation became adversarial, panelists stepped out of the picture and left the matter to some other agency, such as the American Civil Liberties Union, one of the national science teacher associations, or the Committee of Correspondence.

In one instance, the panel learned that a creationist group in one of the state's area education districts was arranging an appearance by Richard Bliss, director of curriculum development for the Institute for Creation Research. Bliss's sponsors asked the district administration to cosponsor the meeting and to invite the area teachers to attend. The district science consultant planned to have Bliss address one meeting, then to have a second meeting at which pro-evolutionists would present their point of view. Bliss was not happy with this arrangement; he wanted a debate or direct confrontation with the evolutionists. Panelists reminded the consultant that Iowa's Department of Public Instruction (DPI) and the Academy of Science had both taken the position that evolution was legitimate science while creationism was not.[23] The panel would be glad to send a team of scientists to the district to explain the sense of the scientific community, but they would not debate creationists. Thereupon, the consultant decided to call off the whole thing and not sponsor any meetings at all. There was no publicity in this affair, no dispute, no massing of public opinion, just quiet discussion.

As another example, in a second Iowa town a creationist activist was demanding introduction of creationism into the school curriculum and censorship of books in the school libraries. The issues, which were dividing the town, received considerable publicity.[24] A few of the citizens opposed to creationism and censorship organized a public meeting at which the panel and several other pro-evolution groups were represented. The highlight of the meeting was a long question and discussion period, after which a vote was taken. Of 125 people in attendance at the meeting, approximately 80 voted against censorship and for evolution. They were astonished by their unity and their numbers. The meeting and the vote served as a kind of catharsis, and the issues and the divisions within the community evaporated. The lesson here is that scientists and other rationalists have great potential strength in American society, but only if they organize themselves—as creationists have been doing for years.

I noted above that the panel entered a community or school district only upon invitation; however, some of its early invitations came about indirectly. After the defeat of one creationist legislative bill, the sponsor, State Senator John Jensen of District 19, sent a letter to all school districts in the state asking them to teach creationism. School officials were puzzled by this document. Since the letter was written on Senate letterhead, although on Senator

Jensen's sole initiative, what authority did it carry? What must the schools do about the request? They addressed inquiries to the Department of Public Instruction, which responded by referring to its position paper opposing the teaching of creationism.[25] The panel took this correspondence as an invitation to offer its advisory services to the various school districts.

Activities of the panel described here were "easy" cases. The more difficult cases involve teachers—like those, for example, who were unwilling to talk to *Time*'s Madeleine Nash—who are inhibited by community pressure from teaching evolution and who are afraid to complain about their situations. The panel had little success in reaching these individuals directly. It was thought that in time, as word got around the state that the panel could resolve confrontations without causing convulsions in the community or getting teachers fired, apprehensive teachers might stand forth and reveal their predicaments publicly.

Committees of Correspondence

The Iowa Committee of Correspondence is part of a nationwide communications network among pro-evolution groups. The name is evocative of the Committees of Correspondence that functioned in the thirteen colonies at the time of the American Revolution. The first two C/Cs were organized in October 1980 in Iowa and in New York. (Chapters 8 and 9 also briefly discuss the rationale and development of the committees.) By 1985, the network had grown to fifty-seven committees in forty-eight states, the District of Columbia, and five Canadian provinces. Each state committee is independent and autonomous, yet in contact with other C/Cs. Committees in South Carolina, Georgia, California, Minnesota, Kentucky, and Alabama antedate the formation of the network but have affiliated with it, and several still retain their original names—for example, the Citizens' Curriculum Coalition of South Carolina.

Committee members are primarily scientists, but teachers, engineers, clergy, other professionals, parents, and others also belong. Like the creationists, the C/Cs use essentially the same public education and civil action tactics that have proven effective for various special-interest groups. The C/Cs have had a considerable measure of success—quiet successes, in the main, rather than spectacular cases. They have helped keep creationism out of the school systems, and evolution in, for example, in Scarsdale, New York; Medford, Oregon; Radnor, Pennsylvania; Clear Lake and Atlantic, Iowa; Huntsville, Alabama; West Bend, Wisconsin; Glen Rock, Wyoming; Lexington, Kentucky; Dodge City, Kansas; and Livermore, California. They have defended the status of evolution in a museum in Milwaukee and a zoo in Providence. And they have supplied information that helped defeat creationist bills in some twenty cities.

The relationships of the C/Cs with each other and with other organizations are flexible and informal. They cooperate with such groups as the National Academy of Sciences, the American Association for the Advancement of Science, the National Science Teachers Association, the National Association of Biology Teachers, the American Civil Liberties Union, the American Humanist Association, the state academies of science, and the like. The C/Cs do not duplicate or compete with these or other pro-evolution societies of national scope; rather they supplement at state and local levels functions that the more visible groups carry out at the national level. Thus, the American Association of Physical Anthropologists has urged all its members to join their state C/Cs as a way to give their pro-evolution concerns a practical turn, and many anthropologists have responded. The C/Cs have no magic formula, but they do offer a realistic medium through which scientists, and nonscientists who have a regard for scientific rationalism, can become involved.

It is the thesis of this chapter that direct personal involvement at the local level is the key to a successful response to the threat of creationism. The Iowa C/C had a cooperative arrangement with two state-level groups—the Iowa Academy of Science and the Department of Public Instruction—to monitor and respond to creationist initiatives. Still other agencies—the Iowa Freedom Foundation, the Iowa State Education Association, the Iowa Library Association, the Iowa Civil Liberties Union, and church groups and committees of clergy—were also in contact with the three originating groups. In addition, the Department of Public Instruction distributes information concerning the cooperative arrangement to all teachers in the state.[26] Iowa had perhaps a unique arrangement in which substantially all pro-evolution groups in the state were in touch with each other as well as with all teachers in the state's school system.

Addendum I: 1985

In the three years since this chapter was written, significant changes have affected the evolution-creation faceoff. In July 1981, in a closing legislative session, a "balanced treatment" bill similar to the unconstitutional Arkansas statute (see Appendixes A and B) slipped through the Louisiana legislature and was signed by the governor. The State Education Department refused to obey the new law on the ground that curricular decisions were the prerogative of the Board of Elementary and Secondary Education, not of the legislature.

The impasse led to three years of litigation in federal and state courts, which was resolved—at least temporarily—in January, 1985, when Federal Judge Adrian Duplantier handed down a summary judgment.[27] The court held that the "balanced treatment" statute was unconstitutional in that it fostered a religious intrusion into the public schools—essentially the same holding as Judge Overton's in the Arkansas McLean case. Judge Duplantier further held that the basis for the judgment was so clear that it did not justify wasting public money on a prolonged trial. Attorney General William J. Guste, Jr., has said he will appeal; whether he actually does so is in some doubt.

Guste, a New Orleans Catholic, is up for reelection. His southern Louisiana constituents, who tend to be liberal on the creation-evolution question, generally seem to accept the Duplantier ruling. But Guste also needs support in the more conservative, fundamentalist, northern part of the state; and he is pressed by both sides on the creation-evolution issue. Creationists, of course, want him to do everything possible to overturn the court's decision. Pro-evolutionists are using the "money" argument to dissuade him. The argument is made more forceful by Judge Overton's ruling in Arkansas that the state not only had to pay its own costs, but also had to reimburse the winning plaintiff, ACLU, for trial expenses. The Duplantier decision intimated that should the suit be pressed, the Arkansas precedent might well be followed. At this writing Guste is on the horns of a dilemma, and it remains to be seen how he gets off. Political considerations of this kind are a normal part of many creation-evolution disputes.

Another test of strength developed in Texas in 1983. This wealthy commonwealth replaces all public school textbooks at state expense every five or six years. The practice makes Texas the most lucrative textbook market in the nation, with an annual expenditure of about $60 million. Consequently, all textbook publishers vie for Texas adoptions and Texas business. Books are edited specifically to meet Texas requirements, and these become the books that are offered to all the nation's schools. Unfortunately, the state's textbook standards have been in some degree troglodytic. For example, there have been severe limitations on the teaching of evolution. Thus, it was required that

> Textbooks that treat the theory of evolution shall identify it as only one of several explanations of the origin of humankind. . . . Textbooks . . . which treat the subject of evolution substantively . . . shall be edited . . . to clarify that the treatment is theoretical rather than factually verifiable. Furthermore, each textbook must carry a statement on an introductory page that any material on evolution included in the book is clearly presented as theory rather than fact.[28] (This last clause is sometimes called the "Texas stamp.")

Elaborate adoption procedures further limited the possibility of acquiring high-quality science textbooks. Thus, any Texas citizen could protest, in writing and through personal appearance, any title offered for adoption. The protesters—more often than not, devoted Fundamentalists and creationists— were given ample time to voice their objections; Mel and Norma Gabler, the nation's leading textbook censors, often took hours to present their long lists of objections. Until 1983, only a book's publisher could respond to protests against it; nobody else could speak in defense of the book.[29]

In 1982 a comparatively new national organization, People for the

American Way (PFAW), initiated a cooperative project to modify the restrictive and obscurantist Texas textbook adoption procedures. PFAW organized a coalition of which the Texas Committee of Correspondence was a member; it held conferences, called for and made presentations at State Board of Education hearings, and generated extensive publicity within Texas and throughout the nation.[30] The coalition's campaign was surprisingly successful.

The 1984 textbook hearings were more open, and fairer, than hearings had been in the past. All speakers were given equal time; the Gablers were no longer able to dominate the proceedings. The long-standing anti-evolution rule and the "Texas stamp" rule were rescinded. All biology textbooks accepted in the 1984 statewide adoption process contained adequate treatments of evolution. Creationist protests against these measures were listened to politely—and ignored. The Commissioner of Education and the Chairman of the State Board of Education resigned. The rest of the board was replaced, and the new board proved to be much less high-handed than its predecessor, more forthcoming, and more responsive to professional recommendations.[31] Clearly, the creationists had been routed, and they seemed ready to accept the reality that action at the state level in Texas is no longer a feasible strategy for them.

But the creationists are far from giving up. On the significant local or grass-roots level, creationist activity continues unabated—or may even be increasing—in Texas, in Iowa (see next section), and nationwide. Following are some examples of creationist activities:

In a western state a high school teacher has been harassed by creationists for two years for using Helena Curtis's fine, evolution-oriented textbook[32] in an advanced biology course. Protests, carried as high as the state superintendent of education, have demanded that the teacher be removed from the course, that the textbook be replaced, or that the state subvention to the school district be withdrawn. All such protests have been denied, and the teacher still teaches the course and uses the book.

In a small town in another western state the reluctant school board is being pressured by a massive drive to introduce creationism into the high school curriculum.

In a college in Appalachia the professor of anthropology is systematically heckled in class by creationist students who seem to attend for the specific purpose of objecting to the inclusion of human evolution in the instruction.[33]

On campuses of major universities, lectures and debates by speakers from the Institute for Creation Research—fountainhead of American creationism—are on the increase.[34] Advisedly, these and other similar efforts are mainly low key and out of the limelight; they do not draw public attention as do dramatic court cases and spectacular legislative battles. Consequently, the response of the scientific community frequently is just to ignore them. Thus in many parts of the United States—and in Canada as well—there is no visible and effective pro-evolution presence. In September 1984 a spokesman for the Ontario Committee of Correspondence wrote: "I am fully aware that even though the scientists may be giving up a little these days, the creationists certainly aren't, and this is the time for utmost care and attention."

What of the schools throughout the nation? In the expanding, private, so-called "Christian" schools, creationism is invariably taught and evolution is disparaged.[35] In public secondary schools creationism is taught rather rarely, but often not much evolution is taught either. The fact that the biology textbook has a chapter on evolution does not necessarily mean that the chapter will be taught; cautious teachers shy away from this booby-trapped subject. The situation feeds on itself. High school students who have learned little about evolution grow into voting adults who see nothing inappropriate in equating creationism with science or in deleting evolution from the curriculum.

Nationally, on the positive side, no state has enacted a creationist or "equal time" law since the Louisiana bill in 1981. In many states pro-evolution groups are still active and effective. These include branches of the American Civil Liberties Union and People for the American Way, as well as Committees of Correspondence in the United States and Canada. In 1983 the C/C network was incorporated as the not-for-profit National Center for Science Education (NCSE). While this is a nationwide organization, it operates on a very shaky financial base; it has no office and no paid employees. NCSE has received small grants from a few scientific societies, but its principal source of support is the private resources of its members. Efforts to generate support from the larger scientific societies, from science-oriented corporations, and from foundations have not been successful.

NCSE's financial dilemma also poses a dilemma for the scientific world: Operations at the grass roots appear to be the most effective way, at least in the political sector, to counter the creationist threat to scientific integrity. But if the science establishment has no mechanism for supporting such activities, can the efforts be expected to have any long-term results?

In the long run education is likely to stimulate acceptance of evolution and rejection of creationism more profoundly and more permanently than are confrontations, whether in courts and legislatures, or in school board meetings and other community forums.[36] The educational process must begin with good science teaching in school and must continue with public information programs aimed at adults. The science community is aware of the need for these measures and has begun to promote them. This volume, and the symposium from which it stems, reflect the concern of AAAS for improving public understanding of science. A 1984 symposium, "Science as a Way of Knowing," initiated a long-term project of the American Society of Zoologists also aimed at improved public understanding.[37] The National Academy of Sciences has produced an excellent brochure on science and creationism, of which 40,000 copies were distributed free to schools and other agencies.[38] In 1982–1984 scientists published at least thirty semi-popular books critical of creationism[39]—an unprecedented outpouring. Many of these volumes, as well as the symposia just mentioned, unfortunately often tended to be above the general public's reading and comprehension levels. But trial and error should enable programs such as these to find appropriate levels; the important thing is that the initiatives continue.

Addendum II: Events in Iowa

No creationist or "equal time" bill has been proposed in the Iowa legislature since 1982. Apparently, in Iowa as well as nationally legislation is now seen as a futile tactic. Yet the state's creationists retain their enthusiasm despite years of continued defeat. They have, however, shifted their attention from DPI and the legislature to local schools, libraries, parents, and officials.

In 1982 Harry Bert Wagoner, Jr., a leading activist, initiated a massive program of local petitions to introduce a list of sixteen creationist books plus other materials into school libraries in sixty communities. The Creation Science Research Center in San Diego jubilantly announced: "After seven years labor Bert Wagoner has finally struck pay dirt in Iowa".[40] But the "pay dirt" turned out to be dross. The campaign was vigorously opposed throughout Iowa by the state's pro-evolution coalition. The Iowa C/C's principal contribution to the coalition was to prepare—with IAS financial support—a paperback book reviewing the sixteen titles on Wagoner's list along with an equal number of additional creationist classics.[41] The paperback was distributed free to educational agencies in Iowa and was then put on sale nationally; it has been distributed in forty-seven states. In Iowa the creationist effort failed dismally in about twenty-five school districts, and the rest of the campaign was quietly dropped.[42]

Wagoner then submitted to the Iowa Civil Rights Commission a complaint against leaders of the C/C and the IAS Panel, alleging that their actions in blocking the placement of creationist books in school libraries constituted religious discrimination.[43] When this complaint was rejected, Wagoner sued the commission in state district court. He contended that it is irrelevant whether creationism is religion or science; in either case it is a minority viewpoint that is entitled to be represented in the schools, and denial of such representation violates the creationists' civil rights. This novel and bizarre legal approach has never been tested. In January 1985 the suit is still pending, and it is possible that Wagoner's claim may be upheld, at least as far as school libraries are concerned. It is doubtful, however, whether even this holding would open the schools generally to "equal time" for creationism.

Meanwhile, creationism continues to make inroads; it is already being taught—sometimes *sub rosa*—in various Iowa schools. In two college towns where this is happening, the school boards, although disapproving, find it prudent to ignore the creationist activity in their schools.

The state's educational and scientific establishments, rather than responding to the creeping progress of creationism, have instead relaxed their initiatives. Over several years Iowa's pro-evolution coalition had achieved substantial recognition, both within the state and nationally.[44] The Panel on Controversial Issues had had cordial relations with IAS, its parent body; yet uneasiness crept into these relations. In April 1983 the IAS Board of Directors abruptly abolished the panel. The ostensible reason was a perception that the panel had been acting as a single-issue agency; yet a feeling seemed to exist among IAS leaders that the panel, though demonstrably successful in its chosen area, had been excessively activist and insufficiently decorous and disciplined.[45] The IAS replaced the panel with a new Committee on Controversial Issues (CCI) under somewhat different guidelines. In its first year the new committee has shown little visible activity with respect to creation-evolution.

The Iowa C/C, the panel's *alter ego*, also became inactive; by 1984 it was little more than a name. The Iowa Freedom Foundation, which had been a strong member of the pro-evolution coalition, ran into funding problems and disappeared from the scene. The coalition itself has not met since 1982 and in effect is dissolved. Thus by late 1984 there was no coherent organization in Iowa with a demonstrated capacity to meet creationist challenges. The high hopes of several years back that creationist aggressions in Iowa would finally be contained had faded.

Donald M. Huffman, a pro-evolution activist, is also a former IAS president, a founding member of the IAS Panel, and first chairman of the new CCI. Early on, Huffman broached as a major objective the setting up of a broad public information program in the state leading to better understanding of science, including understanding of evolution.[46] This was not feasible while pro-evolutionists were busy responding to creationist fire alarms. In 1984–1985 there has been a superficial lull, with no open creation-evolution hostilities—an appropriate time for initiating such a program. But Huffman is out of state for the academic year on a teaching exchange, and nothing has been done. Developing a broad-based program for public understanding of science is arguably the most useful thing that Iowa scientists and evolutionists could now do for the defense of their discipline.

Conclusions

Creationism is a religious movement that attempts to impose fundamentalist positions on public school curricula, and thus poses an enduring threat to our public schools, to the role of scientific rationalism in American public life, and, ultimately, to institutions concerned with scientific research. "Creation science," a defensive reaction to creationist defeats in the courts, attempts to disguise the religious nature of the movement. The response of the scientific community at the national level has been largely ineffective because of the long-standing inertia and noninvolvement of many scientists, but especially because the creationist movement has successfully mobilized public opinion at the community level. As scientists have become more aware of the threat to science that creationism poses, they have become more involved; and some are effectively engaging themselves at the community level. More important, scientists and their professional organizations have begun to develop public information programs to increase popular awareness and understanding of science.

Iowa has been a focus of "scientific creationism" activity; and Iowa scientists have responded to this threat to a greater degree than have scientific communities in most other states. Effective leadership has been exercised by the Iowa Academy of Science, particularly through its Panel on Controversial Issues. The Committees of Correspondence, the nationwide pro-evolution movement that began in Iowa and New York, have also had considerable success in recruiting and involving both scientists and their nonscientist supporters, and in meeting creationist initiatives. Together, these organized responses provide prototypes for effective defense strategies in other states and communities.

In the three years since the paper on which this chapter is based was written, there have been significant evolutionist victories in Texas and Louisiana, while the situations in Iowa and in certain other states have deteriorated. Developments both in Iowa and on the national level suggest that the science establishment has not yet resolved the problem of how to incorporate into its organizational structure and its operating style the kinds of tactics and organizations that can successfully confront the creationists in grass-roots encounters.

Notes

1. C. D. Darlington, "The Origins of Darwinism," *Scientific American*, May 1959, p. 60.

2. Stewart G. Cole, *History of Fundamentalism* (1931; reprint, New York: R. R. Smith, 1971).

3. See L. Sprague de Camp, *The Great Monkey Trial* (New York: Doubleday, 1968); John T. Scopes and James Presley, *Center of the Storm: Memoirs of John T. Scopes* (New York: Holt, Rinehart and Winston, 1967); Jerry R. Tompkins, ed., *D-Days at Dayton: Reflections on the Scopes Trial* (Baton Rouge: LSU Press, 1965); and Jerry R. Tomkins, "Memoirs of a Belated Hero," *American Biology Teacher* 34 (October 1972): p. 383.

4. Maynard Shipley, *The War on Modern Science* (New York: Alfred Knopf, 1927); Richard David Wilhelm, A Chronology and Analysis of Regulatory Actions

Relating to the Teaching of Evolution in Public Schools (Ph.D. dissertation, University of Texas, 1978), pp. 57–59.

5. Oscar Riddle, *The Teaching of Biology in the Secondary Schools of the United States* (Washington, D.C.: Union of American Biological Societies, 1942).

6. George W. Hunter, *A Civic Biology* (New York: American Book Company, 1914).

7. George W. Hunter, *New Civic Biology* (New York: American Book Company, 1926).

8. Judith D. Grabiner and Peter D. Miller, "Effects of the Scopes Trial," *Science* 185 (6 September 1974): 832.

9. See Kenneth Saladin, Chapter 8, this volume.

10. Stephen Jay Gould, "A Visit to Dayton," *Natural History*, October 1981, p. 8.

11. *Epperson* v. *Arkansas*, 393 U.S. 97 (1967).

12. Wendell R. Bird, "Freedom of Religion and Science Instruction in Public Schools," *Yale Law Journal* 87 (January 1978): 515.

13. *McLean* v. *Arkansas Board of Education*, U.S. District Court, Eastern District of Arkansas, Western Division (No. LR C 81 322, 1982). See Appendix B, this volume.

14. *Daniel* v. *Waters*, 515 F. 2d 485 (6th Circuit, 1975); *Hendren* v. *Campbell*, Superior Court No. 5, Marion County, Ind. (1977); both reprinted in National Association of Biology Teachers, *A Compendium of Information on the Theory of Evolution and the Evolution/Creationism Controversy* (Reston, Va.: NABT, June 1977).

15. Jack A. Gerlovich et al., "Creationism in Iowa," letter, *Science* 208 (13 June 1980): 1210; Jack A. Gerlovich and Stanley L. Weinberg. "The Battle in Iowa: Qualified Success," in *Did the Devil Make Darwin Do It?*, David B. Wilson, ed. (Ames: Iowa State University Press, 1983).

16. George Magrane, science consultant, Iowa Area Education Agency 15, personal communication, 29 January 1977.

17. Kenneth M. Pierce, "Putting Darwin Back in the Dock," *Time*, 16 March 1981, p. 80.

18. Glen E. Peterson, "They Should Stop Shooting Shoemakers Too, Shouldn't They?" *American Biology Teacher*, January 1978, p. 10.

19. Elwood B. Ehrle, "The Quantification of Education in Biology," *BioScience*, 1 April 1971, p. 325; and *U.S. Scientists and Engineers 1980*, NSF Publication 82-314, 1982.

20. Robin Marantz Henig, "Evolution Called a 'Religion,' Creationism Defended as 'Science'," *BioScience* 29 (September 1979): 513.

21. "IAS Panel on Controversial Issues Preparing 'Briefing Papers'," *Iowa Academy of Science Bulletin* 15, no. 3 (September 1981).

22. Stanley L. Weinberg and Robert W. Chapman, *What Is a Committee of Correspondence?* December 1981, available from Stanley L. Weinberg, 156 East Alta Vista, Ottumwa, IA 52501.

23. Jack A. Gerlovich, *Methods for Addressing Creation/Evolution Controversies in Iowa Schools* (Des Moines, Iowa: Department of Public Instruction, January 1982).

24. Willis David Hoover, "School Book Controversy Sparks Furor in Atlantic," *Des Moines Register*, 28 February 1982, p. 1.

25. *Creationism in Iowa Schools* (Des Moines, Iowa: Department of Public Instruction, no date).

26. Ibid.

27. Bridget O'Brien, "Creation Law Invalid, Judge Rules," New Orleans *The Times Picayune/States-Item*, 11 January 1985, Section 1.

28. *Texas Administrative Code*, Section 81.71(a)(5) (Austin: Texas Education Agency, May 1983).

29. Stanley L. Weinberg, "Two Views on the Textbook Watchers," *The American Biology Teacher* 40, no. 9 (December 1978): 541; Steven Schafersman, "Censorship of Evolution in Texas," *Creation/Evolution*, Issue X, (Fall 1982): 30.

30. Ellie McGrath, "Showdown in Texas," *Time*, 23 August 1982, p. 47.

31. Michael Hudson, news release, "Creationist Demands Ignored in Textbook Recommendations," 8 November 1984; Wayne Moyer, staff memorandum, "Education Is Back on the Agenda in Texas," 13 November 1984 (both Austin, Texas: People for the American Way).

32. Helena Curtis, *Biology*, 3rd ed. (New York: Worth Publications, 1979).

33. Reports to Committees of Correspondence, September 1984–January 1985.

34. "Speakers' Schedule," *Acts and Facts/Institute for Creation Research*, 14, no. 1 (January 1985): 4.

35. See, for example, *High School Science*, series (Pensacola: A Beka Book Publications). As listed in the publisher's catalog: "This series presents the universe as the direct creation of God and refutes evolution." Beka is reported to supply 50 percent of the textbook and curricular materials market for Christian schools. The publishing firm describes itself as "A textbook ministry for Christian schools" and as an affiliate of Pensacola Christian College and School.

36. Weinberg, *op. cit.*, note 29.

37. *American Zoologist* 24, no. 2 (1984).

38. James D. Ebert et al., *Science and Creationism: A View from the National Academy of Sciences* (Washington: National Academy Press, 1984).

39. James H. Shea, "A List of Selected References on Creationism," *Journal of Geological Education* 32 (1984): 43–49; Stanley L. Weinberg, "Books Critical of Creationism, 1982–84," *Memorandum to Committees of Correspondence* (available in Creation-Evolution Archive, Special Collections, Iowa State University Library) November–December 1983, pp. 7–8.

40. *Creation Science Report* (San Diego: Creation Science Research Center, September 1982) unpaged.

41. Stan(ley L.) Weinberg, ed., *Reviews of Thirty-One Creationist Books* (Ottumwa, Iowa: National Center for Science Education, 1984).

42. *Memorandum to Committees of Correspondence*, September 1982, p. 2; November 1982, p. 4; January 1983, p. 4; March 1983, p. 6; May 1983, p. 5; July/August, p. 4.

43. Iowa Civil Rights Commission, *Charge of Discrimination* NJ #725, Des Moines, 14 March 1983.

44. For press coverage see, for example, *New York Times*, 25 November 1979; *Wall Street Journal*, 15 June 1979; *U.S. News and World Report*, 9 June 1980; *Kansas City Times*, 9 June 1980. Also see Roger Lewin, "A Response to Creationism Evolves," *Science* 214 (6 November 1981): 635–37; Kim McDonald, "Forced Teaching of Creationism Threatens Integrity of Education, Science Group Says," *The Chronicle of Higher Education* XXIII, no. 18 (13 January 1982): 1. In April 1982 IAS gave its Distinguished Service Award to the coordinator of the IAS Panel "for his effective role in championing the defense of legitimate science."

45. Iowa Academy of Science, Board of Directors, *Minutes*, 10 October 1982, p. 5, para. 5.6. Duane C. Anderson, IAS President: "I object to the idea that one must choose between a formal, prudent, conservative organization, and a feisty, free-wheeling, swift-footed [one]. . . . Somewhere in the middle of this continuum there must be an even-handed, well-balanced, and organized approach to problem solving. . . ." personal communication, 19 November 1983.

46. Based on Huffman-Weinberg discussions, 1981–1984; confirmed by personal communications, Donald M. Huffman and Peter De Jong, both 21 January 1985.

CHAPTER 6

Creationism in Kentucky: The Response of High School Biology Teachers

William E. Ellis

Eastern Kentucky University

For several years I have been interested in the evolution/creation conflict both from the perspective of an historian and as one concerned about the consequences of mandating the teaching of "scientific creationism." I have studied earlier clashes over evolution, including the anti-evolution agitation in Kentucky in 1922 which marked the beginning of that nationwide effort, and also the travail of Edgar Young Mullins, a moderate Southern Baptist leader who did more than any other southern religious leader to limit anti-evolution gains in the 1920s. I have been especially interested in those branches of American religious history known as evangelicalism and fundamentalism.[1]

My interest increased in mid-1980 when a group of creationists proposed introduction of their views into the curricula of the Fayette County (Kentucky) Public Schools. By this time the "scientific creationism" movement had spread across the nation, but had achieved only limited success in having the Biblical creation story taught in biology classes.

The Assumptions of Evolutionists and Creationists

"Scientific creationists," anti-evolutionists, and other so-called "conservatives" seem to take for granted that biology teachers heavily stress the theory of

72

evolution, that evolution is taught as fact, and that this instruction is consequently antireligious and part of the general trend of secular humanism in public education. Moreover, they find explicit evidence for this indictment in public school textbooks. On the other hand, many scientists, civil libertarians, and other so-called "liberals" appear to believe that teachers have been inhibited by anti-evolutionism since the Scopes trial and, therefore, place little if any emphasis on evolution. Too, members of this second group frequently claim that only with development and use of the Biological Sciences Curriculum Study (BSCS) materials in the early 1960s did evolution begin to receive adequate treatment in high school texts. Admittedly, these statements are oversimplified, but I think they do offer a convenient frame of reference for taking a look at some of the very complex issues implicit in the evolution/creation conflict.[2]

Recent studies such as Dorothy Nelkin's *Science Textbook Controversies and the Politics of Equal Time* and a 1974 *Science* article, "Effects of the Scopes Trial," give us some direction for thought, but we need more quantitative measures to help us decide which of the suppositions above is closer to the true state of affairs.[3] Much of the existing literature is disappointing because there are lapses into polemics; moreover, there are few descriptions of what is actually taking place in the science classroom.

The Survey of Kentucky Biology Teachers

In late 1980, after extensive background study of secondary material and with the advice of colleagues from several disciplines, I developed an exploratory questionnaire addressed to high school biology teachers.[4] The final version of the questionnaire consisted of three sections (see Appendix 6-1b, this chapter). Section one requested general personal information from the respondent, including education, professional attainments, and religious preference. The second section specifically addressed the expected problems of teaching the theory of evolution. The most important items questioned the level of emphasis that the teacher placed on evolution instruction and the reactions of students, parents, and school administrators. Section three offered teachers a forum to express opinions about key issues related to the teaching of evolution/creation.

Eastern Kentucky University provided an Institutional Research Grant which made it possible to poll all 794 of the state's biology teachers. In mid-February 1981, the questionnaire and cover letter (Appendix 6-1a) were mailed to all public school biology teachers on the list provided by the Kentucky Department of Public Instruction. Forty-four percent (350) of the teachers returned the questionnaire, the results of which are given in detail in Appendix 6-1b. Although anonymity was promised, nearly one-third of the respondents signed their names and an even larger percentage wrote comments on the questionnaire.

Kentucky's Biology Teachers: A Profile

Section one revealed an interesting profile of the respondents. Nearly three-quarters of these biology teachers had a master's degree in science or education or Rank I status (MA plus a thirty-hour planned program). Slightly more than three-quarters had majored in biology and nearly 55 percent had completed a minimum of thirteen graduate hours in biology. Moreover, almost a third had eight to twelve years of teaching experience, and nearly forty percent of the teachers who responded taught five biology classes daily.

These figures indicate that the respondents generally had more than adequate undergraduate and professional training for their assigned tasks and that they had substantial teaching experience—only 6.3 percent had been teaching three or fewer years. We do not know that the group that responded was a representative cross-section of all the state's high school biology teachers, however. It is possible that the "cream of the crop" might have dominated the survey results. Several verification tests of typicality were attempted by comparing the respondents with all Kentucky biology teachers and with all Kentucky secondary teachers, using the information provided by the Department of Public Instruction. With regard to training, these comparisons indicate that those who responded were only slightly better trained than the average Kentucky biology teacher.[5]

Of the respondents, 41 percent reported teaching in a school system with a rural-urban mixture of students. The size of school populations as described by the teachers ranged from the very small (50–125 pupils) to the very large (more than 1500 students), but the largest number of instructors taught in schools with 500 to 1500 students. Most of these schools are large enough to have a science chairperson while maintaining Kentucky's highest accreditation standards.

Section one closed with a request for teachers to mark a religious preference. One-third chose the Baptist column. Methodists ranked second with a representation of 21.5 percent. The Catholic, Disciples of Christ, and Presbyterian persuasions all hovered around the 7 percent level. Nearly 12 percent fell into the "other" category, with the various churches of Christ, Churches of God, and Christian Churches predominating. Only 9 percent marked "no preference." While one cannot judge the religious fervor of Kentucky's high school biology teachers, it is noteworthy that fully 91 percent of the respondents (43 percent of all of the biology teachers in the state) listed a religious preference. Indeed, more teachers listed a religious choice than did the general population in the latest religious census of Kentucky.[6] Interestingly, the statewide Southern Baptist affiliation was about the same percentage as on the teacher survey. Kentucky's high school biology teachers apparently do consider religion a serious matter, and they make no apologies about their affiliation with these institutions.

Textbooks Used and Level of Emphasis on Evolution

The items in section two of the questionnaire focused directly on classroom experiences related to teaching the theory of evolution. Teachers first checked the one or more texts that they used, selecting from a list of ten on the State Multiple List of Textbooks. Many teachers marked more than one text because they teach two or more levels of biology. For example, some used the "old standard," Otto and Towle, *Modern Biology*, for their tenth grade general biology classes and the BSCS Green Version for their advanced classes. The survey indicated that *Modern Biology* leads the way, with nearly two-thirds of the respondents using the book. A representative of Holt, Rinehart, and Winston confirmed that the book has about 65 percent of the Southern market, almost exactly equaling the Kentucky figures.[7] The three forms of the BSCS texts account for slightly over 11 percent, the next highest percentage on the survey.

Kentucky teachers have wide latitude in choosing textbooks. Every five years the State Textbook Commission adopts a list of books,[8] apparently more for the convenience of publishers than for any other reason. However, the adoption process varies from one district to another throughout the state. Only a few teachers expressed total dissatisfaction with the texts that they used. However, in their written comments and in some interviews many teachers complained about a trend toward "watering down" or simplification of reading material, particularly in such texts as that by Otto and Towle. Criticisms of the BSCS volumes ranged from "too difficult for students to understand" to "too research-oriented." Nearly 84 percent of those answering the question found an adequate emphasis on evolution in the texts they used.

The responses to two other items in section two will be of particular interest to proponents of teaching the theory of evolution. Nearly 80 percent of respondents believed themselves qualified to teach evolution. There was little direct pressure reported at the local level—only about 7 percent of the teachers indicated a school policy on the teaching of evolution. None of these individuals elaborated on the subject, however, and the exact wording of these policies is unknown.[9]

For item 16, perhaps the most important part of the questionnaire ("emphasis placed on evolution in your instruction"), the responses are shown in Table 6–1. That some 53 percent of those responding chose the third category was most interesting, and I immediately began to consider retesting this item with a supplementary questionnaire. (The results of that second questionnaire will be discussed subsequently.)

The thirty-two teachers who marked "no emphasis" also replied to a list of possible explanations for their omission of the theory of evolution in their classes. Nearly a third said that they did not believe that teaching about

Table 6-1. Level of Emphasis on Evolution

Amount of Emphasis	Number of Respondents	Percentage of Those Responding
1. No emphasis	32	9.2
2. Little emphasis	108	31.1
3. Moderate emphasis	183	52.7
4. Strong emphasis	24	6.9
Total	347	99.9

evolution was necessary for a high school biology course. Nine said they did not place any emphasis on evolution because they did not believe in it, and five others expressed a firm belief in the Biblical creationist view of life.

Items 18–23 were concerned with student, administrative, and public acceptance of evolution instruction. Nearly half of the teachers indicated that their students responded indifferently to instruction on evolution, but over 42 percent found a positive reaction and only about 9 percent reported a negative attitude. More than half of the teachers indicated that they "frequently" encouraged students to offer opposing views to evolution and about the same number replied that pupils "occasionally" did so. Nearly 80 percent of the respondents maintained that they had never had complaints from parents. Obviously, the teaching of evolution is not viewed as a problem in the classrooms of these teachers, and they reported little if any adverse reaction from school officials. Over 90 percent had never received reprimands from administrators, and 97 percent had never had complaints from a superintendent or school board member. These responses suggest that, for this group of teachers at least, negative classroom or public response to their teaching about the theory of evolution is rare.[10]

Teacher Opinions about the Teaching of Evolution/Creation

Section three of the questionnaire afforded teachers the opportunity to voice opinions about issues related to teaching evolution/creation. In the first item they were asked whether or not they favored KRS 158.177, the 1976 Kentucky statute that sanctions voluntary use of the Biblical account of creation by an instructor if evolution is also taught. By a large majority—78.9 percent—the teachers approved this law.

The next item in the survey concerned a policy statement by Superintendent of Public Instruction Raymond Barber. After the initial phase of creationist agitation in Fayette County in mid-1980, Barber issued a memorandum to all public school superintendents stating that local districts could use some optional state funds if they so chose "to purchase supplemental books and materials setting forth a scientific creationism theory."[11] In effect, this appeared to be official sanction of creationism by the Commonwealth of Kentucky's Department of Education. Teachers responded to this item less decisively, but 57 percent disapproved spending state funds for creationist materials.

On the issue of academic freedom, teachers were asked who should make decisions about what theories are taught. Nearly 55 percent declared that the individual teacher should make this determination. Only about 11 percent wanted this decision made by the state legislature, with the remainder of respondents preferring to have the decision made by the State Superintendent and Board of Education (12 percent), the local superintendent and board of education (17.2 percent), or the school administration (4.8 percent).

The next items confronted the central issue directly: should "scientific creationism" be taught when evolution is and should its teaching be mandated by law if the theory of evolution is taught? Of those responding, over two-thirds said that "scientific creationism" should receive emphasis equal to that placed on the theory of evolution. However, over 76 percent were opposed to *mandating* instruction on "scientific creationism." The Kentucky teachers who responded to the poll clearly do not want to be forced to teach creationism, although a substantial number are willing to teach it. However, presumably because of their strong belief in academic freedom on instructional matters, they accept the open-endedness of KRS 158.177.

The poll on the last item in the survey was revealing and somewhat contradictory. When asked if they considered teaching a "Biblically based concept like scientific creationism" to be a violation of the First Amendment, only 35.2 percent responded "yes." Apparently, many of these teachers do not have a clear understanding of the separation of church and state dictum.

After the responses to the initial survey had been studied, I decided to administer a supplementary survey to seek additional information about some points. I selected 20 percent of the original list of 794 to receive the second questionnaire. Names were selected so that the ratio of teachers per area was the same as those polled in the original survey; otherwise, the selection of names for the "subsample" was random. A cover letter (Appendix 6–2a) explained the purpose of the supplement. Teachers responded at a slightly higher rate (44.4 percent) than in the original survey.

Specifically, I asked for teacher input on three key items (see Appendix 6–2b). First, the subsample was asked how they related evolution and creationism in the classroom—rather than as abstract public issues. Choices ranged from emphasizing only the theory of evolution to stressing only "scientific creationism." Table 6–2 shows the wide range of responses, with options 2 ("some mention should be made of scientific creationism") and 3 ("scientific creationism should receive equal emphasis") together being chosen by 67 percent of the respondents. Roughly the same percentage supported "equal emphasis" as had supported mandating creationism on the original survey. If

Table 6–2. Question Concerning Creationism/Evolution Emphasis (Supplement I).

	Number Responding	Percentage
With which do you agree?		
1. Only the theory of evolution should be emphasized in high school biology courses.	13	18
2. The theory of evolution should be emphasized in high school biology courses, but some mention should be made of scientific creationism, a Biblically based concept, as an alternative theory.	28	38.9
3. The theory of evolution and the theory of scientific creationism should receive equal emphasis in high school biology courses.	20	27.8
4. The theory of scientific creationism should be emphasized in high school biology courses, but some mention should be made of evolution as an alternative theory.	3	4.1
5. Only the theory of scientific creationism should be emphasized in high school biology courses.	1	1.3
6. Neither the theory of evolution nor the theory of scientific creationism should be emphasized in high school biology courses.	4	5.5
7. None of the above	3	4.1
Total	72	99.7

we look at the opposite ends of the item, only one person opted for complete stress on "scientific creationism" while 18 percent preferred total emphasis on evolution.

To test further the teaching of "scientific creationism" and evolution in classroom instruction, teachers in the subsample were asked to indicate with which they felt more "comfortable" (see item 2, Appendix 6-2b). Nearly half said they were more comfortable teaching the theory of evolution than the theory of "scientific creationism." This seems to reinforce both the response to item 1 in the supplementary questionnaire and the opposition to mandating creationism in the original poll.

In an attempt to develop further the information obtained in the original survey, I also decided to retest item 16 of the original survey as item 3 on the supplement. The same categories were used, but each was accompanied by an explicit statement of the scope of the category. Table 6–3 indicates the results.

The percentage of the subsample respondents choosing the moderate option was 43 percent, compared to nearly 53 percent on the first survey, a

Table 6–3. Level of Emphasis on Evolution (Supplement I)

	Number Responding	Percentage
How much do you emphasize the theory of evolution in your instruction of biology?		
1. No emphasis (I never initiate and avoid use of the theory of evolution whenever possible.)	2	2.8
2. Little emphasis (I rarely mention evolution except in response to student inquiry or a general textbook assignment.)	15	20.8
3. Moderate emphasis (I teach at least one unit about the theory of evolution and never avoid usage.	31	43
4. Strong emphasis (I stress the theory of evolution throughout the course as tying together the study of biology.)	22	30.5
5. Other	2	2.8
Total	72	99.9

decline of about 10 percent. However, those choosing the "strong" category increased to about 30 percent, compared to a response on the original survey of about 7 percent. A cause of this shift may be that the meaning of the category was understood differently by the second group. It is also possible that the respondents to the second category simply differed substantially from the original sample in their opinions on this item. Neither survey is generalizable, of course, but both suggest that, of the teachers responding, a majority moderately stress the theory of evolution and that this instruction is more heavily weighted toward the "strong" rather than the "little" category. In their written comments on the questionnaires and in personal interviews teachers indicate that they place more stress on the theory of evolution in classes containing more capable students.

Conclusions

This survey of Kentucky's high school biology teachers has given us some interesting information about the 44 percent who returned the questionnaire and answered the various questions. When it is supplemented with generalizable surveys, in Kentucky and in other states, we will have a better basis for drawing conclusions about the level of emphasis on evolution in the nation's classrooms. However, we can suggest certain possibilities based on this survey alone. A partial reply can be made to the "liberal" and "conservative" contentions about the role of the theory of evolution in high school biology instruction. At least in the classrooms of those responding to the survey questions, evolution receives less emphasis than conservatives appear to believe, and it stressed more than liberals tend to assume. I suspect that neither group will be especially elated with this state of affairs.

In Kentucky conservatives have not been successful in eliminating evolution from these high school biology classrooms, but neither have those supporting the teaching of evolution won the day. The Kentucky biology teachers who answered this survey appeared to have worked out an accommodation between what they see as their responsibility to science education on the one hand and to the religious beliefs of their constituents on the other. The scientific training and orientation of these respondents (many of whom stressed in their comments that they are scientists and not just teachers of science) seems to militate against their leaving out an important underlying principle of modern science. In written comments and personal interviews many repeatedly emphasized that they teach evolution as a theory not as a fact. At an appropriate time they may bring the Biblical account of creation into discussion in response to students who ask about it. But this exchange takes place in a friendly atmosphere, and the religious faith of students is not ridiculed. And, as noted above, the vast majority of the teachers responding to this survey appear to have some religious commitment.[12]

One intangible item that can never be measured is the level of rapport between student and teacher. Some teachers can handle a controversial topic with aplomb, whereas other instructors, regardless of their professional preparation, mismanage such situations. After several embarrassing incidents the latter tend studiously to avoid anything that would cause dissension. Teachers often alluded to both experiences in their written comments. In interviews and observations one can sometimes sense that some individuals have an innate ability to deal constructively with divisive issues while others do not.[13]

I find a clear message from the survey respondents, based on my own interpretation of both surveys, the teachers' written comments, and some personal interviews. In composite form, their majority position might be stated as follows:

> We teach the theory of evolution because it has been proven to be an integral part of the modern study of biology. We teach evolution as a theory, not as an indisputable fact. While we moderately stress the theory of evolution, we often mention the Biblical account of creation at an appropriate time. Students are encouraged to offer opposing views to evolution and they often do so. The teaching of evolution and/or creation is not presently an issue in my classroom. Let us do our job without outside interference. Science education is already hindered by lack of funds and flagging public interest. Do not complicate our task by bringing religious issues into the schools. Above all, do not mandate instruction of "scientific creationism" either by local school board edict or by legislation.

Appendix 6–1a

EASTERN KENTUCKY UNIVERSITY
Richmond, Kentucky 40475

COLLEGE OF SOCIAL AND BEHAVIORAL SCIENCES
Department of History

201 University Building
606-622-2016

Dear Fellow Teacher:

I am presently involved in a study of the instruction of evolution in Kentucky high school biology classes. I have published several articles on previous conflicts over the teaching of evolution in Kentucky in the 1920s and I intend to write several pieces about the current evolution/creation controversy.

I ask your help in my project. I am interested in the level of emphasis that you place on evolution in the classroom. You will also be asked your opinions of evolution and the anti-evolution movement known as "scientific creationism." Supporters of scientific creationism accept the Biblical account of creation and oppose the theory of evolution.

Please respond to the enclosed questionnaire and return in the self-addressed envelope. These responses will be transferred to a data card. Your reply will be entirely anonymous.

You might keep in mind the following developments as you mark this instrument. In 1976, the Kentucky General Assembly passed KRS 158.177 which includes the following:

In any public school instruction concerning the theories of the creation of man and the earth, and which involves the theory thereon commonly known as evolution, any teacher so desiring may include as a portion of such instruction the theory of creation as presented in the Bible, and may accordingly read such passages in the Bible as are deemed necessary for instruction on the theory of creation, thereby affording students a choice as to which such theory to accept.

For those students receiving such instruction, and who accept the Bible theory of creation, credit shall be permitted on any examination in which adherence to such theory is propounded provided the response is correct according to the instruction received.

As a result of increasing pressure from supporters of "scientific creationism," Superintendent of Public Instruction Raymond Barber issued the following policy statement on July 25, 1980, based on KRS 158.177 and KRS 156.447, a law regulating optional purchase of supplementary materials:

It is hereby declared to be the policy of the Department of Education that local districts may voluntarily choose to present a theory of scientific creationism and purchase necessary teaching supplies. School Districts may voluntarily choose to include one or more theories in teaching about creation. If districts so choose they may legally use state textbook funds to purchase . . . supplemental textbooks, materials, and equipment propounding, and for use in propounding, the "scientific creationism" theory of the origin of man and the earth. . . .

A bill mandating the teaching of scientific creationism if evolution is taught failed to pass the 1980 General Assembly. Similar bills may be introduced in the 1982 session of the General

Assembly. The debate over teaching evolution and/or scientific creation intensified in August 1980 in Fayette County.

Results of this study will be made public in late 1981 or early 1982. Thank you for helping in this research project. Best wishes for a successful school year.

Sincerely,

SIGNATURE

William E. Ellis
Professor of History

Appendix 6–1b   Kentucky Biology Teachers Questionnaire[a]

Question	Number Responding	Percentage
Section I		
1. What is your highest educational attainment?		
1. Rank I	94	27.6
2. M.A. in Education	131	38.5
3. M.S.	27	7.9
4. B.A. plus 15 to 30 hours	11	3.2
5. B.A. plus 3 to 14 hours	13	3.8
6. B.S. plus 15 to 30 hours	29	8.5
7. B.S. plus 3 to 14 hours	16	4.7
8. B.S.	16	4.7
9. B.A.	3	0.8
Total	340	99.7
2. Did you major in biology in your baccalaureate program of study?		
1. Yes	263	75.5
2. No	85	24.5
Total	348	100.00
3. How many graduate hours have you completed in biology?		
1. None	71	20.5
2. 1–3	22	6.3
3. 4–12	62	18.0
4. 13–20	73	21.0
5. 21 or more	117	33.8
Total	345	99.6

[a]794 questionnaires send out; 350 (44%) returned.

Question	Number Responding	Percentage
4. How many years of teaching experience do you have?		
1. 1–3	22	6.3
2. 4–7	59	17.0
3. 8–12	110	31.6
4. 13–17	73	21.0
5. 18–25	61	17.5
6. More than 25	23	6.6
Total	348	100.0
5. How many biology classes do you teach? This number should include any courses directly related to the biological sciences such as anatomy, mini-courses, etc.		
1. One	20	5.8
2. Two	61	17.5
3. Three	56	16.1
4. Four	71	20.5
5. Five	137	39.5
Total	345	99.4
6. What is the size of the high school in which you teach?		
1. 50–250 students	14	4.0
2. 251–500	42	12.1
3. 501–750	56	16.1
4. 751–1000	80	23.0
5. 1001–1500	100	28.8
6. More than 1500	55	15.8
Total	347	99.8
7. What is the accreditation level of the school in which you teach?		
1. Comprehensive	209	64.0
2. Standard	98	30.1
3. Basic	5	1.5
4. Provisional	10	3.0
5. Emergency	3	0.9
Total	325	99.5
8. From which environment do most of your students come?		
1. Urban	76	21.8
2. Rural	129	37.0
3. Rural-urban mixture	143	41.0
Total	348	99.8

Question	Number Responding	Percentage
9. Does your school have a science department chairperson?		
1. Yes	285	82.3
2. No	61	17.6
Total	346	99.9
10. How many teachers in your school teach one or more biology classes?		
1. 1–3	176	50.5
2. 4–6	134	38.5
3. 7–10	32	9.1
4. More than 10	3	0.8
Total	345	98.9
11. What is your religious preference?		
1. Baptist	117	34.2
2. Catholic	25	7.3
3. Disciples of Christ	26	7.6
4. Episcopalian	2	0.5
5. Lutheran	3	0.8
6. Methodist	73	21.3
7. Presbyterian	24	7.0
8. Other	41	11.9
9. No preference	31	9.0
Total	342	99.6

Section II

Question	Number Responding	Percentage
12. Which textbook do you use in your biology classes?		
1. Weinberg, *Biology: Inquiry into Nature of Life*	7	1.9
2. Goldman, *Biological Science*	3	0.8
3. Morholt, *Biology: Patterns in Living Things*	8	2.2
4. Cunningham, *Biology: You and Your Environment*	2	0.5
5. Towle, *Modern Biology*	228	65.0
6. Fabiano, *Life: Activities and Explorations*	1	
7. Oram, *Biology: Living Systems*	21	6.0
8. Wong Dolmatz, *IIS: Biology*	27	7.7
9. BSCS staff, all versions	40	11.4
10. Smallwood, *Biology*	15	4.2
Total	352[b]	99.9

[b]Several teachers marked more than one text and several did not mark any. The total of 352 is therefore 2 greater than the total number of respondents.

Question	Number Responding	Percentage
13. What is your opinion of the treatment of evolution in the text you use?		
1. Too much emphasis on evolution	21	6.1
2. Adequate emphasis on evolution	287	83.4
3. Not enough emphasis on evolution	36	10.4
Total	344	99.9
14. Do you feel qualified to teach about evolution?		
1. Yes	276	79.7
2. No	24	6.9
3. Not sure	46	13.2
Total	346	99.8
15. Does your school have a policy on teaching evolution dictated by the board of education?		
1. Yes	24	6.9
2. No	243	70.6
3. Not sure	77	22.3
Total	344	99.8
16. How much do you emphasize the theory of evolution in your instruction of biology?		
1. No emphasis	32	9.2
2. Little emphasis	108	31.1
3. Moderate emphasis	183	52.7
4. Strong emphasis	24	6.9
Total	347	99.9

If you marked number 1 in item 16, please answer item 17. (If you marked number 2, 3, or 4, do not respond to item 17.) If you marked number 2, 3, or 4 in item 16, please respond to the following. (If you marked number 1 in item 16, do not answer items 18–23.)

Question	Number Responding	Percentage
17. Why do you not place any emphasis on the theory of evolution?		
1. I do not believe in the theory of evolution.	9	28.1
2. I do not feel comfortable teaching about evolution.	0	0
3. I do not believe teaching about evolution is necessary for a high school biology course.	10	31.3
4. I do not teach about evolution because of opposition from parents	3	9.0
5. I do not teach about evolution because of opposition from the superintendent or board of education.	0	0
6. I believe in the Biblical creationist view of life and teach this in my biology class.	5	15.6
7. Other	5	15.6
Total	32	99.6

Question	Number Responding	Percentage
18. How do your students most often respond to instruction about evolution?		
1. Indifferently	152	48.7
2. Positively	132	42.3
3. Negatively	28	8.9
Total	312	99.9
19. Do students offer opposing views of evolution in the classroom?		
1. Never	19	6
2. Very rarely	87	27.5
3. Occasionally	162	51.2
4. Frequently	48	15.1
Total	316	99.8
20. Do you encourage students to offer opposing views about evolution?		
1. Very rarely	34	10.8
2. Never	12	3.8
3. Frequently	168	53.6
4. Occasionally	98	31.3
Total	312	99.5
21. Do you receive complaints from parents or other citizens about teaching evolution?		
1. Frequently	2	0.6
2. Very rarely	46	14.5
3. Occasionally	19	6.1
4. Never	249	78.8
Total	316	100.0
22. Do you receive complaints from administrators about teaching evolution?		
1. Occasionally	5	1.5
2. Never	286	90.5
3. Frequently	0	0
4. Very rarely	25	7.9
Total	316	99.9
23. Do you receive complaints from the superintendent or school board about teaching evolution?		
1. Never	307	97.0
2. Very rarely	8	2.5
3. Occasionally	1	0.3
4. Frequently	0	0
Total	316	99.8

Question	Number Responding	Percentage

Section III

24. Do you favor KRS 158.177 which allows teachers to include a Biblical account of the creation of man and the earth?

1. Yes	267	78.9
2. No	70	20.7
Total	337	99.6

25. Do you favor expenditure of state funds to purchase materials that offer a scientific creationist (Biblical) explanation of man and the earth?

1. Yes	147	43.2
2. No	193	56.7
Total	340	99.9

26. Who should decide whether or not any specific theory is taught in Kentucky high school biology classes?

1. Kentucky General Assembly	36	10.9
2. State Superintendent and Board of Education	40	12.1
3. Local superintendent and board of education	57	17.2
4. School administration	16	4.8
5. The individual teacher	181	54.8
Total	330	99.8

27. With which of the following do you agree?

1. If evolution is taught in biology classes, scientific creationism should receive equal emphasis.	203	67.0
2. Only the theory of evolution should be emphasized in explaining the origin of life.	95	30.1
3. Only scientific creationism should be emphasized in explaining the origin of life.	5	1.6
Total	303	98.7

28. Are you in favor of a state law mandating the instruction of scientific creationism if the theory of evolution is taught in high school biology classes?

1. Yes	79	23.0
2. No	261	76.3
Total	340	99.3

Question	Number Responding	Percentage
29. Do you believe that the teaching of a Biblically based concept like scientific creationism in Kentucky high school biology classes violates the U.S. Constitution which guarantees the separation of church and state?		
1. Yes	119	35.2
2. No	217	64.2
Total	336	99.4

Appendix 6–2a

EASTERN KENTUCKY UNIVERSITY
Richmond, Kentucky 40475

COLLEGE OF SOCIAL AND BEHAVIORAL SCIENCES
Department of History

201 University Building
606-622-2016

Dear Fellow Teacher:

A few weeks ago I mailed a questionnaire to all high school biology teachers in Kentucky. You may recall filling out this instrument. Of 800 quiestionnaires mailed out since early February, over 40 percent have been returned to this office. By any test this is an excellent response, proving that Kentucky's high school biology teachers really care about their profession. Later this year I will publish the results of my research.

While most of the respondees and I were generally satisfied with the original questionnaire, one glaring fault is apparent. Many teachers did not feel comfortable about marking item number 27 which asked the following:

_____ With which of the following do you agree?

1. If evolution is taught in biology classes, scientific creationism should receive equal emphasis.
2. Only the theory of evolution should be emphasized in explaining the origin of life.
3. Only scientific creationism should be emphasized in explaining the origin of life.

Obviously, I did not make the range of responses wide enough for the tastes of most Kentucky biology teachers. In order to get more accurate data for this item and two others, I am asking a random sample of Kentucky high school biology teachers to respond to the enclosed questionnaire.

Please respond to the questionnaire and return in the self-addressed stamped envelope at your earliest convenience. Thanks again for your help. Best wishes for a successful school year.

Sincerely,

SIGNATURE

William E. Ellis

Appendix 6–2b   Kentucky Biology Teachers Questionnaire   Supplement I[a]

Question	Number Responding	Percentage
1. With which of the following statements do you agree?		
1. Only the theory of evolution should be emphasized in high school biology courses.	13	18.0
2. The theory of evolution should be emphasized in high school biology courses, but some mention should be made of scientific creationism, a Biblically based concept, as an alternative theory.	28	38.9
3. The theory of evolution and the theory of scientific creationism should receive equal emphasis in high school biology courses.	20	27.8
4. The theory of scientific creationism should be emphasized in high school biology courses, but some mention should be made of evolution as an alternative theory.	3	4.1
5. Only the theory of scientific creationism should be emphasized in high school biology courses.	1	1.3
6. Neither the theory of evolution nor the theory of scientific creationism should be emphasized in high school biology courses.	4	5.5
7. None of the above	3	4.1
Total	72	99.7
2. With which of the following do you agree?		
1. I am more comfortable teaching the theory of scientific creationism than the theory of evolution.	11	15.3
2. I am more comfortable teaching the theory of evolution than the theory of scientific creationism.	35	48.6
3. I am not comfortable teaching either the theory of evolution or the theory of scientific creationism.	9	12.5
4. Other	17	23.6
Total	72	100.0

(Of the 17 who marked the "other" category, 12 (16.6%) made the written comment that they were comfortable teaching either evolution or creationism.)

[a]162 questionnaires sent out (20% of biology teachers on state list); 72 (44%) responded.

Question	Number Responding	Percentage
3. How much do you emphasize the theory of evolution in your instruction of biology?		
1. No emphasis (I never initiate and avoid use of the theory of evolution whenever possible.	2	2.8
2. Little emphasis (I rarely mention evolution except in response to student inquiry or a general textbook assignment.)	15	20.8
3. Moderate emphasis (I teach at least one unit about the theory of evolution and never avoid usage.)	31	43.0
4. Strong emphasis (I stress the theory of evolution throughout the course as tying together the study of biology.)	2	2.8
Total	72	99.9

Notes

1. Ellis, "Evolution, Fundamentalism, and the Historians: An Historiographical Review," *The Historian* XLIV (November 1982): 15–35.

2. The sources for these attitudes are voluminous. Perhaps Henry Morris, ed., *Scientific Creation* (San Diego: Creation-Life Publishers, 1977) and Dorothy Nelkin, *Science Textbook Controversies and the Politics of Equal Time* (Cambridge: MIT Press, 1977), 27–103, best represent the two sides of the controversy. Public opinion studies indicate that a majority of Americans probably favor creationism over evolution and endorse the teaching of "scientific creationism." See, for example, UK New Information Services, News Release, 30 April 1981; Stanley L. Weinberg, "Two Views on the Textbook Watchers," *American Biology Teacher* 40 (December 1978): 541–45; Gerald Skoog, "Legal Issues Involved in Evolution vs. Creationism," *Educational Leadership* 38 (November 1980): 154–156; *Lexington Herald*, 18 November 1981.

3. Nelkin, *Science Textbook Controversies*; Judith V. Grabiner and Peter D. Miller, "Effects of the Scopes Trial," *Science* 185 (6 September 1974): 832–37.

4. Those with whom I conferred included Wayne A. Moyer, Executive Director, National Association of Biology Teachers; Frank Howard, Science Consultant, Kentucky Department of Education; Rudolph Prins, Biology Professor, Western Kentucky University; Wallace C. Dixon, Associate Dean, College of Natural and Mathematical Sciences, Eastern Kentucky University; and Branley A. Branson, Biology Professor, Eastern Kentucky University.

5. Frank Howard to the author, 18 January 1981; Clara DeMoss to the author, 15 October 1981. Both Howard and DeMoss are with the Division of Teacher Education and Certification, Bureau of Instruction, Kentucky Department of Education.

6. P. P. Karan and Cotton Mather, *Atlas of Kentucky* (Lexington: University Press of Kentucky, 1977), 30.

7. James Boyd, sales representative for Holt, Rinehart, and Winston, to the author, 9, 21 September 1981.

8. "The State Multiple List of Textbooks and the 1977 Textbook Adoption for the Public Elementary and High Schools of Kentucky, The 1977–1982 Period of Adoption Group III, Science (1–12)—Health (1–12)."

9. The author also mailed a questionnaire to the 184 Kentucky public school superintendents in early April 1981. Of the 44 percent who replied, five superintendents indicated some form of school board policy governing the teaching of evolution/creation, but they did not say what the policies were. The Jefferson County system, the state's largest, has a science curriculum guide which includes the "creationist theory" as a suggested part of the study of variation and diversity. (*Science* 210, 211, 212, 213 [Guidelines for Curriculum] 1975, Department of Curriculum Development and Supervision, Jefferson County Public Schools.) However, several Jefferson County biology teachers indicated in personal interviews that this suggestion is generally ignored by biology teachers.

10. Of those who added comments on their questionnaire forms, only two teachers reported any major difficulties for having taught the theory of evolution. One instructor "got into trouble with a board member whose daughter was in the class," but apparently was not publicly reprimanded. Another teacher reported that local opposition to evolution has discouraged their "usual treatment of evolution."

11. Letter from Fred Schultz, Deputy Superintendent, Elementary and Secondary Education, Kentucky Department of Education, 2 December 1980.

12. The written comments on the questionnaire forms and personal interviews have given life to a set of sometimes rather dull figures. The composite statement at the end of this paper is a distilled version of many teacher comments. These ranged from the humorous to quite ill-tempered ones. For example, one teacher replied to the religious preference question by printing in bold red letters, "NONE OF YOUR DAMN BUSINESS."

13. I believe that controversial topics can sometimes be less troublesome in the smaller districts and schools than in the larger ones. In some of the comments and interviews a subtle characteristic emerges that relates educational experiences to the community. Teachers of the small systems are an integral part of the community. As one teacher explained, he is known by many parents. They see him at school functions, go to church with him, and "see him in the supermarket." They trust him, and he returns that confidence by carefully handling the theory of evolution. Moreover, he maintains that he heavily stresses evolution throughout his teaching and has never had any problems. This contact with the "community" is often lost in large urban school systems, particularly where the teacher turnover rate is high.

A Two-Model Creation versus Evolution Course

William M. Thwaites
San Diego State University

In the fall of 1977, Dr. Frank Awbrey of the Department of Biology, San Diego State University, and I decided to debate two professional debaters from the Institute for Creation Research (ICR), located in the nearby community of El Cajon, California. Having witnessed a previous debate involving ICR personnel, we knew that simply supporting evolution would not win the debate. Instead we would have to read what the creationists were saying and then find a simple way to refute each of these assertions. We think we won the debate, but as with all such debates with the ICR, there were no official judges.

After the debate it occurred to us that we had gone to an enormous amount of work for a mere four-hour show. We also recalled that before the debate we had been told by creationist students that science "has no answers to the creationist challenges against evolution." It seemed entirely logical to offer a course in which we would give some of those answers that the scientific community supposedly didn't have. Additional motivation for a creation/evolution course came in the form of a report from a colleague who had permitted a student to present evidence for fiat creation in a senior seminar course in biology. The results shocked us. According to the report, all but a handful of the class members were deeply impressed with the "evidence" given for creation. Several students said that they no longer believed in evolution, and most of the remainder said they still believed evolution was correct, but they could not explain why they still thought so. No one in the class was able to see the obvious flaws in the creationist assumptions and reasoning. The conclusion was inescapable: these university graduates were not prepared to deal with even the most elementary challenges to the underlying principle of biological studies. They had learned countless conclusions, but apparently knew nothing of the reasoning behind them. The creationists had pointed out, perhaps inadvertently, some major deficiencies in science education.

Once we had decided to go ahead with the course, we ran into some of the standard responses of the academic community, the most typical being, "Why would you wish to give those religious fanatics a platform?" Another was, "Does anyone really still believe in that nonsense?" We eventually offered the course under an "experimental topics" umbrella. With the increase in public awareness of the creation controversy, we have found that most of the objections from our academic colleagues have vanished. We even receive a small volume of what could be construed as fan mail. And the symposium upon which this volume is based is further evidence that the traditional academic response to creationism is changing.

The Course Format: Equal Time for Creationists

The first time we offered the course we made the mistake of writing all of the exams and of taking the bulk of the lecture time to refute the few creationists whom we invited to lecture. We found that this format gave some of the students reason to suspect that we were biasing the course in our favor out of timidity, that evolutionary theory needed a handicap in order to compete with creationism. In subsequent courses we tried to dispel this erroneous impression by giving the creationist speakers 50 percent of the lecture time and inviting them to make up 50 percent of the exam questions. We also invited the creationists to choose their own lecture schedule, topics, and speakers. It seemed to us that this was now very similar to the "two-model" course the creationists say they want in the public schools. We would find out just how well creationism would do in the open market place of ideas.

Topics Covered

During the semesters the creation/evolution course has been taught we have had speakers from the Institute for Creation Research (ICR), El Cajon, California, the Georesearch Institute of Loma Linda University, Loma Linda, California, and the Creation-Science Research Center (CSRC), San Diego, California. We asked the creationists to choose whatever topics they thought would put their suppositions in the most favorable light. In the course of the semester they presented talks attempting to establish the following points:

1. The second law of thermodynamics prevents macroevolution—what they refer to as "vertical evolution in the upward direction."
2. Many physical observations of the earth and the universe suggest ages that are many times shorter than the commonly accepted 4.6 billion-year age for the earth and the 10 to 20 billion-year age for the universe, and radiometric dating is unreliable.
3. The earth never had a reducing atmosphere and even if it had, the fundamental components of life (amino acids, etc.) would not have formed.
4. The geological record shows that the earth's history has been punctuated by many catastrophies, perhaps even a worldwide flood.
5. The fossil record shows sudden shifts in life-form morphology, not gradual change; therefore, many evolutionists are abandoning Darwin's ideas as totally unworkable. The logical alternative would be creationism, but evolutionists have a "religious" commitment to evolution and thus cannot accept the obvious.
6. Most of life, especially biochemistry, is too intricate and interdependent to have evolved. The intermediate stages would not have been viable; thus creative design is seen at all levels of organization.
7. The probability of getting even the simplest self-replicating systems purely by chance is essentially zero.

The contributions from the Loma Linda University speakers usually did not contain many of the foregoing items but instead consisted of attempts to establish two main concepts: (1) some of the geological features commonly understood to have formed in a desert or near-desert environment may have formed under water; and (2) being a Biblical literalist does not prevent one from doing credible science; it might even help. However many of the creation speakers from both the ICR and Loma Linda University denied that their suppositions had any connection to the Biblical scenario.

We started our presentation with a clarification of what is really meant by "creation" and by "evolution." We mentioned that the belief that a theistic power somehow guided the course of evolution (the theistic evolutionist's position) is a belief upon which science can shed no light at the present time and that such a belief is certainly not a belief in supernatural creation. Several times we have found students who thought they were creationists only to discover at this point in the course that they were really theistic evolutionists by our definition.

We have found that general agreement on the meaning of many nonscientific terms used in the creation/evolution debate is virtually nonexistent. We have received letters from colleagues who argue that there really is no conflict between religion and evolution, but it is clear to us that what they are saying is that there is no conflict between *their* religion and evolution. In our course it became obvious that we were in fact conflicting with the kind of narrow religious beliefs that deny the obvious conclusions reached by the study of genetics, embryology, the fossil record, radiometric dating, stratigraphy, and astronomy. We have made an effort to define the word belief as it is used in science and as it is used in everyday life. We suggested that a belief outside of science usually represents a rather static final conclusion about something, whereas within science a belief is usually a much more tentative conclusion about the relative validity of a hypothesis.

On the seven points presented by the creationist speakers, we found that they never really defined their hypotheses. They preferred to intimate that there is something fundamentally wrong with evolutionary theory and that creationism is the logical alternative. Exactly what is meant by creationism is more or less left up to the student's imagination as far as class presentation is concerned. In the absence of definitions from the creationist speakers, we attempted to expose this ambiguity by presenting a creation model derived from creationist books written by Dr. Henry Morris, director of the ICR, and by Morris and John C. Whitcomb.[2] It consists of the following:

  I . The Creation
      A. Accomplished by a supernatural being
      B. Everything created from nothing relatively recently
      C. The Earth was perfectly designed for life
          1. Protected by a vapor layer
              a. Uniform warm climate
              b. Cosmic radiation could not penetrate
          2. No wind or rain
          3. The land irrigated by water from underground
      D. All kinds created separately
          1. Each kind is unique and fixed
          2. Each kind is genetically highly variable
      E. Humans were uniquely created
      F. No decay occurred
 II. The Fall
      A. The second law of thermodynamics invoked
          1. Perfect order began to deteriorate
          2. Death, decay, and disorder began
      B. People began to populate the Earth; all humans descended from the original couple
      C. The vapor barrier enabled great longevity
III. The Flood
      A. Simultaneous, worldwide cataclysm

    B. All land was covered within forty days
    C. Flood water had two sources
        1. The vapor barrier
        2. Underground reservoirs
    D. The Flood began 1656 years after creation
    E. The Flood formed and deposited the geologic column
    F. The Flood split the land mass into the present continents.
    G. The only survivors were aboard one boat
        1. Eight humans
        2. One pair of most kinds of animals
        3. All were aboard the boat for 371 days

IV. The Post-Flood Period
    A. Leftover Flood energy caused the ice ages
    B. Flood survivors repopulated the Earth
    C. All living species are descendants of the survivors
        1. The animals had great original genetic variability
        2. They were modified by horizontal change to fill the Earth
    D. The vapor barrier was destroyed—longevity decreased
    E. All species degenerate since disorder *must* increase
    F. Present geological processes are different from those of the Flood

The presentation of this model in class has provoked some interesting responses. The most unexpected was the interest of some of the ICR personnel. Apparently none of them had ever seen the entire creation model presented in one place in such a succinct fashion. One of the faculty from ICR visited our campus just to obtain copies of the model. Other staff members also asked for copies. At least one claimed that we had made some errors, but he has declined to point them out in spite of our repeated requests to do so. The general consensus among the creationists seems to be that our model is actually the Biblical model of creation, rather than the scientific model, and thus is not suitable for classroom discussion in a secular setting.

Our general impression is that most of the professional creationists and most of the creationist students cannot accept the whole of our reconstituted creation model. Rather they pick and choose from it. We point out to the students that good scientists reduce all theories to their most fundamental postulates since these can usually be tested. We also emphasize that evolutionists not only welcome the close analysis of the underlying postulates of evolution, they insist on it.

In this context we were able to introduce the underlying postulates of evolutionary theory. We borrowed a set of Darwin's original postulates from the writings of Professor Ralph W. Lewis.[3] These postulates are as follows:

I. Theory of descent with modification
    A. All life evolved from one simple kind of organism or from a few simple kinds.
    B. Each species, fossil or living, arose from another species that preceded it in time.

C. Evolutionary changes were gradual and of long duration.

D. Over long periods of time new genera, new families, new orders, new classes, and new phyla arose by a continuation of the kind of evolution that produced new species.

E. Each species originated in a single geographic location.

F. The greater the similarity between two groups of organisms, the closer is their relationship and the closer in geologic time is their common ancestral group.

G. Extinction of old forms (species, etc.) is a consequence of the production of new forms or of environmental change.

H. Once a species or other group has become extinct it never reappears.

I. Evolution continues today in generally the same manner as during preceding geologic eras.

J. The geologic record is very incomplete.

II. The theory of natural selection

A. A population of organisms has the tendency and the potential to increase at a geometric rate.

B. In the short run the number of individuals in a population remains fairly constant.

C. The conditions of life are limited.

D. The environments of most organisms have been in constant change throughout geologic time.

E. Only a fraction of the offspring in a population will live to produce offspring.

F. Individuals in a population are not all the same: some have heritable variations (variable traits).

G. Life activities (struggle for existence) determine which traits are favorable or unfavorable by determining the success of the individuals who possess the traits.

H. Individuals having favorable traits (favorable variations) will, on the average, produce more offspring, and those with unfavorable traits will produce fewer offspring. (Natural selection is the term used to encompass statements G and H.)

I. Natural selection causes the accumulation of new variations and the loss of unfavorable variations to the extent that new species may arise.

After introducing Darwin's postulates we show that at least one, gradualism (postulate I-C), is being actively investigated by a growing number of evolutionists. We also alert students to the fact that many creationist arguments concerning the fossil record do nothing more than cast doubt on this one postulate that is not currently accepted by many evolutionists. Obviously, fiat creation is not the only alternative to gradualism. The logical alternative is something such as "punctuated equilibrium."[4] The creationists would have us throw out the proverbial baby with the bathwater, but one does not need to throw out an entire system of theories just because one of the postulates is currently undergoing modification.

While talking about postulates and theories, we introduce some of the elements of hypothetico-deductive reasoning and talk about testing and falsifying hypotheses. This requirement for testability of hypotheses is what makes creationist "hypotheses" about a supernatural creator unscientific. By definition we cannot use the methods of *natural* science to test or measure something supernatural. If science cannot test or measure the supernatural, then neither can it disprove the supernatural. The supernatural simply falls outside the realm of scientific inquiry. But we go on from this point and say that creationist hypotheses could be partly scientific if one would just substitute something like "an unknown creative force or entity" for the creationist "supernatural Creator." We go on with our testing of the creation hypotheses as if our opponents had modified the creation model to make it scientifically acceptable.

Another item that gets heavy emphasis is the nature of scientific evidence. Much of the creationists' "evidence" consists of written opinions of evolutionist writers. Much has been written regarding the fairness of these quotes, whether indeed many of these may be quoted out of context. Regardless of how many times the creationists have taken quotes out of context, we know of some examples where the quotes by creationists do, in fact, convey the same impression as the context. Our point, however, is that *opinion* is not *evidence*, no matter what the source of the opinion. Evidence is found in the results section of a scientific paper, not in the introduction or the discussion.

We advocate the advantages of empiricism, or checking things out for yourself. One example of this approach is the demonstration of back mutation production and selection in class. The creationists argue again and again that the second law of thermodynamics prevents the accumulation of "order" (i.e., useful biological information) through a random process like mutation. We counter by saying that mutation is indeed a random process, but selection is anything but random. In the back mutations demonstration we take a strain of yeast that lacks a functional urease. The original urease mutuation was caused by ultraviolet light. We expose the mutant yeast to even more mutagenic ultraviolet light and within a week or so we see colonies composed of the descendants of the lucky survivors that happened to mutate in a very unlikely way so that their urease gene was again functional. If the creationist interpretation of the second law of thermodynamics were valid, such back mutations would be impossible.

Another classroom demonstration dealt with an argument often used in public debates by one of the ICR speakers. The subject was the Bombardier beetle and the supposed impossibility of its evolution. The argument goes something like this. The beetle uses hydrogen peroxide and hydroquinone to produce an explosion (with the help of catalase and peroxidase enzymes). The beetle needs an inhibitor to stop these chemicals from exploding on contact. The chemicals are of no use without each other but would blow up if both were present. The inhibitor likewise would have no function by itself. So evolution would require that all three ingredients (and the structures necessary for their production, storage, and utilization) would have to have evolved simultaneously. This is impossible; therefore, the beetle must have been created by an intelligent, possibly supernatural being.

From the literature we show that hydrogen peroxide, hydroquinone, catalase, peroxidase, and all the structures found in the beetle's defense glands are common in the phylum Arthropoda. The enzymes involved are found in most life forms. The beetle had nothing unique, and all the components had other functions that might have been selected individually. The only unsolved problem was the supposed inhibitor which would prevent the explosion. We decided to mix hydrogen peroxide with hydroquinone to see if they would explode. In fact, we tried this first in a private experiment on the outside chance that our creationist friend was correct; he is a biochemist. The mixture turned brown. When we brought the demonstration to the class, we first played a tape of the creationist telling his audience "If you or I mixed these chemicals together in the laboratory, they would explode!" Then we had the first rows move to the back of the lecture hall. We set up a safety screen, donned protective clothing, and watched the solution slowly turn brown, the color of spent photographic developer. Although the creationist claimed to have had trouble reading the original paper since it was written in German, he has continued to use the same argument in public debates.

We spend two or three class periods trying to explain radiometric dating. The subject is quite difficult for most nonscience majors, but we present the subject as simply as possible. We critique Slusher's "Critique of Radiometric Dating" and show how the author failed to understand many aspects of what he was attempting to invalidate.[5] We have never been addressed by this author, but we think we understand why he has not come forth to defend his critique. We also understand that there are individuals within the creationist camp who are embarrassed by this publication in particular. Another scientist from ICR claims that radiometric dating depends on the willingness of radiochronologists to throw out any dates that do not fit with their preconceptions. An excellent monograph by G. Brent Dalrimple summarizes his answers to creationist accusations that radiometric dating does not work.[6] We plan to use some of this material in our classroom encounters with the creationists in the future.

We have developed rather elaborate handouts refuting the creationist claim that the fossil record shows no intermediates. These handouts go into considerable detail to demonstrate that *Archaeopteryx* was a dinosaur that had feathers and could fly. The creationist critique of *Archaeopteryx*, on the other hand, deals only with the feathers, which, they argue, make the fossil "100 percent bird." Of course, this really only reflects the taxonomic convention that feathers are characteristic of birds and not that *Archaeopteryx* was anything like a modern bird.

At times it does get repetitious hearing many of the same creationist arguments, but overall, the course is more exciting than any other that either of us has taught before. It has also shown us that it is urgent that students be taught how scientific conclusions are reached.

Observations and Course Evaluation

One striking observation concerns the lack of general agreement among the creationists: they disagree about almost everything. Certainly there is much dissension among standard scientific ranks, but creationists are, almost by definition, absolutists. And when absolutists confront disagreement, there is little room for compromise. It is not surprising, then, to find that ICR and CSRC used to be a single entity. The original organization apparently was torn apart over a difference in philosophy as to just how the cause of creationism should be advanced. And the conflict continues. For example, the CSRC was the instigator of the recent "Scopes II" case in California, while ICR publications frequently point out that this type of direct confrontation is far less desirable than grass-roots efforts such as ICR's. It appears to us that ICR personnel may deal with the potential for conflict by trying to ignore the existence of differences within creationist ranks.

A Loma Linda speaker told us that supernatural hypotheses were not part of science, yet the director of the ICR, Dr. Henry Morris, always makes it perfectly clear to his listeners and readers that he includes God in all his scientific thinking. And a similar dichotomy was also seen within the ranks of the ICR. One of their speakers, when asked if his speculations about catastrophism could include the Noachian Flood, replied that he had not come out to give a Sunday school lesson—the implication being that he had come to talk about science, not Bible stories.

Creationists also differ widely on scientific matters. One ICR scientist told us that amino acids would not form spontaneously under any conditions that could occur in nature. To form at all they would require conditions that could only be met in the biochemist's laboratory. This was his major point. he said that this was why the Miller-Urey origin-of-life experiment was nothing more than a "trivial exercise in organic chemistry." A few weeks later another ICR scientist claimed in our class that the production of amino acids in meteorites and in interstellar space was a thermodynamic necessity.

We are aware of a few cases where we thought we detected a rather wide gap between what a creationist wrote for the faithful and what he was willing to tell our class. This was particularly striking in the case of a speaker who wrote in an ICR religious tract about evidence for the Biblical flood.[7] When he talked to our class, he spoke only in general terms, to the effect that asteroid impacts in the ocean basins could have caused floods much larger than anything documented in history books. He agreed that his hypothesis might account for many less-than-worldwide floods. This did not sound like Biblical literalism to us.

We have often asked ourselves what it is that would cause apparently sincere individuals to be publicly inconsistent with themselves, with each other, and with established scientific practices. As much thought as we have given to their motivations, no single reason seems to explain very much.

Creationists are admittedly in the evangelism business: their job is to change people's beliefs. With this in mind we have conducted surveys in the class in an attempt to measure their success. The survey is a self-evaluation of belief that is filled out during the first and last class periods of each semester. Students do not sign their names, but we are able to pair the before and after ratings with the use of birth dates. We are aware of the many shortcomings of our surveys. I have already mentioned one problem—that some of the students do not know how to define their own beliefs at the beginning of the class. Our survey assumes that the respondent does possess this information. Another obvious fault with our survey is the small sample size, N = 36. Nevertheless, we have allowed ourselves some speculations based on these data.

"Before" and "after" responses were voluntary and anonymous and were paired by birth dates. The numbers refer to the number of respondents having the "before" and "after" responses corresponding to that coordinate position. Thus, numbers above the diagonal line represent students claiming a move toward evolution, while those below the line represent students claiming a move

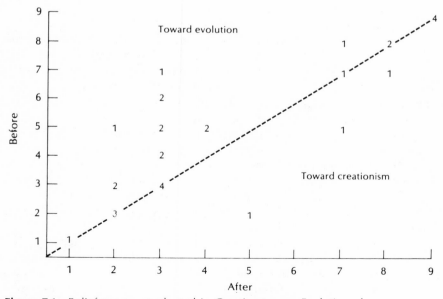

Figure 7.1 Belief survey conducted in Creation versus Evolution class.

toward creationism. These survey results are for the two semesters following the formation of the standard rating scale described in the text. Only the responses of students who were present on the first and last days of classes are included.

We asked students to rate themselves using a scale of 1 to 9 as follows:

9 = Dogmatic creationist—a religious conviction that creationism is absolutely correct.

8 = Creationist—no doubts about the idea

7 = Creationist?—some minor doubts about the idea

6 = Leaning toward creationism—some major doubts about the idea

5 = Fence sitter—both ideas are equally likely

4 = Leaning toward evolution—some major doubts about the validity of evolution

3 = Evolutionist—some minor doubts about the idea

2 = Evolutionist—no doubts about the idea

1 = Dogmatic evolutionist—a religious-like conviction that evolution is absolutely correct

The results of this survey from two semesters are shown in Fig. 7-1. The data are not particularly surprising, in that students who enter the class with strong opinions tend to keep those opinions, while those who initially claim some ambivalence are more likely to change. On the other hand, we can see that thirteen individuals changed their opinions in the direction of evolution while three said they moved in the direction of believing what the creationists had to say. It does not appear that the creationists won many converts with their presentations in our classroom.

From our many conversations with students holding all shades of belief, we had gained the impression that most, if not all, of the students regarded the defense of creationism by the creationists as being illogical and strained. Nevertheless, we had not obtained any of these comments in writing. At the conclusion of a recent semester, however, we decided to ask the students taking the survey to comment on how well they thought each side of the debate was represented. The comments from those favoring evolution were positive regarding our presentation of evolution and rather negative about the creationists' attempts to defend their ideas. Of greater interest to us, however, were the comments from students who rated themselves as creationists in the survey. Here there was some support for the defenders of creationism, such as "yes" response by a "dogmatic creationist" to the question "Was each side well represented?" But there were also comments such as that by a biology major who paradoxically claimed to have moved from a "7" to an "8." This student simply wrote, "Evolution was better represented than creation." The same student also commented that the worst part of the course was "listening to the creationists *try* to defend their views—they seemed very defensive and unsure of themselves on the whole." Another dogmatic creationist wrote, "A few [creationists] need to do more homework." While a fellow "9" wrote that creationists are "useful as iconoclasts, [but] theory [was] poorly supported.

Their controversy has led to greater spread of knowledge about evolution in the masses, by accident I'm sure." Concerning the presentation of the evolution side, the student commented, "from a scientific point of view, [it was] better."

While reviewing the comments by creationist students, we were reminded of a recent article by Singer and Benassi, who invited an amateur magician to their classes and then asked what proportion of the class believed that the guest possessed psychic powers.[8] To their surprise many of the students refused to believe that they had only witnessed a clever magic show consisting of nothing but illusions. Many persisted in their belief of psychic powers even though they could correctly respond to questions that logically would have led them to a nonmystical conclusion. It may be that some of our creationist students persist in their supernatural beliefs by faulting professional creationists, not the ideas of creationism.

We think that our course is a useful endeavor. At the conclusion of each semester we ask the students if they think the course should be offered again. We have never received a negative response. But more importantly we have had several serious science students tell us that the course really made them aware of the many logical and emotional pitfalls that threaten logical thinking. They admit that the creationists seem to represent an extreme example of this type of mistake, but a highly instructive extreme nonetheless.

Notes

1. Henry M. Morris, *Scientific Creationism* (San Diego: Creation-Life Publishers, 1974).

2. John C. Whitcomb and Henry M. Morris, *The Genesis Flood* (Nutley, N.J.: The Presbyterian and Reformed Publishing Company, 1961).

3. Ralph W. Lewis, "Evolution: A System of Theories," *Perspectives in Biology and Medicine* 23 (1980): 551–572.

4. Stephen J. Gould and N. Eldredge, "Punctuated Equilibria: The Tempo and Mode of Evolution Reconsidered," *Paleobiology* 3 (1977): 115–151.

5. Harold S. Slusher, *Critique of Radiometric Dating*, ICR Technical Monograph No. 2 (San Diego: Creation-Life Publishers, 1973).

6. G. Brent Dalrimple, *Radiometric Dating, Geologic Time, and the Age of the Earth*, preprint, 1981. Available from the U.S. Geological Survey, 345 Middlefield Road, Mail Stop 19, Menlo Park, CA 94025.

7. S. Austin, "Origin of Limestone Caves," *Impact* (El Cajon, Calif.: Institute for Creation Research), no. 79. A subscription to the *Impact* and *Acts and Facts* series of publications can be obtained by writing to ICR at 2100 Greenfield Drive, El Cajon, CA 92021. Back issues are available from the same address. As of this writing, there was no charge for these publications.

8. Barry Singer and Victor A. Benassi, "Occult Beliefs," *American Scientist* 69 (1981): 49–55.

CHAPTER 8

Educational Approaches to Creationist Politics in Georgia

Kenneth S. Saladin

Georgia College

The 1920s and 1930s stand out as a period of especially visible anti-evolutionary crusades and attenuation of evolutionary content in biology text-books. Grabiner and Miller attributed this in part to the fact that professional scientists were little aware of the state of public education and did not exert pressure on publishers not to yield to sectarian interests; scientists responded forcefully to the prosecution of John Scopes, they said, but "failed to follow through."[1]

History may remember the 1960s to 1980s as a time when the Fundamentalist attack on evolution was far better orchestrated than in the era of William Jennings Bryan. Whether scientists will follow through this time remains to be seen, but they have responded more vigorously in the past few years than they did sixty years ago. Fundamentalism is not merely attacking science now, but attempting to imitate it and legislate its way into legitimacy. Science seems especially to resent imposters. Scientists have emerged from the ivory tower, established Committees of Correspondence (see Chapter 5), lobbied their legislators, and confronted creationists in the grass-roots arena. Unaccustomed to such organized opposition from scientists, creationist authors may now be realizing that their attempts at political coercion are counterproductive to their evangelistic aims.

Political opposition to creationism is, however, only a stopgap measure. Weinberg cites the need for a two-pronged attack: "first, a public educational program; second, frank political action."[2] Science educators lately have fallen into a paroxysm of self-recrimination, wondering, like the parents of a juvenile delinquent, "Where did we go wrong?" What did we do to produce a public that so grossly misunderstands science and willingly embraces a motley pot-pourri of pseudo-intellectual cults? The depth of our guilt is debatable, although it would certainly be beneficial to begin a more conscientious effort to give students a better sense of the fundamental nature of science. Our students today will very soon be the arbiters of public policy in a society that is obviously becoming ever more technological and dependent on science.

This chapter describes a collegiate educational counterattack on "scientific creationism." I was stimulated to develop such an approach by a four-year spate of creationist legislation in Georgia. This, in turn, is part of a sixty-year history of basically anti-evolutionary legislation in the state. Since this constitutes the cause and historical backdrop of the teaching approach, I briefly recapitulate that history in this chapter. I have elsewhere done so in more detail,[3] but I take this opportunity to correct a few points in that report and to add a description of the creationist crusade at the local school board level. The emphasis here, however, is on the methods and effects of dealing with creationism in the college classroom.

Sixty Years of Creationist Legislation

Seven states passed anti-evolution laws and resolutions from 1921 to 1929. Bryan campaigned for such a law in the Georgia legislature, but none was ever enacted. Georgia House Resolution 93 of 1923 and House Bill 731 of 1924 both passed the House Education Committee and inspired rather colorful rhetoric by their supporters,[4] but neither bill was brought to a floor vote. Shipley[5] and Johnson[6] cited unsuccessful measures to prohibit the teaching of evolution in Georgia in 1925–1927, but I have not been able to confirm either report. Evolution was an eagerly seized-upon topic in the *Atlanta Constitution* through the 1920s but this newspaper apparently mentioned no such legislation here after 1924, and two searches of state archives revealed only the 1923 and 1924 measures.[7]

On the whole, creationist politics went into remission nationally after 1930, and emerged again in the late 1950s for reasons analyzed by Nelkin.[8] Local crusades against evolutionary teaching were vigorous and sometimes violent in the 1960s. The legislative approach, however, was not resurrected until the U.S. Supreme Court overturned the forty-one-year-old Rotenberry Act in Arkansas in 1968, and Mississippi repealed its anti-evolution law, the last in the country, in 1969.

Soon afterward, creationists began to promote "equal time" for Genesis in courses teaching evolution. Six states considered "Genesis bills" in 1973, including Georgia. Tennessee was the only state to enact such a law, and it was abrogated in 1975. The Georgia Senate passed S.B. 276 in 1973 "to assure academic freedom by requiring the teaching and presentation of special creation in public schools if the theory of evolution is taught."[9] The bill went to a ten-member House committee, which conducted hearings throughout the state and heard testimony from teachers, students, clergy, the State Board of Education, and the public. The committee rejected the bill in 1974 on two grounds.[10] First, "the Committee has found that most Georgians, while desiring the availability of information on the various theories of creation in the public schools, do not feel that it is necessary that the subject be mandated by law." Second, the committee learned that the state board had recently adopted the creationist text, *Biology: A Search for Order in Complexity*,[11] "which gives extensive treatment to the theory of special creation, as well as other theories of creation." State adoption permitted local school boards to receive state funds to defray a portion of the cost of locally adopting the text. The committee concluded that local districts thus had the reasonable option of presenting creationism without the need of legislation. While rejecting the bill, the committee recommended that the state board continue to identify creationist textbooks and bring these to the attention of local boards for consideration. The above text remained on the state list of approved biology textbooks through 1983, despite the 1977 case of *Hendren Vs. Campbell* wherein the Superior Court of Marion County, Indiana, found its use to be unconstitutional.[12] Ten more creationist textbooks were subsequently added to the list in Georgia, all published by the Institute for Creation Research (ICR) and the Creation-Science Research Center (CSRC).

"Scientific creationism," the next legislative ploy, owes much of its current progress to Atlanta attorney Wendell Bird. Most such legislation can be traced to a "Resolution for a Balanced Presentation of Evolution and Scientific Creationism" written by him in 1979 for the ICR.[13] Bird joined the ICR the following year for a two-year "ministry" as staff attorney. Although thwarted in his intent to lead the defense team in the 1981 trial on the Arkansas statute, he currently leads the defense in Louisiana. He left the ICR in 1983 to join a Christian law firm in Atlanta,[14] and continues to engage local authorities in debate on creationist legislation.

South Carolina lay evangelist Paul Ellwanger ignored an ICR caveat against using the Bird resolution as legislation—a caveat the ICR itself has apparently abandoned—and drafted a series of derivative state and federal "model bills." These became the basis of the 1981 statutes in Arkansas and Louisiana and 1980–1982 legislation in Georgia and many other states. Several authors have recently traced the peregrinations and sectarian sponsorship of these bills.[15] (See also Appendix A.)

The career of "creation-science" legislation in Georgia is typical. A Baptist church in Atlanta held a 1974 symposium arranged by the ICR. The featured speaker was the ICR's executive director, Dr. Henry Morris, who was billed as "one of the greatest scientific minds of this century." Science teachers were invited to attend and were encouraged to make the symposium a student exercise. As prescribed by Morris, local citizens formed an organization they called "Citizens for Another Voice in Education" (CAVE).[16] CAVE acquired a Bryanesque spokesman, Judge Braswell Deen, Jr., of the Georgia Court of Appeals. Deen courted and received prodigious media attention. Trailed everywhere by television cameras, he denounced evolution as the cause of everything from prophylactics to pollution.[17] Invited by a sympathizer in the Department of Continuing Education at Oglethorpe University, Deen taught a noncredit anti-evolutionary course for one quarter until discovered by an astonished and irate science faculty. They severed the university's association with Deen, but he had assumed a title for himself— Adjunct Professor of Scientific Origins—and used this in public addresses, letters to newspapers, and so forth. CAVE had some success in introducing creationism into an Atlanta school district, but was unable to get the Georgia Department of Education (DOE) to sanction statewide adoption. In 1978, CAVE took its case to the legislature.

Mr. Tommy Smith had just been elected to the House, at the age of twenty-seven, on a government morality platform. He was known in his district mainly for his leadership of Methodist youth and lay witness missions[18] and listed his occupation in the membership director of the General Assembly as "Christian lay activities." Smith was appointed to the education committee and was sought by CAVE as a sponsor. They apparently convinced him of scientific weaknesses in evolution and of the merit of creationism, and Smith rewrote the 1973 "Genesis" bill, substituting "scientific creationism" for "special creation." He introduced this in 1979 as House Bill 690.

The bill was referred by a skeptical education committee chairman to a subcommittee chaired by Representative Cas Robinson, whose career previous to the legislature had included eight years in the Presbyterian ministry followed by administrative work in church evangelism. Robinson took immediate exception to the bill. He objected to its narrow sectarian viewpoint, to the legislation of curriculum, and to the cost of implementation. His subcommittee heard testimony from thirty-three individuals on both sides of the controversy including a representative of ICR, and issued a thorough and multifaceted report in 1980.[19]

House Bill 690, Robinson said, was a crusade promoted by a California religious group interested in a lucrative textbook market. (The ICR and its publishing arm are subsidiaries of the Scott Memorial Baptist Church in San Diego.) At the subcommittee's behest, the Georgia DOE prepared a first-year cost estimate of implementing H.B. 690. The total exceeded $4.9

million, and of this, $1,778,221 would go for textbooks of which the ICR was named as sole supplier. Smith acknowledged that he did not think teachers who disbelieved creationism would present it as science even if H.B. 690 were enacted.[20] His primary objective, he said, was to create a market for ICR textbooks so George school children would have that viewpoint in hand regardless of what the teacher might say. Smith especially promotes *Scientific Creationism* by Henry Morris.[21] The cost of implementation served as a very powerful argument against the bill. Morris has cited this as a major reason that creationist legislation was stalled in Georgia.[22]

Robinson was asked by a majority of his colleagues in the House to keep the bill in committee. Many apparently considered it bad legislation but said it would be politically unaffordable to vote against it if it came to a floor vote. Robinson braved considerable public vilification for stalling the bill through most of the 1980 legislative session, but the committee was finally forced to release it under threat of attachment to another bill on the floor of the House. A bland and patently unconstitutional bill was voted out of committee on the agreement that its supporters would not amend it on the floor of the House or in the Senate. It was, however, subsequently amended in both places "to put the teeth back into the bill." Elsewhere I have described the debates over the bill.[23] It passed the House by 139 to 30 and the Senate by 46 to 7 in 1980, but parliamentary maneuvering kept the bill tied up in a conference committee during most of the final day of the session. The General Assembly had adopted a joint resolution to adjourn *sine die* at 11:30 P.M. on 8 March. The Smith bill emerged from conference committee with less than a half hour on the clock and was preceded on the agenda by a speech from the governor and discussion of another conference committee bill. Opponents of H.B. 690 had been prepared to filibuster, but this was unnecessary. On the previous bill, complex questions and follow-up discussions suddenly sprang up everywhere. Smith was allowed to take the well with thirty seconds remaining, and just as he was about to call for a vote on H.B. 690, the 1980 legislative session was gaveled to adjournment.[24]

Teachers, parents, scientists, and others were alarmed by the narrowness of this defeat, as well as by the discovery that scientific creationism had already been taught in some Atlanta schools without parents' knowledge. They organized in 1980 as the Georgia Citizens' Educational Coalition. This group subsequently joined the network of Committees of Correspondence (Chapter 5) and became a nonprofit state corporation, the Georgia Council for Science Education (GCSE). Also rising against the bill after 1980 were the Georgia School Boards Association, the Georgia Association of Educators, the Georgia Civil Liberties Union, and the American Association of University Professors. A group of Atlanta clergy established the Georgia Committee for Religious Liberty, and the Georgia Academy of Science established a Legislative Guidance Committee, both in response to H.B. 690. In 1981, and again in 1982, Smith introduced a draft of H.B. 690 identical to the Arkansas statute written by Ellwanger, but neither emerged from the Education Committee. Smith attributed its failure to mounting and better organized opposition to the bill from the outside. Of perhaps still greater importance, the bill was increasingly effectively opposed within the legislature, especially by education committee chairman Ben Ross and Speaker of the House Thomas Murphy. Also, the Overton opinion of early 1982 certainly inhibited the progress of such legislation in Georgia and other states that year.

Smith decided not to introduce the bill in 1983, but to await the outcome of litigation against Louisiana's similar statute. Not only because he has reportedly grown tired of the issue, but also because of the unfavorable ruling dealt to the Louisiana statute,[25] it is unlikely that such legislation will soon arise again. As the creationists shift their tactics away from the legislatures, the Committees of Correspondence are turning their attention to putting out numerous creationist "brush fires" and rebuilding the partially razed edifice of science education. The GCSE continues to work on problems with local school boards (below), to "lobby the public" through local print and broadcast media, to provide or assist speakers and debaters in Georgia and elsewhere, and to explore long-range means of support and service to public school teachers.

School Board Actions and Opinions

Georgia has 187 school districts, making it difficult to know what is happening with respect to creationism and evolution statewide. If the mounting influence of adverse court decisions leads creationists to abandon legislative efforts in favor of a redoubled campaign at the local level, both their task and the task of the GCSE face formidable difficulties.

When Representative Smith first introduced Georgia H.B. 690, "he stated that the demand has been so great and the pressure on local school systems has been so heavy, without response by local boards of education, that he felt the need to introduce this legislation. . . . Furthermore, he contend[ed] that evolution is taught exclusively and dogmatically in the public schools. . . ."[26] Research suggests that here, as in Arkansas (see Appendix B), the sponsoring legislator undertook no authentic fact-finding effort in his own state. The Georgia House Education Subcommittee of 1979–1980 had asked the DOE to survey all Georgia school districts on H.B. 690 in 1979. One hundred eleven (59 percent) of the districts responded, and of these ninety reported they had never been asked to teach creationism, nor had they taken any initiative to do so; two had adopted creationism without being asked; twelve had declined to implement creationism despite being asked to do so; and seven had adopted creationism in response to requests. Thus 83 percent of the reporting school districts had received no requests to teach creationism. On 11

November 1979, the subcommittee met with the Georgia Association of School Superintendents. The superintendents almost unanimously said H.B. 690 would create "an unbelievable workload on the local school system," requiring a major overhaul of the curriculum with little financial support from the General Assembly or curriculum guidance from the DOE.[27]

Although nine school districts reported that they had decided to teach creationism, all but two of them apparently abandoned the idea. Representative Smith, for example, reported that his home county of Bacon was one of these but that it had abandoned "scientific creationism" for lack of DOE guidelines.[28] It seems typical that school districts are reluctant to implement such a broad and sensitive curriculum change without direction from the upper echelons of the state educational system. Only two systems in Georgia, both in metropolitan Atlanta, are known to have proceeded without such guidance.

In the course of Judge Deen's highly publicized crusade against evolution, it was inevitable that some school board members would respond. As described by Paula G. Eglin, a science teacher at Lassiter High School in Cobb County, Fundamentalist board member John McClure led the rest of the board, with little debate and by a vote of 7 to 0, to adopt a "balanced treatment" resolution it believed McClure had written. The board, having little knowledge of the scope or California sponsorship of the "creation-science" crusade, spent $7600 on materials from the ICR and distributed these to the schools. Science teachers complained to administrators about the gross misrepresentations of science in these materials, and the school board agreed to reconsider its action. Science department chairpersons testified to the board and pointed out that McClure's resolution had been plagiarized from ICR literature. The school board was not highly impressed with the legal, educational, or philosophical objections to "creation science," but they were impressed with the fact that McClure had sponsored a resolution originally published by Henry Morris and that the school system had subsequently purchased nearly $8000 worth of material from an institution controlled by Morris.

The board voted 5 to 2 in December 1979 not to require the teaching of creationism in the science classes, but this was no real victory for proponents of good education. The board also voted to prohibit the teaching of evolution below the ninth grade; to permit students with religious objections to evolution to substitute another science course for biology; and to implement a course, "Theories of Origins," to be offered as an elective outside the science departments. This course failed for lack of enrollment and was dropped from the curriculum. In the summer of 1982, however, curriculum guides also dropped the last euphemistic vestige of evolution, "speciation."[29]

In December 1984, the Cobb County superintendent's office issued a policy memorandum to teachers itemizing nine "controversial topics," of which two were never to be introduced for discussion by teachers and seven were to be "handled carefully." Evolution was among the latter. For most subjects, teachers "are encouraged to use outside sources of their own selection which they believe to be appropriate for their classroom situations." Teachers were not granted the same professional discretion regarding evolution, however. "[M]aterial related to [evolution] should be limited to that selected and purchased through county procedures." The GCSE complained to the assistant superintendent for curriculum, "Since evolution is no longer covered, mentioned, or even hinted at in *any* of the biology course guides for high school science, and is specifically excluded from middle and elementary school science, [we] fail to see how it can be required to be handled carefully, while not being handled at all." The GCSE foresees an arduous task in not only getting evolution removed from the Cobb County *Index Librorum Prohibitorum*, but getting it reinstated to the curriculum guide.

DeKalb County schools have an excellent national reputation, but long taught "scientific creationism" under Fundamentalist superintendent Robert Freeman. This policy was initiated in 1978 under orders from then-superintendent James Hinson and continued until 1980 without the knowledge of parents. Hinson ordered science teachers to show an ICR audiovisual program[30] and to refrain from criticizing it. He was fired by the board of education in 1980 for unrelated reasons and replaced by Freeman. Freeman made the ICR program optional and lifted the prohibition on criticism, but otherwise sustained the requirement to present "scientific creationism" despite appeals from the GCSE and the DeKalb County Community Relations Commission, which also had complaints about other church-state entanglements under Freeman's administration. In 1984, however, the creationism requirement was quietly dropped from the county's curriculum guide.

Evolutionary Education in Georgia

Others have so cogently argued the necessity of evolutionary theory to meaningful education in biology there is no need to belabor the point here. Teaching biology without it seems tantamount to teaching chemistry without the periodic table. Yet one south Georgia school superintendent remarked in the midst of our 1980 legislative controversy that his district spends "part of one class period of one day" on evolution. Eglin conducted a survey of Georgia science teachers in April 1982, receiving 128 responses geographically distributed in close approximation to the state population distribution. Sixty-two percent said they thought there was no scientific basis for creationism, and 59 percent thought it should be excluded from science courses that deal with origins. Thirty percent thought it should be included, and 11 percent were undecided.[31]

If they were directed to teach creationism as science, about 8 percent said they would refuse and 6 percent said they would simply ignore the order.

Thirty-four percent would teach it, but only as a religious belief, and 29 percent would teach it as a science, as ordered. (The rest did not respond to this item.) Eglin found that only 39 percent of the responding teachers present only evolution in their courses, 27 percent teach both creationism and evolution, and 31 percent teach neither. These data belie Representative Smith's assertion that H.B. 690 was needed because evolution is taught "exclusively and dogmatically" in Georgia.

I have asked college freshmen in recent years about their religous attitudes and how they perceive evolution. I gave the same questionnaire to 166 students in five classes. The questionnaire included both multiple-choice and open-ended items, some based on student responses to prototype questionnaires of earlier years. Students answered the survey questions at the beginning of each course, before the first lecture period, and with no prior discussion of evolution or the creationism controversy. In explanation I said only that I was interested in student opinions on a certain controversial subject in biology. All responses were anonymous.

Some characteristics of the institution and the students may add meaning to the survey answers. Georgia College is a four-year, public college with about 3700 students drawn primarily from a 50-mile radius. Admission requirements include a high school grade-point average of 1.80 and combined Scholastic Aptitude Test score of 530 (the 1983 mean was 892). There are about 120 biology majors, a biology faculty of nine, and usually about six to ten M.S. and M.Ed. candidates. There is no doctoral program. The students in this survey were predominantly freshman nonscience majors taking a two-quarter biology course. Their modal age was eighteen to nineteen (mean 18.8, range seventeen to twenty-six).

Of particular interest at this point of discussion (other data are given later in the chapter) are student responses to the item, "Write what you believe to be a correct definition of the biological theory of evolution." Some of the submitted definitions, with verbatim spelling and composition, seem to reflect the fact that Georgia is the lowest-ranking state in the United States in per capita spending for public education:

- [Man] evolved from some other animal (apes?) who just were here by some scientific majic without any such thing as God as the creator.
- The theory of evolution is basically that man resolve from an ape. I think that the theory could be true in some cases.
- Man developed from a lower case animal.
- It's a theory that considers the changes in life to determine what comes first and what comes last. A theory that man cannot determine with his head, it takes on scientific meaning with a little help from the space.
- The biological theory of evolution is that man has more than one life. When someone dies they will come back as something else.

- The means of mind being able to compute the gases and chemical compounds of structures together.
- Evolution is the term meaning the time period of making a completedness and starting again. Evolution is like the time it takes for the earth to completely revolve until it is back at the same position as when it started.
- It is based on that people are cycled around a certain growth span and it hav taken hundred of years to learn knowledge that we have today.
- The biological theory of evolution is dealing with biology in a sense. It has to do with the beginning of the sciences, I guess.
- The theory of evolution in my opinion is something like the Big Bang theory is where the universe is began and how it functions and feature start.
- It is the way and time that the earth changes. It may be in the rotation or the way the sun heats. It also has to deal with living things.
- That God created Adam & Eve exzactly as we appear today & he created the heavens & the earth in 6 days.
- Evolution is the process of living things evolving over a period of time. That is a very rough but nevertheless a general definition of this lunacy called evolution.
- The theory of evolution is that which science believes in.
- I don't know. I don't understand what an evolution is.

Of the 166 students giving a definition, 29.5 percent defined evolution strictly in terms of the development of human beings from a lower animal, generally an ape; 26.5 percent defined it in terms of natural selection or the appearance of organisms of increasing complexity; 10.2 percent equated it to the Genesis account of Adam and Eve and 6.6 percent to theistic evolution; 4.2 percent defined it in terms of the Big Bang; 3.0 percent said they did not know what evolution is; and 20.0 percent submitted definitions too obscure to classify, such as some of those quoted above.

Such responses are probably not attributable entirely to insufficient treatment of evolution in middle or high school. In freshman biology courses it is frequently difficult to find anyone in class who has ever heard of a fungus, a jellyfish, or a dragonfly, much less a mitochondrion or trilobite. I have taught courses for high school biology teachers and have often found that even they have no comprehension of such basic terms as "mitochondrion," "ATP," or even "extract." An appalling number of students say they have never had to write a term paper, take an essay examination, or do homework. One recently said she had never read an entire book.

If these claims are true, we should not be surprised at the current controversy or at the vulnerability of many facets of the scientific enterprise to political whim. Such statements should compel us to take a searching look at our own educational methods and to accept some responsibility for bringing the present controversy upon ourselves.

The Uses of Creationism in College Education

Creationists tend to assume that those who oppose their political aims are desperate to prevent students from being exposed to creationist ideas. Yet many of the educators most actively involved in the controversy also most avidly introduce creationism into their own classrooms. They do not oppose (and indeed should encourage) the critical examination of evolution and creationism. But educators do justifiably oppose creationism being misrepresented as a science, being imposed on teachers by law or school board fiat, and becoming a red herring that diverts educators from the real business of teaching science.

Students can be taught a great many factual details of biology and geology, and more importantly, can develop a better understanding of the intellectual habits and constraints of science, by analyzing the claim of creationism that it is scientifically supportable. Several college courses do this (including the course at San Diego State University described in Chapter 7). In Georgia, such courses have been taught at Columbus College by David Schwimmer,[32] at Mercer University of Atlanta by Dan May, and at Georgia College by Everette Barman and me. The balance of this chapter describes the methods and some results of my approach at Georgia College.

A Priori Student Attitudes

Before embarking on any course that deals critically with such a divisive issue, it is important to understand the attitudes students bring with them. Thus I have administered anonymous questionnaires, as described above, not only in freshman biology courses that touch very little on creationism, but also in seminars for biology majors where the controversy is studied in depth.

Two hundred seventy-nine students have responded anonymously to one item in which they chose one of four statements—basically unlabeled definitions of theism, pantheism, agnosticism, and atheism—that most closely agreed with their personal beliefs. There were 75.6 percent theists, 20.1 percent pantheists, and 4.3 percent agnostics and atheists. Out of 275 students, 29.5 percent said they attend church once or more than once every week, 24.7 percent attend at least once a month but not every week, and 45.8 percent attend rarely or never, or only under parental influence when living at home. Thus the respondents include about 211 theists, but 126 who seldom go to church on their own initiative. Students seem to retain their emotional commitment to Biblical theism longer than their commitment to institutional religious observance. Several interpretations might be placed on this, and are best left to students of religion. Patterns of church participation, and the total of 24.4 percent of those students who do not seem to believe in a personal god, but at most in a supernatural "something out there," perhaps reflect the uncertainty and philosophical metamorphosis one would expect of college students.

Table 8-1 suggests that biology majors are less conservative than nonscience majors in some religious values. It must be pointed out, however, that the 25 to 26 biology majors responding to item 1–3, and about 22 percent of those responding to item 4, were juniors and seniors, whereas the nonscience majors were predominantly freshmen in their first quarter or two of college. Age and experience alone may contribute as much to these results as the choice of major.

The tabulated data and error probabilities show that biology majors pray to a personal god no less frequently than nonmajors. Substantially fewer biology majors, however, believe in personal afterlife, a question on which their biology curriculum may have some bearing. Belief in Biblical inerrancy is directly relevant to the credibility one would accord to creationism. Biology majors show somewhat less tendency toward Biblical literalism, especially in the greater fraction who regard the Bible as "a purely human anthology of stories, poems, letters, fables, etc., inevitably containing many errors and differences of opinion."

Item 4 in Table 8-1 shows, surprisingly, that substantially equal percentages of biology and nonbiology students entirely reject evolution. Biology

Table 8-1. Comparative Religious and Evolutionary Attitudes in Nonscience Majors versus Biology Majors[a]

	Biology Majors	Nonscience Majors	p[b]
1. Students who pray "occasionally or often"	(26)	(116)	
	92.3%	93.1%	0.900
2. Students who believe in personal afterlife	(26)	(114)	
	76.9%	94.7%	0.005
3. Students who accept that scripture contains:	(25)	(113)	
No errors	28.0%	42.5%	0.104
Minor errors and contradictions	60.0%	53.1%	0.501
Numerous errors and contradictions	12.0%	4.4%	0.011
4. Students who regard evolution as:	(120)	(155)	
Totally untrue	21.7%	27.1%	0.117
True except for humans	12.5%	21.9%	0.005
True and divinely guided	52.5%	45.2%	0.095
True and naturalistic	13.3%	5.8%	0.005

[a]Given as percentages of the parenthetically indicated sample sizes.
[b]Error probabilities (P) are based on chi-square tests.

majors are, however, significantly more inclined to accept naturalistic evolution in which God plays no necessary part, and they are less inclined to exempt humans from a natural process to which all other life is subject. (I find a surprising number of biology professors who accept evolution for everything else but draw the line at humans, who they believe were specially created—a peculiar dominion of emotion over reason.) Among both science and nonscience students, theistic evolution emerges as a comfortable and popular compromise.

A Senior Seminar on Creationism

I have taught a creationism seminar to junior and senior biology majors three times in the last two years. At least one seminar course is required of all our biology majors, to develop student communication and analytic skills through a combination of written papers and oral classroom presentations. The theme of the seminar varies among instructors, but I find that creationism lends itself very well to these general purposes and gives the course added dimensions described below.

I have thirty hours of classroom contact with the students: one-hour periods three times a week for ten weeks. The content and format of my course differ to some degree every quarter,[33] but I have always begun with a few didactic lectures on the history of evolution as an intellectual controversy from Ionia to the present. I emphasize the recent politics and rhetoric of "scientific creationism," ending my historical overview around the third week with the ICR audiovisual program described earlier[34] as an example of the current methods and stance of the "scientific creationists." The class discusses the program's content and techniques of persuasion; and this leads into basic questions about the respective criteria of science and religion, the scientific and lay meanings of "fact" and "theory," and similar broad issues. I have routinely followed this with an anticreationist audio-filmstrip that treats creationism as an extension of the Copernican controversy and discusses the issues of supernaturalism, the criteria and processes of science, and the failure of creationism to qualify as science.[35]

Some approaches used in past quarters have been changed not because they failed in their purpose but to create time to experiment with other methods. For example, in the first two seminars the next student assignment was to give a ten-minute class presentation on other religious controversies over science as detailed by White.[36] I find students often know of creationism only from the news media but may look upon it as a trivial and transient oddity. Many have never heard of the Scopes trial. They do not know who Giordano Bruno was and why he was burned alive, or why Galileo was censured. White's volumes, though nearly a century old, place the present conflict in historical perspective. From this perspective, it seems students could scarcely help but see that Fundamentalist opposition to teaching evolution is about as rational as its opposition to lightning rods, vaccination, and psychiatry.

In past quarters I found Appleman's anthology on Darwinism a very suitable textbook for conveying the broad social and philosophical relevance of evolutionary theory.[37] It gives students, perhaps, a memorable awakening to the importance of the subject matter beyond the laboratory bench. Its 174 pages from Darwin's key books provide the most exposure to Darwin's writing that most students will ever have. In subsequent seminars, and with somewhat less satisfaction, I have used Kitcher's recent critique of creationism as a text.[38] Textbooks and memorization are not meant to become dominant tasks in a seminar, so I have generally scheduled readings and encouraged their completion by means of either take-home or open-book examination.

In the past I have centered few class periods on explicit criticisms of creationist arguments, giving at most three or four lectures on such issues as the creationist interpretations of *Archaeopteryx*, the Paluxy River tracks, stratigraphy, and radiometric dating. The current use of Kitcher's book somewhat dictates the use of more class time on such criticism. I have been circumspect toward students' religious beliefs and have spent little class time on the Biblical aspect of creationism. I have, however, usually spent one period on the first and second chapters of Genesis. Most students are, until then, unaware that there are two distinct accounts of creation (not to mention fragments of a third and perhaps fourth) and have amalgamated the story of Adam and Eve into the same scenario as the six-day creation week. I defer to works by Gilkey[9] and Moody[40] and I use a tape by Skehan[41] to provide students with a theological perspective on the issue. Skehan's lecture in particular brings visible relief to many students who apparently did not yet see that the overwhelming evidence of science does not call for a repudiation of the important elements of Christian faith.

I have used two methods, a term paper and class debate, every time I have offered the course. In past quarters I have suggested a broad range of term-paper topics and have made available to students about a dozen creationist books (especially Morris, *Scientific Creationism*), three creationist periodicals, and three loose-leaf collections of literature: one of assorted creationist material, one of anticreationist papers, and one of relatively objective historical treatments and court decisions on creationism. I have gotten generally quite good papers on scientific, legal, historical, philosophical, theological, and biographical aspects of the controversy. I have also experimented with Schwimmer's method, assigning each student one issue of the ICR *Impact* bulletin—most of which are four-page technical polemics against evolution— as the basis for a critical term paper.[42]

Class debates are an especially interesting and productive teaching method. At the outset of the course, I always distribute copies of Smith's Georgia House Bill 690 (roughly the same as Arkansas' Act 590) for overnight study and ask students to return the next day with a straw vote on the bill. Usually about half the class favors it. From their early remarks in class, reports from the White volumes, and so forth, I assess how articulate and confident each student seems to be. By the fourth week of the course, I divide the class into two to four teams of three or four students each, attempting to balance the teams with respect to their attitudes toward H.B. 690 and their verbal skills. Students have the rest of the quarter to prepare for an end-of-term debate on the proposition that any teacher in Georgia who presents evolution be required by law to give equal treatment and respect to "scientific creationism." An especially useful element in these debates is that each team takes the creationist position on one day and then, usually after a day or two of self-assessment and preparation, takes the anticreationist position. This deflects any potential charge of bias against a student's personal beliefs, but more importantly, it cultivates more skill in self-expression than if students were only to argue a point with which they actually agree. The debates are usually judged by additional faculty, the biology honors society, or students from other courses who are offered a little extra credit for the task (which spreads the educational effect a little beyond those enrolled in the seminar). About 2 percent of the course grade is based on winning debates, seldom enough to affect the final grade but enough to stimulate a vigorous effort that is always enjoyable to watch. A good, articulate team can and often does win the debate regardless of which position it takes.

Effects of the Use of Creationism in College Education

Using creationism in such a seminar, as well as my more limited uses of it in freshman biology and zoology and an interdepartmental honors seminar, has had four especially noticeable effects: (1) class discussions are especially animated and thought-provoking; (2) students gain appreciable self-directed education in the natural sciences, philosophy, law, and other areas; (3) creationism loses credibility, at least as a science; and (4) students question principles they have never before doubted. Let me elaborate on these.

Liveliness of Class Discussions. Considering what subject to use as the basis of a ten-week seminar brings to mind several timely and controversial issues in science. I have tried, to a limited degree, such topics as sociobiology, genetic engineering, heritability of intelligence, and others, but the creationism controversy has been by far the most fruitful. The political influence wielded by the creationists, the annual introduction of creationist legislation in the state, and the prolific media coverage of this subject all make this a more timely and urgent issue to students and instructors. Moreover, virtually all students feel they have an emotional stake in the outcome of this political conflict. As several educators, both creationist and anticreationist, have commented, this by itself makes class discussions more animated and thought-provoking than one is likely to see in many other courses.

Academic credit and grades tend to recede in importance. The course is a forum for students to express themselves on a vitally important issue to them, and for them to hear the thoughts of other students and instructors. In a word, it is fun.

Self-directed Education. Creationism is a stimulating subject for a biology course because it touches upon so many areas in addition to biological knowledge. Students are led to read, explore, and think on the interface between biology and theology, constitutional law, the legislative process, history, philosophy, and other sciences such as geology, astronomy, and physics. The debate method, in particular, forces students to become broadly versed in these areas. It is difficult to defend any position against the specious arguments of pseudo-intellectual opposition. Evolution is especially difficult to defend because it requires such a broad technical knowledge; even professional scientists used to fare poorly against professional anti-evolutionary debaters. In class debates, the creationist team may vacuously argue that radioactive decay rates may have varied over the course of earth history, that there are vanishingly few good examples of transitional fossil species, or that laws of probability dictate against the original formation of organic molecules such as nucleotides and peptides. The anti-creationist team must either artfully show an audience of judges—largely biology students not enrolled in the seminar—that these do not bear importantly on the real issue of the debate, or they must know and skillfully express the errors in these very wide-ranging creationist arguments. But they cannot evade the issue. Lack of knowledge, logic, organization, or oratory skill is fatal to the debate and compromises the grades of every student on the team. The educational value of this approach has been quite impressive. Anyone who has followed the last several years of creationist polemics and has tried to identify in his or her own mind the errors in their arguments will understand this point very well.

Creationism's Loss of Scientific Credibility. I have both quantitative and impressionistic indications that such a course causes creationism to fall in esteem among students, at least in its effort to masquerade as science. I have usually given my students an identical, anonymous questionnaire before and after the course; the results from two classes are shown in Table 8-2. By the end of the seminar about twice as many students felt creationism is contradicted by the evidence of science as at the beginning. More than half the class at the outset thought creationism should be given equal time with evolution in science classes, but only one-quarter thought so at the end. Half the class supported H.B. 690 at the beginning, one-fifth at the end. Many students professed to be Biblical creationists but said they could see only harm in forcing science teachers to present creationism.

Students naturally tend to conform to what they think the professor wants to hear, and such data may certainly be criticized on that point. To counteract this as much as possible I have emphasized that I am much more

Table 8–2. Student Attitudes before and after a Senior Biology Seminar on Creationism.[a]

	Before	After
1. Creationism:	(26)	(25)
Is contradicted by science	30.8%	60.0%
May have some scientific support	50.0%	32.0%
Is thoroughly consistent with the evidence of science	19.2%	8.0%
2. High school biology courses should teach:	(24)	(24)
Only evolution	11.5%	16.7%
Evolution; mention creationism as religion	26.9%	58.3%
Equal time and credence as science	61.5%	25.0%
Creationism; mention evolution briefly	0.0%	0.0%
Only creationism	0.0%	0.0%
3. Should Georgia enact H.B. 690?	(24)	(25)
Yes	50.0%	20.0%
No	50.0%	80.0%

[a]Parentheses indicate the number of students responding, pooled from two classes taught in 1982. The results are significant on all three questions at the 0.01 level of confidence (chi-square).

interested in students who might disagree with me but who express their opinions well than in students who blandly agree. I have stressed that there is no real satisfaction in merely converting students to my opinion; moreover, to convert someone to evolution is about as meaningless a notion to me as to convert someone to physiology. I have also pointed out that, statistically, creationist and noncreationist students have received equivalent grades in the course. The mean ± standard deviation of the grades of eight creationist students to date are 88 ± 5.96, and those of eight noncreationist students 92 ± 3.18. The difference is insignificant (Student's t = 1.67, p greater than 0.10). (The rest of my students were graded by a different system and so cannot be included in this comparison.) In this small department and college, my views are well known, and if students sought merely to appease their instructor one would expect less support for creationism even in the preseminar survey. I have always tried to understate my own viewpoint and be circumspect toward students' religious values. Class discussions have been candid, and I think there is no reason to believe students have felt inhibited about expressing views contrary to the instructor's in class, much less on anonymous questionnaires.

Such criticism may also be answered from the perspective afforded by Thwaites (Chapter 7), who has the advantage of teaching in the same city as some leading creationist institutions. Thwaites shows that creationism loses credibility among students even when notable creationists themselves are given 50 percent of the classroom time and examination questions. In my own classes, the creationist literature has been clearly self-discrediting. I need only provide students with the publications of Henry Morris, Duane Gish, and others, and they soon enough discover for themselves that these writers—billed as the world's leading creation "scientists," the "greatest scientific mind[s] of the century"—seriously contend that plants are not alive because they were created two days before "living creatures" (Genesis 1:12), and furthermore were eaten long before death was first visited upon the world; that the light of the stars was created, and already on its way to earth, before the stars themselves; that the fossils are stratified in complexity because the more advanced animals ran uphill faster than their slow, primitive comrades and escaped Noah's flood longer. There is little need for the instructor to add to that!

An instructive incident occurred in 1982 when I taught an interdepartmental seminar for honors students, which featured five guest speakers on various aspects of the creationist controversy. The first week's speaker was a history professor who gave a rather dispassionate overview of the development of the conflict. Audience response led us to believe there was an appreciable number of creationists in the group, arguing for "fairness" and "equal time." The next speaker, two weeks later, was Representative Smith, who began by passing out the bill he had so long sponsored in the state legislature. Exposed to this bill for the first time, students read through it, grew surprisingly cynical, and gave Smith an altogether difficult evening. He commented afterwards that our students were even worse than Atlanta journalists! These were not primarily science majors, and only two people in the audience of fifty were in my concurrent biology seminar on creationism.

These general results seem to occur whenever creationist literature is submitted to the scrutiny of students with two or three years of college education behind them. To be sure, creationist literature wins a handful of converts. I have had two or three students in my seminars more favorably disposed toward "scientific creationism" at the end, as have Thwaites and Awbrey (Chapter 7). But in general, creationism does not fare well when it is subjected to the same rationalistic, skeptical treatment that must be endured by any authentic science.

The Wisdom of Uncertainty. Finally, such courses tend to make students a little more skeptical and open-minded, and a little less dogmatic, on issues broader than just "scientific creationism." It is an inexhaustible source of wonder that beginning college students exhibit so little experience of the world and so little spirit of inquiry and healthy skepticism. Several of my students in freshman human physiology have thought that women have one rib more than men, and apparently never thought to count. Many accept the Bible as historically and scientifically unquestionable, but apparently have not read it very well. Nearly all of my seminar students agree that the Bible says the world was created in six days, with Adam as the first man and Eve created later from his rib. They are astonished when I ask them to read Genesis 1 and 2 and draw up a list of the order of creation, discovering that the order of events and even the mode of human creation is so markedly different in the two narratives, and that Adam and Eve have no connection with the six-day creation week. It was probably a typical student who wrote, in an anonymous evaluation of the seminar,

> This course has confused me more than anything else. I've always believed in the creation and have never given any thought to an alternative. I believe there are variations within a species but am not quite sure what standpoint I take. Can [I] believe in both—somehow?

This is the kind of student who has found my recording of Skehan's AAAS lecture (see also Chapter 2) such a welcome answer to a pressing intellectual and religious dilemma.

A colleague who teaches a similar seminar has remarked that he will know he is doing his job when he begins to convert the Fundamentalists themselves. At Georgia College, Professor Barman (Department of Biological and Environmental Sciences) and I have each taught a young Fundamentalist minister who, despairing of a livelihood in that profession, returned to college for a chemistry degree. He came to us avowing the infallibility of Scripture and bristling at any suggestion of evolution in our courses. He took Barman's general biology course in which there is strong emphasis on scientific method and on the evolutionary underpinnings of all biology, and then my general zoology course. I treat freshman zoology from a phylogenetic and thoroughly evolutionary and adaptational perspective. I use audio-filmstrip adaptations of David Attenborough's television series Life on Earth to dramatize the major evolutionary themes of vertebrate development.[43] By the time he completed these courses he said he was no longer certain what he believed. He could not dismiss the cogent weight of biological evidence, and he felt the "scientific creationists" go to excess in their denunciation of evolution, but neither could he accept that "God would have made a mistake when He wrote Genesis." He said he simply considered his mind open on the issue. Carrying his coals to Newcastle one day, he came excitedly into my office to say he had read some thought-provoking essays in Natural History. He wondered if I had ever heard of a writer named Stephen Jay Gould.

So it is little wonder that the "scientific creationists," barely beneath the surface, are profoundly anti-intellectual. Their doctrine cannot withstand intellectual scrutiny. Walter Lammerts, first president of the Creation Research Society, has understandably declared:

> Science in more ways than evolution must be completely reorganized. In fact, our whole civilization needs a going over. Mechanization and all its horrible consequences—air pollution, highway networks, college and university courses, federal bureaucracy—need to be done away with.[44]

College is not supposed to be a comfortable haven where sacred ideas go unchallenged. Students who have never given serious thought to alternatives to their cherished suppositions ought to find college a soul-searching experience. Higher education should instill skepticism and uncertainty. This is not an iconoclastic assault on faith and hope, but an effort to replace a blind faith with an informed and malleable one, to give hope not grounded in mental escapism. If education has a disquieting effect on hitherto unquestioning students, it has done its job. Doubt, uncertainty, skepticism, insecurity—these are the first steps toward greater wisdom, compassion, tolerance, and constructive social responsibility.

Conclusion and Recommendations

It is most unfortunate that so many scientists continue to scoff at the "scientific-creationists" as if they were merely another harmless lunatic fringe, as if opposing creationism would be as worthless as mounting a crusade against astrology. Regardless of the intellectual vacuity of "scientific creationism," its proponents wield tremendous political power and cannot be taken lightly. Science and education are funded by public officials who generally have little understanding of either one and who may be quite willing to yank the rug from under science at the behest of sectarian interests. If we ignore the problem posed by creationist politics, we will be in for a rude awakening.

Consider, for example, that Ellwanger, who got two state legislatures to pass his anti-evolution bills, has promoted a related federal bill with some supporters on Capitol Hill. It would have required that anyone applying for a research grant from the National Science Foundation, for example, sign a statement of adherence to either the creationist or evolutionary model. The NSF would then be required to distribute equal funds to the two factions. The bill would require federally funded museums and parks, such as the Smithsonian and Yellowstone, to match their evolutionary exhibits with creationist ones. It would bar all federal funding of curricula that touch on the origin of life or the cosmos.

It is easy, tempting, and dangerous to laugh this off. But in 1976, Arizona Congressman John Conlan succeeded in having the U.S. House of Representatives pass, by 222 to 174, an amendment to the National Defense Education Act to prohibit federal funding of any curriculum project with evolutionary content or implications. Congress only barely defeated his 1977 bill to require congressional approval of all curriculum projects prior to allocation of NSF funds, including, for example, the Biological Sciences Curriculum Study. Congress did temporarily halt NSF curriculum funds pending review of such programs. In these initiatives, Conlan effectively employed the hoax that teaching evolution is government-sponsored indoctrination in "the religion of secular humanism." Dorothy Nelkin recently reported that the NSF recommends that grant applicants not mention the word "evolution" in their abstracts, which are read by Congress.[45] California Congressman William Dannemayer introduced a bill in 1982 to bring the Smithsonian Institution under congressional review, making it possible to reduce its treatment of evolution. Intimidation of publishers and teachers by Fundamentalists has widely achieved what the legislation of the 1920s was meant to do—eliminate evolution from the classroom. In 1982, for example, an executive of Laidlaw Brothers, a subsidiary of Doubleday & Co., said the firm would not use the word "evolution" in a new biology textbook so that the firm could avoid controversy and "sell thousands of copies."[46]

Barring a successful assault on federal granting agencies—which is by no means inconceivable—creationists will not put an immediate damper on the progress of evolutionary studies. But under their influence, students will become all the more hopelessly out of touch with science—not just its phenomenal progress and successes of the 1970s and 1980s, but with its very premises and methods. One who accepts that an intractable scientific problem may be blithely sacrificed to a supernatural explanation, who accepts as Henry Morris does that the authority of Scripture should put an end to all further questions of, for example, terrestrial chronology, can hardly be expected to make any meaningful contribution to science. And if the current crop of students is strongly persuaded by creationist illogic, we might well expect a stagnation or at least an impediment to scientific progress on the horizon. We can judge the potential productivity of students subjected to this kind of miseducation from the current scientific productivity of the so-called institutions of creationist "research," which is nil. They do not have a *method* for empirically approaching questions about nature. They "solve" everything, and therefore nothing, on Scriptural grounds. We scarcely need elaborate on the Orwellian dangers of revising the curriculum for political, doctrinal reasons rather than educational ones. Such education will simply leave students intellectually behind, ill prepared for college or career, and possibly abandoned by a world in which scientific and technological understanding is fast becoming indispensable.

It is vital that scientists and educators understand creationist politics, acknowledge and confront its real dangers, and undertake emergency political defenses in the grass-roots arena. I need not repeat Weinberg's exhortations and suggested methodology (Chapter 5). But we must also realize that political defense is only a short-term, superficial solution to a deep-seated, long-term problem. It is the treatment of a symptom, not the disease. In the long run, we must acknowledge the educational imperatives raised by this conflict.

I suggest that college educators welcome creationist materials into the classroom, but remember that the science classroom is no place for a doctrine, Biblical or not, to be treated as a sacred cow. Expose creationism to the harsh light of rational criticism. Provide students with a few basic intellectual tools and let them work on the literature themselves. The literature will turn upon itself and discredit its own authors and their cause. The instructor need not personally attack the cause in lectures.

Such courses are uniquely stimulating and enjoyable. They are no substitute for didactic courses, but they are a valuable complement to them. Students can learn a great deal by having to defend their position orally against opposing charges and by having to assemble and convincingly articulate the facts on which this controversy touches. The debate format has probably been the single most valuable element of my own seminars, and I strongly recommend it as a teaching tool. I think the basic approaches described in this chapter could also be productive in areas other than creationism versus the biological and earth sciences. One might, for example, similarly employ von Däniken to teach archeology, Velikovsky to teach astronomy—and geophysics, or naturopathy to teach dietetics.

The creationist controversy brings out the importance of being an *educator* and not merely a lecturer, a *professor* and not merely a fact dispenser. We cannot reach everyone, but we do have the overwhelmingly dominant influence in educating those who will soon be influential makers of public policy. By 1990, a substantial number of those now in our classrooms will be teachers, school board members, legislators, parents, and voters. Now is the time for educators to profess, argue, debate, stand for something. We must make it clear to students that education, reason, and good will are vitally important to the survival and progess of humane society. We must invite our students, implore them, to join with us in the defense of these values against the enemies of the intellect.

Notes

1. J. V. Grabiner and P. D. Miller, "Effects of the Scopes Trial," *Science* 185 (1974): 832–37.
2. S. L. Weinberg, "Two Views of the Textbook Watchers," *American Biology Teacher* 40 (1978): 541–45.
3. K. S. Saladin, "Sixty Years of Creationism in Georgia," *Society* 20, no. 2 (1983): 17–25.
4. Ibid.
5. M. Shipley, "Growth of the Anti-evolution Movement," *Current History* 32 (1930): 330–32.
6. A. W. Johnson, *The Current Status of Church-State Relationships in the United States, with Special Reference to the Public Schools* (Minneapolis: University of Minnesota Press, 1934).
7. Charles Brooks, formerly president of the Georgia Citizens' Educational Coalition, searched the archives in preparation for our presentation to the AAAS symposium, from which this volume is derived, and found only the 1923 and 1924 House actions. After I discovered the Shipley and Johnson reports, Virginia Schadron of the Georgia Department of Archives and History specifically

searched for verification of either one and found none. I am grateful for both their efforts.

8. D. Nelkin, *Science Textbook Controversies and the Politics of Equal Time* (Cambridge: MIT Press, 1977).

9. Incorrectly reported as S.B. 273 in note 3.

10. E. B. Toles et al., *Report of the Committee to Study the Teaching of Divine Creation in the Public Schools* (Atlanta: Georgia General Assembly, 1974).

11. J. N. Moore and H. S. Slusher, eds., *Biology: A Search for Order in Complexity* (Grand Rapids, Mich.: Zondervan Publishing House, 1970).

12. *Hendren et al.* vs. *Campbell et al.* in Superior Court No. 5, Marion County, Indiana, 1977; reprinted in Jerry P. Lightner, ed., *A Compendium of Information on the Theory of Evolution and the Evolution-Creation Controversy* (Reston, Va.: National Association of Biology Teachers, 1978.)

13. W. R. Bird, Resolution for Balanced Presentation of Evolution and Scientific Creationism, *ICR Impact Series* no. 71 (1979).

14. Anonymous, "Wendell Bird Joins Atlanta Law Firm," *Acts & Facts* 11 (11, 1982): 3.

15. W. J. Broad, "Louisiana Puts God into Biology Lessons," *Science* 213 (1981): 628–29; R. Lewin, "A Tale with Many Connections," *Science* 215 (1982): 484–87; R. L. Numbers, "Creationism in Twentieth-Century America," *Science* 218 (1982): 538–44.

16. H. M. Morris, *Introducing Creationism into the Public Schools* (San Diego: Institute for Creation Research, 1975).

17. Saladin, "Sixty Years of Creationism."

18. F. Moore, "What In Creation Is the Fuss About?" *Atlanta Constitution*, 18 February 1982.

19. C. M. Robinson et al., *Report of Interim Subcommittee to Study H.B. 588, H.B. 603, and H.B. 690* (Record Group 37-8-35, Box 11, Location 1855-06, Georgia Department of Archives and History, Atlanta).

20. Tommy Smith, interview with author and class lecture at Georgia College, Milledgeville, 26 April 1982.

21. H. M. Morris, ed., *Scientific Creationism* (Public School Ed.), (San Diego: Creation-Life Publishers, 1974).

22. H. M. Morris, "The Anti-creationists," *Impact*, no. 97 (1981).

23. Saladin, "Sixty Years of Creationism."

24. K. S. Saladin, "Creationist Bill Dies in Georgia Legislature," *The Humanist* 40, no. 3 (1980): 59–60; C. M. Robinson, "A View from Within," paper presented at a symposium titled "How 'Bout Them Dogmas?" Dealing with Creationism in Georgia," University of Georgia, Athens, 28 January 1983.

    To correct misprints in reference 3, H.B. 690 was introduced in 1979, not 1980, and held in subcommittee until 1980, not 1981.

25. Louisiana's creationism law, passed by the state legislature in July 1981, was abrogated by U.S. district court judge Adrian Duplantier on 10 January 1985. He declared that any concept of special creation is inescapably theological and therefore not constitutionally proper content for the science curriculum.

26. Robinson et al., *Report of Interim Subcommittee*.

27. Ibid.

28. T. Smith, interview with the author, 26 April 1982.

29. P. G. Eglin, "Confronting Creationism in the Local School District," paper presented at the symposium "How 'Bout Them Dogmas? Dealing with Creationism in Georgia," University of Georgia, Athens, 28 January 1977.

30. Anonymous, *Creation and Evolution: A Comparison of Two Scientific Models*, audio cassette and 76 slides (San Diego: Institute for Creation Research, 1983).

31. P. G. Eglin, "Creationism versus Evolution: A Study of the Opinions of Georgia Science Teachers," (Ph.D. thesis, Georgia State University, Atlanta, 1983).

32. D. R. Schwimmer, "An Experimental, 'Balanced Treatment' Creation/Evolution Course for College Students: Methods and Results," paper presented at the 59th annual meeting, Georgia Academy of Science, 23–24 April 1982, Columbus, Georgia; also, personal communication.

33. A copy of the syllabus and reading list for this course will be available from the author through December 1988.

34. See note 32.

35. M. D. Stone et al., *Science under Attack: Evolution versus Creationism*, Audio cassettes and filmstrips, 2 parts, 193 frames (Pleasantville, N. Y.: Audiovisual Narrative Arts, 1980).

36. A. D. White, *A History of the Warfare of Science with Theology in Christendom*, 2 vols., 1896 (New York: Dover Publications, 1960).

37. P. Appleman, ed., *Darwin* (New York: W. W. Norton, 1979).

38. P. Kitcher, *Abusing Science: The Case Against Creationism* (Cambridge: MIT Press, 1982).

39. L. Gilkey, "Evolution and the Doctrine of Creation," in *Science and Religion: New Perspectives on the Dialogue*, I. G. Barbour, ed. (New York: Harper and Row, 1968).

40. P. A. Moody, "What of It? An Open Letter to Students," in *Introduction to Evolution*, 3rd ed. (New York: Harper and Row, 1970).

41. J. W. Skehan, "Geological and Theological Perspectives on the Origin of Life on Earth," paper presented at the 148th Annual Meeting, American Association for the Advancement of Science, Washington, D.C., 4 January 1982. Also available as an audiocassette (order no. 82 AAAS/36-37) from Mobiltape Company, Inc., 1741 Gardena Avenue, Glendale, CA 91204. Substantially the same as Chapter 2, this volume.

42. See note 32.

43. D. Attenborough, *Life on Earth: A Natural History* (Boston: Little, Brown, 1979). Audio-filmstrip adaptations from the television series are distributed by Nova Scientific Corporation, Burlington, NC 27215.

44. Quoted in H. P. Zuidema, "Less Evolution, More Creationism in Textbooks," *Educational Leadership* 39 (1981): 217–18.

45. D. Nelkin, personal communication, 24 February 1983.

46. S. Schafersman, "Censorship of Evolution in Texas," *Creation/Evolution* 3(4): 30–34. I spoke on the phone with the same Doubleday/Laidlaw executive and received confirmation of this, which in light of criticism he said had been a "bad judgment" on his part.

Creation, Evolution, or Both?
A Multiple Model Approach

Craig E. Nelson
Indiana University, Bloomington

Science teachers find themselves in the precarious position of being expected by their students, the students'parents, and others to provide expert answers to questions on which prominent experts—or apparent experts—disagree substantially. When these questions are socially controversial, some of the students and their parents can be expected to take exception to any position the teacher presents. Under such conditions, prudence may seem the better part of valor, and the teacher may choose to ignore the issue. This often seems to be the course chosen in the case of "creation, evolution, or both," the origins controversy. My experience with high school teachers in summer biology courses suggests that Indiana's high school biology teachers often do not explicitly teach evolution. Similarly, almost one-fourth of a sample of Kentucky's high school biology teachers rarely or never mention evolution and less than one-third use evolution as a theme tying together the study of biology (Ellis, Chapter 6). Nelkin (Chapter 3) notes that choices by teachers to avoid confrontation by minimizing the treatment of evolution may be the most important impact of the origins controversy. H. J. Muller's classic cry "One hundred years without Darwinism are enough" remains fully relevant.[1]

In talking with Indiana teachers, I find that some feel they have no method of presentation that allows them to deal confidently with all sides. Others find themselves unable to become sufficiently expert to resolve the controversy fully in their own minds. In this chapter I summarize an approach to understanding and presenting socially controversial scientific controversies that addresses both of these concerns. It allows the teacher to present the controversy without having to be an expert, and it facilitates the presentation of the various positions in the controversy. In contrast to Ellis's assertion that "some individuals have an innate ability to deal constructively with divisive issues while others do not," my approach suggests a method whereby all of us—scientists and teachers alike—can learn to analyze and teach controversial issues effectively. I use the "creation, evolution, or both" controversy as an illustration of the approach. At the end of the chapter I will consider further the educational implications.

The approach I suggest has two main parts. The first requires that we explicitly recognize that science is uncertain and that this uncertainty is not just hypothetical or negligible. The second requires us to ask how we can make rational decisions in the face of such uncertainty. This approach is an honest way to teach, because science is, in fact, uncertain. I have found that it is also an effective way to teach, both because it engages the students' interest and because it helps them understand the several sides of each controversy. Further, it can be a safer way to teach, in that it does not put the teacher between the experts. The teacher can say "let's examine this controversy" and then let the experts shoot at each other. On issues where the teacher has a strong opinion, this can be one of those examined. On issues where the teacher does not have (or wish to present) a strong opinion, the students can still learn to understand the issues better by examining all positions. Careful comparison of each position with the criteria of scientific validity will usually allow both the students and the teacher to distinguish positions that are well-justified scientifically from those that are devoid of scientific merit.

The Uncertainty of Science

My first major point is that scientific knowledge is fundamentally uncertain. A basic reason for this uncertainty is that different hypotheses can give identical predictions. Since we can never eliminate all possible alternative explanations, no amount of agreement, not even perfect agreement, between predictions and data ever justifies our believing a hypothesis is certainly true. Popper was an early and effective advocate of the idea that we cannot prove things in science, we can only disprove or falsify them.[2] But he was only half right—we cannot falsify them with certainty either, because in falsifying them we must make other (auxiliary) assumptions, and sometimes these assumptions, rather than the main hypothesis, will be wrong.[3] In his explanation of the fundamentally uncertain nature of science, Bronowski joins this argument with others based on the intrinsically metaphorical nature of language and on Godel's theorem.[4] A good example of uncertainty in science is provided by continental drift.

Continental drift was proposed in the early 1900s on stratigraphic and biological grounds. Geophysicists noted that if continents are going to move, there must be a physical force adequate to move them. They examined the various physical forces (such as tidal and centrifugal forces) that seemed possible and found that all plausible forces were much too weak to move continents. They had thus explicitly falsified continental drift by showing that it was (apparently) physically impossible.[5] That was the proper scientific conclusion. It was exactly what they should have concluded, even though we subsequently discovered that the middle of the sea floor rises, spreads, and pushes the crustal plates along. Hence we now understand a physical force that they could not have examined, and the movement of continents by plate tectonics is regarded as physically inevitable rather than impossible. This illustrates the uncertainty in science that follows from the fact that we can never test all possible alternative explanations. At a minimum, there always remain those that no one has thought of and those that no one presently takes seriously. And sometimes, as in continental drift, one of these is important. Thus, as Kitcher shows, "virtually all of science is an exercise in believing where we cannot prove."[6] Consequently, as Moyer (Chapter 4) notes, each explanation in science must be regarded as only "tentatively true," as "a blueprint of reality, not reality itself," with the clear understanding that for science "absolute truth" and "positive proof" are impossible.

Let us now apply this to the origins controversy. To assert that we know with absolute certainty that evolution by natural selection is what is going on in the real world would be to misrepresent science. It would ignore the inescapable uncertainty that pervades all science. What we need instead is an approach that acknowledges the existence of uncertainty while distinguishing better scientific theories from worse ones.

The existence of uncertainty in a controversy can be understood and presented by making a preliminary list of some alternative choices. Unfortunately, the discussions of many controversies at the interface of science and society are marked by strongly presented but logically flawed dichotomies. The "creation, evolution, or both" controversy is no exception. Creationists often characterize the issue as one of (Christian) creation or (atheistic) evolution. The response of scientists has been too often to contrast (rational) science with (irrational) pseudoscience. The prevalence of these false dichotomies is understandable both in terms of dualistic cognitive structures that assume that certainty is available and that falsehood is evident[7] and, perhaps, in terms of the nature of effective political persuasion. Nevertheless, an essential step in understanding such controversies usually is the delineation of a set of alternative choices. In most cases, several choices are already available and well formulated, although the advocates of the less dichotomous positions may have been less vocal or have received less coverage by the media.

A preliminary list of some possible choices in the creation, evolution, or both controversy is presented in Tables 9-1 and 9-2. Table 9-2 emphasizes positions popular among various divisions of the Judeo-Christian tradition in the United States. Thurman delineates several of these in more detail and

Table 9–1. A Spectrum of Possible Choices for Origins and Some Key Points Related to Each Choice

Atheistic evolution
  1. Atheism on other grounds is often coupled with imperfection in biological systems arguing against a creator.

Nontheistic evolution
  1. Scientific truth is objective and is (or should be) independent of religious assumptions.
  2. Arguments for or against God from natural processes are logically flawed and *vice versa*.

Gradual creation (theistic evolution)
  1. Evolution is God's way of creation (just as gravitation is God's way of controlling the Earth's movement).
  2. Creation is the ultimate origin of the universe and continues at each moment in its maintenance.

Progressive creation (limited evolution)
  1. The great age of the universe, earth, and life are accepted as is the existence of as much evolutionary change as is directly shown by fossils.
  2. New lineages (including humans) are regarded as separate acts of special creation. The complexity of the new forms when created increases progressively through time.

Quick creation ("scientific creationism")
  1. The Earth is only a few thousand years (up to 10,000 years) old.
  2. The geological column was formed in a year-long global flood.
  3. Evolutionary change is only within "kind."

cites a number of books that advocate particular choices.[8] Brief overviews are provided by Cain[9] and Young.[10] A different array of options might be appropriate for some other teacher or for particular audiences. However, the exact content of these lists of options is usually unimportant since their function is to emphasize the breadth of available choices and encourage us to

Table 9–2. Some Bible-based Creation Models

1. *Gradual creation* (theistic evolution): creation by evolution
   a. Gradual creation with *revelation* in six days
   b. Gradual creation with *special creation of humans* (separately or from apes)
   c. Gradual creation with *ruination* at fall of Satan *and recreation* in six days

2. *Progressive creation* (limited evolution): old Earth with numerous acts of special creation *progressing* from primitive to advanced; evolutionary change limited
   a. Progressive creation with *overlapping periods* of creation
   b. Progressive creation with new kinds created only on a few *widely separated creation days or periods*
   c. Progressive creation in distinct episodes, each followed by *catastrophic extinction* with each recreation including more advanced forms

3. *Quick creation* with *apparent age*: creation necessarily involving the appearance of age
   a. *Quick creation* with flood-geology: young Earth, fixed kinds, and geological column formed in one catastrophic *global flood*

SOURCE: Derived in part from L.D. Thurman, *How to Think about Evolution and Other Bible-Science Controversies*, 2d ed. (Downers Grove, Ill.: InterVarsity, 1978).

transcend dichotomies. The lists will often be modified by the discussion of the grounds for choice.

One important conclusion evident from Tables 9-1 and 9-2 is that the available choices in this controversy are both more complex and more congenial than the creation or evolution dichotomy on one hand, or the science or pseudoscience dichotomy on the other. The creation or evolution dichotomy ignores many alternative ways of viewing creation. As Gilkey (Chapter 11) emphasizes, quick creation is a "minor" viewpoint "not even shared by most present-day Christian groups or Churches." On the other hand, the science or pseudoscience dichotomy dismisses the religious element as unimportant. This seems to me to be a serious error as it fails to emphasize the array of Creator-based choices available and thus offers no challenge to the quick creationsts' assertion that evolution is fundamentally atheistic. As Moyer (Chapter 4) stresses, we must make it starkly evident "that there is nothing about science or evolutionary theory that precludes a deep and abiding belief in a Creator God." Presenting a spectrum of choices emphasizes this fundamental point. Treating the origins controversy only as a choice between science or pseudoscience tends to obscure it.

A second important conclusion is evident from Tables 9-1 and 9-2. Although creationists who advocate young-earth and global-flood geology have tried to preempt the label "scientific creation," there is no reason to consider their model either more reflective of a belief in creation by God or as scientific as several of the other models. A more descriptive label than "scientific creation" is clearly needed. Since time is a key difference between the young-earth, global-flood geology position and the other Creator-based positions, the former can be better characterized as "quick creation." Designating two of the other major options as "gradual creation" and "progressive creation" stresses the availability of other choices that include a Creator.

Given a preliminary list of choices, such as that of Table 9-1 or 9-2, an obvious question is, Why does such a wide array exist? That is, why are one or two positions not so persuasive that most careful students of the topic have come to agree? And this leads us from a consideration of the scope of the uncertainty to a consideration of the advantages and disadvantages of the various choices, the second major part of the method proposed here for analyzing and presenting controversies.

Decisions in Uncertainty

My second major point addresses the question, If scientific knowledge is uncertain, then how do we decide anything? This is part of the general question, How do we rationally decide things in uncertainty? If we knew something with absolute certainty, we wouldn't have to worry—we could just believe it. But for those things, like science, that we don't know for sure, rational decisions require more thought. Elementary decision theory provides an instructive model.[11]

First, however, I need to note the myth that what we do in science is simply pick the most likely hypothesis. That this is a myth is most starkly evident at the frontiers of science. When Einstein made a model of the universe, he assumed for philosophical reasons that the universe cannot be infinite. But he thought that if it were finite, it would have already collapsed from gravitation, so, by a wave of his pen, he created an imaginary physical force, that of cosmic repulsion, in order to preserve his initial assumption of finiteness.[12] As Kuhn demonstrated, major schools or paradigms of science differ in their basic assumptions on points such as the relative importance of particular questions, the kinds of data that are relevant, and the properties of good answers.[13] Typically these assumptions cannot be evaluated in terms of their probability but rather form a nexus against which the probability of particular results is evaluated. There is an understandable tendency to pretend or hope that whatever paradigms we personally use are going to persist forever, but a bit of reflection on Euclid, Newton, and other landmarks in the history of science should make us skeptical.[14] Thus, probability alone is insufficient, and we can return to the question of how to make decisions in the face of uncertainty.

Let us start with an example. Suppose we discover a very rusty but apparently intact grenade. Being naturally curious, we wonder if it would go off if we pulled the pin. Should we? Since the grenade is old and rusty, the more probable hypothesis is that it will not go off. The rustier the grenade, the higher the probability that nothing will happen. And yet we are reluctant to pull the pin. This illustrates basic decision theory well. What benefits do we get when we pull the pin if our hypothesis of nonexplosion is true? Only the usual satisfaction of confirming a hypothesis (limited, in this case, by its scientific insignificance). What about the nature and value of the consequences of being wrong? It is clear that these possible consequences are disproportionately large compared with the rewards of being right. Whenever the consequences of being wrong are disproportionately large, we rationally should, and often do, reject very probable hypotheses by not choosing to act as if they were true.

Now let us develop the logic a little more formally. If we want to apply elementary decision theory to make a rational decision in the absence of certainty, we need to know the array of plausible choices or hypotheses (e.g., Tables 9-1 and 9-2, for origins). For each of these we then need to ascertain its relative probability and the relative "costs" of two basic kinds of errors: excess skepticism and excess credulity. To find the costs of skepticism for a hypothesis, we need to estimate the nature and values of the benefits that will accrue if we act as if that hypothesis is the better one and it does turn out retrospectively to have been the better one ("benefits-if-better"). The costs of skepticism are the portion of these benefits that are lost by not accepting the hypothesis now. To find the costs of credulity we need to estimate the nature and values of the consequences that will follow if we act as if the hypothesis is the better one and it turns out retrospectively to have been false ("consequences-if-false"). As a first approximation, the strength of evidence (probability) we demand for accepting a hypothesis is determined by the ratio of the value of the consequences-if-false to the value of the benefits-if-better. This approach is explicit in statistics when the acceptance level is set by a consideration of the relative costs of skepticism and credulity (of type I and II errors).

A couple of caveats are important. I am not suggesting that decision theory provides a complete description of how we usually make decisions, nor am I suggesting that all parties to a controversy must have arrived at their positions by rational means. March ably summarizes the reasons for skepticism on these points.[15] Cole and Withey emphasize the important role played by "perceived" risks and benefits (in contrast to statistically defined risks and benefits).[16] Indeed, in some ways the approach I suggest yields more nearly a rational reconstruction of the controversy than a literal description of it. I am suggesting that analyzing controversies in this way provides a powerful tool for transcending the limits of our own viewpoints, enables us to attain a better understanding of controversies, and facilitates their effective presentation. With these caveats in mind, we can examine the application of this approach to science.

Within a school or paradigm in basic science, we frequently assume that the only benefit of being correct is that of increased knowledge and that the only consequences of being wrong are mild embarrassment and a more cluttered technical literature. Within many paradigms, the tradeoff between these benefits and consequences has traditionally been regarded as equal at a 5 percent chance of being wrong (by falsely rejecting the null hypothesis), and this has been used as the standard of acceptance. Although the arbitrariness of 5 percent and the frequent use of more stringent standards for unexpected results should be noted, the important point here is that 5 percent assumes that there are neither other relevant benefits of being right nor other relevant consequences of being wrong. In applied science, this is typically not the case. For example, more rigorous standards often are appropriate in determining safety. And more lenient standards may be applied in other areas; for example, to the probability of cure required of treatments for otherwise fatal illnesses. Thus, in considering any controversy involving science and society, a key question is, What level of probability is appropriate for acceptance of the scientific hypotheses?

Two important corollaries follow. First, if two of us disagree substantially about the nature and values of either the benefits of a hypothesis or the consequences of prematurely accepting it (if it ultimately should turn out to be false), then this disagreement will frequently lead us to divergent conclusions over a wide range of data—that is, over a wide range of probabilities of the hypothesis being true. This disagreement can be fully rational and appropriate. Second, in cases where the benefits are very large and the consequences of error comparably negligible (or vice versa), the probability of the hypothesis is largely irrelevant. Thus, if the negative consequences of believing a hypothesis prematurely are very large, one must rationally reject the hypothesis unless the benefits are correspondingly large. Since we may not notice likely hypotheses we routinely reject, it may help to recall the rusty grenade example.

The nuclear power controversy also illustrates this point well. Suppose we know that the probability of a very serious accident is, say, one per million plant operating years. Given such a probability, what do we do with it? Some of us focus only on the consequences of the possible accident and say basically that nuclear plants are like rusty grenades—no matter how small the probability, as long as an accident is possible, we do not want them. But nuclear plants are not parallel to rusty grenades because there are substantial benefits from running them, both in terms of electricity and in terms of not running oil or coal plants. So we have to weigh these benefits against the consequences of a possible accident. Even people who agree that there are benefits from nuclear plants often disagree substantially on how important the various benefits and consequences are. For example, how much of an increase in the chances of an accident are we justified in accepting when we take account of keeping capital in this country instead of sending it to the OPEC nations, or when we take account of heavy metals or acid rain from coal plants? If we disagree strongly on these points, then we are going to disagree on decisions regarding nuclear power over a very wide range of data on plant safety.

Let us now try a similar analysis of the origins controversy.

A Decision Theory Approach to the Origins Controversy

In order to apply this approach to the creation, evolution, or both controversy, we will need to examine several questions. First, what are the benefits that would accrue from acceptance of each hypothesis, assuming that it is the better one? Second, what would be the consquences of prematurely accepting each should it ultimately be found to be false? Third, how does the magnitude of the benefits-if-better compare with the magnitude of the consequences-if-false? If these are approximately in balance, then the usual scientific standard of skepticism (the 5 percent level) will suffice. If the consequences are disproportionately large, we will want to remain skeptical even in the face of substantially stronger evidence. If the benefits beyond science are very large and the consequences small, we may reasonably demand less than the usual amount of evidence. Our comparison of the benefits-if-better with the consequences-if-false will thus determine our acceptance level—

that is, how strong the evidence must be before we will provisionally accept any hypothesis as correct. Once we have chosen such an acceptance level, we will ask, What is the nature of the data for each hypothesis and how probable does each seem at present? Comparing this with the levels of acceptance we have chosen will determine which hypothesis, if any, is currently acceptable. Note that these judgments will depend very heavily on which benefits and consequences we regard as relevant and on the relative values we assign them.[17] It will also depend on the array of hypotheses we regard as relevant and on the data which we think support each of these.

In pursuing this analysis further, it will be useful to examine the questions of religious values, scientific values, and scientific evidence sequentially. First, however, we need to delineate further the array of hypotheses we want to examine. From the lists of options we have generated (for example, those in Tables 9-1 and 9-2) we can extract a list of key questions in the controversy. Those I see as most central to the origins controversy are listed in Table 9-3. The relevant hypotheses to be examined are the divergent answers proposed for each of these questions. I will focus here on the various answers provided by the array of Bible-based creation models common among U.S. Christians (Table 9-2). These span the range from full acceptance of evolutionary science by the gradual creation model to rejection of important parts of biology, geology, chemistry, and astronomy by the quick creation model. The array thus allows a consideration of the interactions among religious values, scientific values, and scientific information without spuriously confounding science and atheism. Consequently, it provides a framework for integrating into the education of scientists a consideration of the relationships between science and other aspects of culture as urged by Gilkey (Chapter 11).

For the array of Table 9-2, we are now ready to examine the question raised earlier, that is, Why does such wide disagreement exist, even among the followers of a single major religious tradition? We will look first at religious values, and then turn to scientific values, and, finally, to scientific information.

Religious Values

L. D. Thurman, a professor at Oral Roberts University, discusses the array of creation models found within the U.S. Protestant tradition (Table 9-2) and concludes that "differences among creationists arise mostly because of varying interpretation of the Biblical text."[18] These different interpretations reflect two conflicting sets of religious values.

Consider first the quick-creationist assessments in which evolution is largely dismissed. Within this perspective, premature acceptance of evolution (if it were really false) would involve several very unfortunate consequences, including questioning the argument from design for the existence of a Creator, questioning the literal truth of the Bible ("day," "kinds," "flood," etc.), and questioning original sin as an explanation for evil in the world (see Chapter 3 for further elaboration of this point). When these are considered together, many Fundamentalists believe premature acceptance of evolution would risk disloyalty to God and might even markedly increase our chances of disbelief and, hence, of eternal damnation. In a more extreme view, Morris asserts that the essence of evolution was transmitted to Adam by Satan and that it is responsible for communism, racism, imperialism, militarism, pornography, promiscuity, and perversion and is otherwise responsible for moral and social decay.[19] In contrast, what benefits would be lost by prolonged skepticism as shown by present rejection of evolution, should it eventually turn out to be true? In this framework, nothing would be lost that is at all comparable to eternal damnation or moral decay. You will recall that we are reluctant to pull pins on rusty grenades and thus act so as to minimize the chance of an explosion. It is clear that in comparison with Morris's lists, to say nothing of eternal damnation, a grenade explosion is a scarcely noticeable inconvenience. Thus, if we were to accept the Fundamentalists' assessment of consequences, then rationally we would have to reject evolutionary hypotheses just as we would avoid pulling pins on rusty grenades. Both decisions could be fully rational, given the particular assessments of benefits and consequences, and both follow directly from these assessments and are essentially independent of any evidence on the probability of evolution, in one case, and of rusty grenades exploding, in the other.

Since none of us likely to pursue eternal damnation willfully, it is clear that any disagreement with the quick-creationists' position must include disagreement with the assessments of the benefits and consequences. One such disagreement would question whether the consequences of believing in evolution were it to be false are as extreme as the Fundamentalists assert. Theological disagreements on issues such as how the Bible should be interpreted (and not just for origins), how we should account for evil under a benevolent God, and how we might know that a Creator exists all considerably antedate both the modern synthesis of evolutionary theory and Darwin himself. It could thus be suggested that quick creationists greatly overrate the extent to which a false belief in evolution would increase the likelihood of doubt and damnation. Is design by a Creator necessarily less evident in a big-bang-to-people creation than in quick creation? A second mode of disagreement would be to suggest that the quick-creationist argument, while accurate as far as it goes, overlooks other important religious dimensions. Creationists of all types believe that the natural world is a creation of God. Thus a key question is, How much Biblical guidance is required in interpreting the natural world? A basic idea of natural theology is that the created world can be directly interpreted in its own right. It is this idea on which Skehan (Chapter 2) relies in concluding "there can be ultimately no irresolvable issues between science and religion for the reason that both deal with truth" and that "God, as the author of all truth, cannot contradict himself." Gilkey

Table 9-3. A Comparison of Quick and Gradual Creation on Eight Important Questions.

Question	Answer Given by:		Examples of Evidence and Puzzles	Applications
	Quick Creationists[a]	Gradual Creationists		
1. Origin of universe?	Created: creation week	Created: big bang	Age (below) Expansion 3° background radiation Composition changes *Galaxy puzzle*	?
2. Direction of change?	Decrease in order: from Eden	Decrease in order: from primaeval fireball	Second law of thermo-dynamics Thermodynamic order is property of system not of parts	Second law fundamental to many engineering applications
3. Ages of universe and Earth?	Thousands of years (10,000)	Billions of years (10 billion)	Extent of geological change Size of universe Stellar processes Radioactive dating Plate tectonics Mineral balances	Great age fundamental to most of geology, astronomy, and nuclear physics Plate tectonics now powerful in geological explanation and in mineral exploration
4. Geological record formed?	Quickly: in year-long flood	Slowly: by gradual processes and local catastrophies	Age (especially plate tectonics) Index fossils Pattern of fossil sequence (replacement and expansion) Finely layered sediments Ecological assemblages	Geological explanation Plate tectonics and mineral exploration

5. Origin of life?	Divine intervention	Natural processes[b]	Organic molecules in space Prebiotic syntheses Precambrian fossils *Genetic system puzzle*	?
6. Microevolutionary change?	Occurs	Occurs	Artificial selection Industrial melanism Pesticide and antibiotic resistance	Crop, livestock, and antibiotic improvement Crop protection and medicine
7. Extent of evolutionary change?	Within "kind"	Beyond phylum	Vertebrate morphology and embryology Vestigial structures Sequence of fossils (index, radiometric) Biochemical similarities Physiological Immunological AA, RNA, and DNA sequences *Why progress puzzle*	Fundamental to biological explanation Important applications in medical research
8. Human origins?	Separate creation	From apes[b]	Morphological, embryological, and behavioral similarities African fossils Biochemical and chromosomal similarities	Important in medical research

[a]Quick creation styles itself "scientific creation," but this term applies as well or better to both progressive and gradual creation. Gradual creation is also known as theistic evolution. *Progressive creation* tends to agree with gradual creation on questions 1–4 and with quick creation on questions 5, 7, and 8. All three positions agree on question 6.
[b]Some gradual creationists suggest that God intervened to create life and again in human evolution to infuse souls or the knowledge of good and evil.

(Chapter 11) prefers to argue that the truths of science and religion are on different explanatory levels. Bodat agrees that "Christian tradition has long recognized that the message of the Bible lies in a spiritual plane beyond the literal stories."[20] On these views, the religious consequences of rejecting evolution may be important. Setting religion against the obvious features of the world or the dominant scientific views might lead to questioning or even rejecting religion on grounds that are very peripheral to the central ideas of religion. Interpreting the Bible so as to conflict with the dominant ideas of science would increase the risk of disbelief in the spiritual truths of religion and, therefore, the risk of damnation. If this risk is regarded as commensurate with that cited by the quick creationists, the decisions clearly become harder.

To summarize, three positions are frequently taken on the religious aspects of the origin controversy. We could assert with the quick creationists that a premature belief in evolution engenders a substantially increased risk of disbelief and damnation and that this risk is not balanced by a similarly important benefit. We would then reject evolutionary hypotheses until the evidence became overwhelmingly strong. Alternatively, we could agree that although the risk the creationists see is real, it is largely balanced by risk of disbelief and damnation arising from setting science in conflict with religion. If we were to judge these risks to be largely commensurate, we would focus on the nonreligious benefits and consequences and on the strength of the evidence for the various hypotheses. We could, as a third alternative, arrive at a similar focus on nonreligious aspects of the controversy by concluding that the arguments asserting particular religious consequences from particular scientific positions are tenuous and unreliable. One answer to our question of "why so many models" is thus that there exists considerable disagreement on which interactions between science and religion are important and on the magnitudes of the consequences of making particular mistakes.

It should now be evident why both of the dichotomies that have dominated public discussion of the origins controversy are too restrictive. The issue is not one of evolution or creation. Creation can encompass the full range of scientific theories. Similarly the science or pseudoscience dichotomy is too simple. As Nelkin (Chapter 3) notes, the neutrality and objectivity of science are often overstated. At a minimum, it seems that, explicitly or implicitly, we must assume that the scientific hypotheses we adopt can be adopted without substantially increasing our chances of eternal damnation. This can be because we regard the hypotheses as compatible with our religious beliefs, because we doubt the linkage between scientific beliefs and religious consequences, or because we make the choice of not believing in eternal damnation. Any one of these choices is at least implicitly religious. If we acknowledge this implicit religious element to our scientific positions, it is essential that we also make the distinction between religious assumptions that permit a scientific position and religious assumptions that dictate a scientific position.

The religious assumptions of quick creationists dictate their conclusions on most of the constituent scientific questions in that only one answer is compatible with the religious assumptions. The religious assumptions of the gradual creationists, in contrast, would, if the evidence warranted, permit gradual, episodic, or quick creation. The choice is thus not simply between science or pseudoscience but rather among positions which are very different in the extent to which the religious presumptions dictate the scientific conclusions.

In summary, three key points have emerged from our consideration of the predominant religious values. First, if eternal damnation were to seem to be appreciably and unilaterally increased by particular hypotheses, rationally those hypotheses should be rejected. Second, there is an array of religious considerations, and these lead different individuals to different conclusions. And, third, different positions differ markedly in the extent to which their religious presumptions dictate their scientific conclusions.

If I have been successful thus far, I have delineated the array of religious questions but have left open the choice among the answers. Indeed, a major advantage of the approach I am suggesting here is that the relationship among the religious and social value issues and the scientific issues can be clearly delineated while leaving the personal value choices up to each student, listener, or reader. In a heterogeneous classroom, the teacher can present the religious elements of each position without either advocating or denigrating any. In my own experience, this greatly facilitates an understanding by students of the scientific issues. In contrast, when some positions are dismissed as nonsensical or pseudoscientific, it seems to make it more difficult for many students to understand why most scientists think as they do. And I believe that it is far more important for students to understand why most scientists accept particular ideas than it is for them to agree with those ideas. Let us now look at the values that we apply within science as we decide which hypotheses are scientifically justified.

Scientific Values

There are three main levels of explanation intertwined in the origins controversy: attributions of ultimate cause, summarization of empirical patterns, and explanation and prediction of these patterns by scientifically accessible causes (Table 9-4). Gilkey (Chapter 11) stresses the importance of distinguishing the levels of explanation with which science can deal, from those, such as "ultimate origins" and "supernatural" causes, with which it cannot. Moyer and Saladin also emphasize this point, noting that science can tell us "how" but not "why" (see Chapters 4 and 8). I agree that issues of ultimate cause lie outside the realm of science. The primary values that we use in science to choose among alternative hypotheses reflect the other two levels: com-

Table 9-4.   Three levels of explanation.

LEVELS

Religious
1. Religious affirmation of ultimate cause. (God makes:)

Scientific
2. Summary of patterns of empirical observations. (The planets move in ellipses . . .)
3. Scientifically assessable causes that provide explanation and prediction. (. . . because of inertia and gravitationally warped space.)

Note that these levels might all three be true but that science deals only with 2 and 3.

---

patibility with empirical patterns and power in causal explanation and prediction. I will turn to the patterns of observations in the next section. In this section I want to focus on explanatory and predictive power. Brush (Chapter 10) emphasizes both greater explanatory power and more effective hypothesis generation (which includes predictions) as reasons for giving preference to evolutionary hypotheses. Explanatory power lets us understand what has occurred in contrast with what has not occurred. Predictive power includes what will not occur (or be found) as well as what will occur (or be found). A basic question here is, What are the scientific costs of accepting the evolutionary hypotheses (embodied in gradual creation) if they ultimately turn out to be false? Scientifically there aren't any costs. The evolutionary hypotheses are the most powerful descriptive and explanatory hypotheses we currently have available. Even if parts of the evolutionary hypotheses turn out to be false— and we can be confident they will be substantially modified in time by the progress of science—we do not lose anything *scientifically* by accepting them until a more powerful theory is formulated. On the other hand, if we were to reject them we would lose their considerable explanatory and predictive power.

Let us consider an example. Some whales have internal vestiges of hind limbs, including even some foot bones, and some toothless baleen whales form teeth embryonically but reabsorb them before they erupt.[21] The evolutionary hypotheses explain this as a process of inheritance from a distant ancestor, and such deductions implicitly predicted that most other structural features, even proteins,[22] of whales will be similar to those of other mammals and divergent from fishes.

In contrast, the idea of creation can be treated in two ways. Looked at in one way, the hypothesis of creation is compatible with any state of affairs in the natural world because, in principle, God could have chosen to do anything. Since the idea of creation alone excludes nothing in the natural realm, in the scientific sense it explains nothing and predicts nothing. Further, since it cannot be falsified, it cannot be tested and is thus not scientific— as emphasized by Ayala[3] and Thwaites (Chapter 7). Indeed, the explanatory power of quick creation is scientifically equivalent to that of chance—almost anything that occurs presumably might have happened by chance but attributing something to chance usually has little or no predictive or explanatory power. Neither creation nor chance provides a scientific explanation of foot bones and embryonic teeth in baleen whales, and neither either implicitly or explicitly makes any predictions from these features to others. Thus, when evaluated strictly on scientific values, the evolutionary hypotheses of gradual creation will uniformly be preferred over those of quick creation as long as the latter are formulated essentially as "God did it that way."

An alternative way to treat the idea of creation is to attempt to reformulate it into a more directly scientific form, as many of the quick creationists claim to have done. Such reformulations could compete on purely scientific grounds only if these reformulations had explanatory and predictive power comparable to that of evolutionary hypotheses. This brings us to the questions of scientific evidence, but before turning to these issues, let me note that quick-creationist writings frequently raise a number of issues involving scientific values on which they assert that evolution fails to be scientific. Prominent among these are falsifiability and tautological formulation. Kitcher explains these and several other quick-creationist arguments and shows that each is fundamentally mistaken.[24]

Scientific Evidence

When we turn to the issues of specific patterns of data and scientifically accessible causal explanations, and consider the array of available options (Tables 9-1 and 9-2), it becomes evident that several distinct and basic questions are confounded under the rubric of origins. Eight of the more salient are listed in Table 9-3, which compares the hypotheses usually proposed by quick and gradual creationists.[25] This table also lists some of the important kinds of data and practical applications that are relevant to each question.[26] I will quickly highlight some key points from this table and consider them in the framework of decision theory. I will also suggest that the breadth of acceptance of specific evolutionary hypotheses across the religious spectrum generally reflects the overall strength of the supporting data, the extent of practical applications, and the length of time that these have been evident.

Let us begin with the idea of microevolution, particularly genetic change by the processes of selection (question 6, Table 9-3). The existence of some change by the mechanisms of natural and artificial selection and its important practical applications were integral to Darwin's presentation and have become increasingly manifest since that time. Of the various questions integral to the origins controversy (Table 9-3), the evolutionary answer to this one is most widely accepted and is advanced even by such prominent quick creationists as Morris[27] and Gish.[28]

The existence of an ancient earth (question 3) was evident to Lyell and Darwin from the extent of geological changes. This received strong confirmation from other areas only after World War I.[29] It became of indirect practical importance during and after World War II through nuclear physics, and became integral to important practical applications only after the formulation of plate tectonics in the 1960s and its intensive application to mineral exploration in the 1970s.[30] Further, it was only the mechanisms of plate tectonics—including burial of sediments in trenches and mineral precipitation and enrichment by undersea volcanic and hydrothermal action[31]—that made fully evident the spurious basis of the very young ages suggested by some interpretations of oceanic mineral composition.[32]

The idea of a flood-formed geological column (question 4) is closely related to young-earth models. Like the young-earth models, flood geology was extensively contradicted in practical applications by plate tectonics in the 1970s, although the other data for an old earth, the progressive nature of the fossil record, and many aspects of sedimentary geology and fossil communities had led much earlier to its general rejection by the scientific community.[33] Similarly, a young earth and flood geology are rejected across a broad spectrum of Bible-based creation models (Table 9-2). Indeed, progressive-creation models differ from the quick-creation models primarily on the two issues of age and formation of the geological record.

As the "scientific" quick-creationists ask, we can consider these young-earth and flood-formed geological column ideas as scientific hypotheses. In doing so, it is informative to remember that these theories were popular among much of the scientific community a century and a half ago. Over the past century, these hypotheses have been repeatedly falsified: by an understanding of geological processes, by index fossils, by the discovery that light takes time to travel and hence that a large universe is an old universe, by radiometric dating, by stellar dynamics, by paleomagnetism, by sea-floor spreading and plate tectonics, and by detailed stratigraphic sequences showing literally millions of apparently annually deposited layers in continuous vertical sequence.[34] In so far as any scientific theories are falsifiable, those of a very young earth and flood geology have been thoroughly falsified.

The considerable difficulties for quick creationists posed by the data for an ancient universe and a gradually accumulated fossil record are evident in their proposals of ad hoc and untestable hypotheses to explain away the data. Three examples will suffice. The vast size of the universe and the time light takes to travel together suggest that the universe must be at least several billion years old. Morris and others argue that this need not be so—God could have created the light en route to the earth separately from the stars.[35] Similarly, Morris suggests that the heavily cratered moon need not be old, but instead that the surface may reflect "some kind of heavenly catastrophe" that occurred either during Satan's rebellion or during subsequent battles between Satan and Michael and his angels.[36] Finally, for radiometric dating, Morris admits that some rocks appear to be billions of years old but argues that the Creator could have chosen to create the daughter and parent elements in just the right proportions to make the rocks have consistent apparent ages.[37] As Gilkey (Chapter 11) notes, such explanations are intrinsically non-scientific. In Kitcher's terms, the auxiliary hypotheses made to "save" quick creation from falsification are not independently testable.[38] More precisely, Morris's reactions show that when the data become a sufficiently strong embarrassment to a "scientific" model of quick creation, its advocates revert to a non-scientific "God-did-it-that-way" explanation. It is evident that there are no scientific criteria that would lead us to prefer Morris's ad hoc and scientifically inaccessible hypotheses to those of normal science.

Let us briefly note how these ideas illustrate the process of gradual assimilation of scientific findings by religious groups. These first three questions (change by selection, age, and formation of the geological record) share three important features. For each the evolutionary hypothesis is strongly supported by multiple lines of evidence which have been available for several decades, for each the evolutionary hypothesis has important practical corollaries, and for each the evolutionary hypothesis is directly contradictory to quick-creationist hypotheses. In the case of microevolution, which has been solidly established the longest, leading "scientific" quick creationists accept the evolutionary hypotheses. In the case of age and geological record the progressive creationists (who are generally conservative on religious issues) accept the evolutionary hypothesis while leading advocates of "scientific" quick creation posit ad hoc "God-did-it-that-way" explanations of creation with "apparently" evolutionary features. Thus, among these three questions, the evolutionary answer which has been solidly established for the longest time is most broadly accepted. The evolutionary answers for the other two have been established on a multidisciplinary base more recently and are accepted somewhat less broadly across the religious spectrum. The remaining questions (Table 9–3) will provide further insight.

Consider next the questions of the origin of the universe and the direction of change (questions 1 and 2, Table 9–3). The basic ideas of thermodynamics were well established before 1900 and have many common and important engineering applications. The quick creationists accept thermodynamics but assert that the evolutionary view of the universe contradicts the second law of thermodynamics. Prior to the postwar flowering of molecular biology, the compatibility of life with the second law of thermodynamics was not understood, and life was sometimes cited as a miraculous exception to the second law by prominent scientists. It is now evident that the existence, origin and evolution of life are all compatible with the second law.[39] Similarly, until the discovery and acceptance of the 3°K background radiation in the 1960s, it was far from evident how the history of the universe (question 1) related to the second law. The now prevalent big-bang model views the universe as having started at a very high level of thermodynamic order which has been dissipated at each stage in the subsequent development of the universe and at each moment in the processes of life.[40] One of the intriguing paradoxes of the origins controversy is that the emphasis by quick creationists on thermodynamic order and the second law has occurred after thermodynamic understanding advanced to the point where the scientific questions were settled and it became evident that a big-bang creation would have much more initial thermodynamic order than an earthly Eden. Thus those aspects of thermodynamics which have been established the longest and which have important practical applications are accepted widely across the religious spectrum. In contrast, the more recent and less practical extensions of thermodynamics to cosmology and life processes are rejected by quick creationists and by some progressive creationists. This illustrates both decision theory (practical applications accepted) and cultural lag (older evidence accommodated, recent rejected).

Continuing with our exploration of the questions in Table 9–3, the evolutionary hypotheses which answer two of the remaining questions have been clearly supported by diverse lines of evidence only within the last two or three decades. As in the case of the compatibility of biological evolution with thermodynamics, much of the support came from molecular biology. Headway in understanding the abiotic origin of biological systems (question 5) has largely occurred since Miller's now classic 1951 experiments.[41] Direct paleontological evidence that the extent of evolutionary change (question 7) has extended as far as classes is limited to a few key examples such as *Archaeopteryx* and the reptile-to-mammal transition.[42] Moreover, morphological and embryological evidence showing relationships at levels above class is often based on a small number of characters and subject to divergent interpretations. The advent of amino acid and DNA sequencing and microcomplement immunology and their application as molecular clocks in deducing phyletic relationships provided a powerful new source of information.[43] The confirmation of the geological sequence by radiometric dating and the discovery and characterization of an extensive series of Precambrian fossils, and with it the demonstration of the gradual increase in structural complexity, has also occurred predominantly within the last two decades.[44] Thus relatively strong scientific demonstration of big-bang origins, of the compatibility of cosmic and biological evolution with the second law, of plausible prebiotic origins, and of large-scale evolutionary change are all comparatively recent.

The evolutionary answers to these four questions also share two additional key features in which they differ from those for the first three questions we considered. At present none of this group of four has any major direct economic applications. Further, each includes some fairly impressive remaining scientific challenges. Present models for a big-bang origin (question 1) predict a structure so homogeneous that no galaxies could have formed (the "galaxy puzzle" in Table 9–3),[45] and the existence of a universe presently dominated by matter (rather than being half matter and half antimatter) is just now being understood as a reflection of the same processes that gave rise to the nonconservation of parity.[46] In our hypotheses for the origin of life (question 5), we still lack a reasonably detailed and plausible model for the origin of a self-replicating system and its transformation into an indirect coding system, a difficulty that is compounded by the difficulties encountered in finding plausible prebiotic syntheses for some of the essential nucleic acids (the "genetic system puzzle" in Table 9–3).[47] Consequently, it is not yet evident whether we should regard the origin of genetic systems as essentially inevitable, like prebiotic syntheses of amino acids; as so improbable as to have probably occurred only a few times; or as so improbable as to be essentially or literally miraculous.[48] In the history of life, gaps remain a prominent feature. The recent flowering of theories of punctuated equilibria takes its roots in the ubiquitousness of gaps between species. Although transitions at intermediate taxonomic levels are common and some transitions among classes are evident, many classes and almost all phyla remain without described transitional types.[49] The proposal that the Calichordata link the echinoderm and chordate phyla may provide an anthropocentrically important exception.[50] Further, molecular analysis of affinities still has to be extended to many of the classes and phyla of organisms so that an assertion that the data will be compatible with a single common origin presently requires considerable extrapolation. Finally, although evolutionary progress does not contradict the second law of thermodynamics, we have no strong scientific explanation of why life increased in complexity from bacteria to flowering plants, beetles, and mammals during the last 3 billion years (the "why progress puzzle" in Table 9–3).

These questions (big-bang, origin of life, compatibility with the second law, evolutionary progress) thus contrast with the first group considered (microevolution, age, geological formation) in three important ways. Strong lines of relevant scientific evidence are relatively recent, no major direct economic applications have yet developed, and each includes some impressive remaining scientific challenges. In decision theory terms, somewhat less scientific power is lost by remaining skeptical of the evolutionary answers for these four questions (and the benefits from their acceptance are lower) than for those of microevolution, age, and geological formation. In terms of my suggestion of gradual assimilation of scientific hypotheses by religious groups, the emphasis of progressive creationists on separate creation thus reflects, in part, the relatively recent nature of relevant scientific evidence, the greater remaining uncertainty, and the lack of practical importance.

The evolutionary answer to the one remaining question in Table 9–3, that of human origins (question 8), is a partial exception to the pattern of gradual assimilation of well-documented scientific ideas and can be best illuminated as part of a summary of some interactions of values and evidence.

Values and Evidence

Let us now summarize the interactions among the religious and scientific values and the scientific evidence.

The quick-creationist positions are based on a set of religious assumptions within which premature acceptance of evolutionary hypotheses carries a substantial risk of disloyalty to God or even of eternal damnation that is not seen to be offset by comparable risks for skepticism. Such value assumptions rationally require extreme skepticism of evolutionary hypotheses even when these are supported by fairly strong evidence. In this system, religious value choices overwhelm scientific considerations whenever there is a conflict between them. However, prominent quick creationists now are willing to accept a substantial amount of evolutionary change within "kind" and, more generally, are attempting to find scientific validation for their views. This suggests that they are also trying to address the risks to faith that might come from a direct conflict between science and religious beliefs. The particular evolutionary hypothesis they accept (change by selection) and the nature of many of their arguments against other evolutionary hypotheses (outdated interpretations of the second law, for example) are suggestive of a cultural lag between scientific discovery and religious assimilation.

The progressive-creation positions reflect a more even balance between a fairly direct interpretation of Genesis (and the religious positions this permits) and attempts to avoid a substantial conflict with science (and the religious disadvantages that can flow from such a conflict). This follows from or permits a much greater acceptance of the scientific values of explanation and prediction. Again the particular evolutionary hypotheses accepted by progressive creationists (change in kind, great age, and ancient geological record) can be seen as an assimilation by religious groups of scientific findings which have been solidly established for several decades.

Finally, most of the elements of the gradual-creationist positions can be interpreted as emphasizing the advantages of concentrating on a core of religious insights, avoiding the disadvantages of conflicts with science on peripheral issues, and exploiting the full power of science in nonreligious areas. The assumption that one can choose among the full array of scientific theories without thereby risking eternal damnation as advanced by gradual creation is shared, at least implicitly, by nontheistic evolution.

Let us now examine the question of human origins (question 8, Table 9–3). The morphological, embryological, and behavioral evidence that Darwin cited for a common ancestry of humans and apes was quite strong. Further, our affinities with other mammals has had important practical applications in medical research for some decades. If the assimilation of scientific findings by religion depended simply on the strength of scientific evidence and the extent of practical applications, we would expect the evolutionary origin of humans to be very broadly accepted. On the contrary, however, the evolutionary hypothesis for human origins is the greatest stumbling block to general public acceptance of evolutionary theory. The Tennessee law that gave rise to the Scopes trial banned the teaching of "human evolution" and William Jennings Bryan, who aided the prosecution, had no objection to "evolution before man" except that it might "raise a presumption in behalf of evolution to include man."[51] The same concern remains intense today. Saladin (Chapter 8) notes of college biology majors that "a surprising number . . . subscribe to a separate creation for humans and [to] the exemption of humans from the evolutionary process." As a further example, Young concludes that evolution "apart from the question of the origin of man, is not necessarily anti-Christian or unbiblical" but emphasizes that he believes that "man as God's image bearer" and "our sinful estate" cannot be accounted for by evolution.[52] Clearly, the issue of human evolution is different from that of evolution in general.

Two factors contribute to this difference. First, strong confirmation of Darwin's idea on human origins by evidence from independent areas has occurred relatively recently—by the discovery of a substantial fossil record for hominids and by detailed biochemical and chromosomal studies.[53] Multiple confirmations and the time they have been available are important in the assimilation of science. However, as the quotes in the preceding paragraph and the special emphasis given human origins by some variant positions spanning the spectrum from gradual to quick creation (Table 9–2) make clear, much of the resistance to human evolution reflects the more central position of ideas such as "in God's image," soul, and original sin in theological explanations. Indeed, a decision-theory model predicts that we will require more rigorous scientific support for modifications more central to our theological ideas.

The special consideration often given to human origins makes clear the difference between decisions based simply on scientific values and decisions for which values, benefits, and consequences outside science are seen as relevant. It also suggests that the issue of human origins requires special educational attention. Since there is more initial skepticism, we need to present more evidence, with emphasis on multiple confirmation, than for points which appear roughly equivalent on scientific criteria alone. However, the special scrutiny given human origins arises from religious considerations rather than from an absence of scientific evidence. Consequently, apperception of the scientific content often will depend as much on finding a way to accommodate the science with religion as on the strength of the scientific evidence presented. We can probably facilitate this accommodation by providing a range of options. For example, an important degree of freedom comes by stressing that students always have the option of learning "this is what most scientists now believe, and these are the data and scientific criteria on which they base their decisions." When elementary decision theory has been one of the evaluative frameworks presented, one can stress that we will rationally be more skeptical of those hypotheses that we believe to have serious consequences. Other alternatives can be elicited from the class (or audience) or presented as questions to think about. To what extent would a requirement for "man as God's image bearer" be satisfied by God's foreknowledge of evolutionary processes and results? Would it be satisfactory to interpret "our sinful estate" as a lack of a strong inherent tendency always to do right rather than as literal guilt? Could special creation of humans be by intervention in the evolutionary process as by the infusion of souls) at the threshold of human evolution?[54] If so, could this achieve both "God's image" and "sinful estate"? As I leave this topic, let me stress two points. First, it is, of course, as important to emphasize that such alternatives are not part of science as it is to note that they may facilitate a better understanding both of ideas and data that are part of science and of the fact that science is not intrinsically antireligious. Second, I regard it as absolutely essential for the protection of religious pluralism that any consideration of such issues be done in a way that neither advances nor denigrates any particular religious choice.

In this section I have analyzed the origins controversy primarily from a decision theory perspective. I have used these issues as an example of how this perspective can help us better to understand and present controversies by examining the ways in which scientific evidence, scientific values, and other social values interact to produce an array of positions. I also suggested a second explanation of the array in this particular case, that of gradual assimilation of scientific findings by other parts of our society. Cultural-lag explanations seem to be most powerful when considered in conjunction with differences in values.

Educational Implications

In classroom presentations of natural science, many teachers largely or entirely ignore questions of how scientific ideas might relate to religious ideas. Before we consider alternatives to this traditional approach, we should examine the basic rationales that underlie it. We can do this by asking why we have not generally emphasized the possibility of direct divine intervention or causation. This question is particularly pertinent when scientific explanations are presently lacking or nebulous, as for the ultimate origin of the universe. Some would argue that we ignore the religious dimension because we are inherently antireligious. Insofar as philosophies such as logical positivism and Marxism are antireligious, there is, perhaps, a degree of truth in this for some members of the scientific community. Some of the essays of Julian Huxley[55] and Stephen Jay Gould[56] might support such an interpretation. In other cases, as Gilkey implies in Chapter 11, some of us may not mention other religious interpretations because of the assumption that science supports our own "religion of naturalistic humanism." I agree with Gilkey, Hanson (Chapter 1), and Nelkin (Chapter 3) that it is important that we avoid implicitly or explicitly teaching naturalistic humanism under the guise of neutral science. However, neither antireligious nor naturalistic assumptions provide a general explanation. I find that many of my faculty colleagues in biology believe in a Creator, belong to religious organizations and participate regularly in their activities, and otherwise demonstrate that religion is important to them personally. Most of them also usually set the religious elements aside in their classrooms. Several factors apparently contribute to this.

One common rationale is the too-little-time argument: scientific knowledge grows exponentially but class time stays fixed. Consequently, we, as teachers, must continually trim out very good science in order to insert newer and (we hope) better science. Any time we devote to religious, social, and practical ramifications further reduces the amount of good basic science we can present. Moreover, helping students understand and master the methods and values of science is, in itself, a substantial challenge. Different methods and additional value dimensions typify practical, social, and religious issues. If we were to deal with these aspects, we would need to help the students develop the frameworks to do so constructively. This intensifies the time dilemma. Further, many of us may be (appropriately) wary of our own competence to teach such nonscientific aspects effectively. However, neither time constraints nor the necessity for becoming competent in new areas keep us from adding important new materials to our courses. Thus we must either regard religion as relatively unimportant or have important reasons for *not* addressing religious issues. I am going to suggest two important reasons that may explain why we have tacitly or explicitly chosen not to address directly those aspects of religion which appear related to the science we teach.

One strong reason for not addressing religion in science classes reflects our basic approach as scientists. As I noted above, the objectives of science are to delineate empirical patterns and to find scientifically accessible causes that explain and predict them. Recognizing (or misperceiving) ultimate causes is at best irrelevant in science and can be hurtful by obscuring the need for scientifically assessable explanations. Any alternative educational strategy clearly must address this important objection.

I think that a second very important reason why many of us have not considered religious dimensions as we teach science has been our deep respect for religion and religious pluralism. If we discuss only the currently dominant scientific ideas, the student whose religion teaches otherwise is challenged by options only in the area of science. Such a student then has choices, such as learning that "this is what most scientists now believe." Religious issues are left to the home and church and to discussions outside of class. If, in contrast, the student is presented with an array of religion and science options as in Tables 9–1 and 9–2, those advocated by his or her faith will be listed among many others without any special emphasis or validation except for their scientific advantages or disadvantages. As Saladin (Chapter 8) notes, this may contribute to an undermining of some students' religious beliefs. In accord with "the usual exemption of religious faith from scientific scrutiny" which he notes, I once would have argued strongly that focusing solely on the scientific issues best served the interests of both science and religion. I still think that any other approach should be adopted with extreme care.

As we decide how to react to the demands of the quick creationists, it is essential that we keep our respect for religion and religious pluralism clearly in mind. In my judgment, it is religious values more than scientific values that are threatened by the quick creationists' pleas for parallel treatment. Science itself may be little damaged (but for a contrary view, see Kitcher[57]). I think that the quick creationists have blundered in assuming that equal time means standard evolution presentations accompanied by a quick-creationist critique of evolutionary science and by a presentation of the quick-creation model. Such a presentation would clearly be irresponsibly unbalanced. Two missing elements are a critique by evolutionists of quick creationists' assertions and attempted rebuttals of both critiques. Furthermore, the comparisons in science classes must be in terms of scientific values such as agreement with data, explanatory and predictive power, and potential testability. Indeed, the courses described by Thwaites (Chapter 7) and Saladin (Chapter 8) coincide with my own approach in emphasizing presentations of quick-creation arguments together with scientific data that explicitly challenge those arguments and in using the contrast to sharpen the students' understanding of the bases for scientific judgments. Thwaites, Saladin, and I all find that under these conditions few college students are swayed toward quick creation. The predominant reaction of my students after reading and discussing one of Morris' books[58] is that his thesis "is much weaker than I thought." From those who were initially inclined towards quick creation, there are accusations that I did not pick a competent quick creationist (Morris is director of the Institute for Creation Research and the most prominent "scientific" quick creationist).[59] It thus seems that two-model, science-or-pseudoscience, and multiple-model approaches, when adopted voluntarily by teachers, may adequately protect science as long as they emphasize discussions of the objectives of science and include a critique of quick creationists' assertions.[60] I have found that a consideration of the origins controversy increases both students' interest in science and their understanding of the nature and limits of science, as also noted by Bergman,[61] Thwaites (Chapter 7) and Saladin (Chapter 8).

My misgivings with approaches that are literally two-model or science-or-pseudoscience remain intense, however. I have argued above that these approaches implicitly acquiesce in the quick creationists' attempts to confound all forms of belief in a Creator with quick creation. These approaches also give undue emphasis to the beliefs of some sects and are a basic affront to religious pluralism. They also make it easy for students mistakenly to conclude that science and religion are necessarily antithetical. Gilkey (Chapter 11) argues forcefully that the naive conclusion by both quick creationists and some scientists that evolution and Genesis are comparable and antithetical is the key confusion in the origins controversy. As he stresses, such a conclusion spuriously taken is likely to be detrimental to both religion and science.

In this context, one further agreement between the approach I advocate and those used by Thwaites and Saladin is important. I emphasize the availability of an array of creation alternatives. Thwaites starts his course with an emphasis on theistic evolution (gradual creation) as an alternative to quick creation. Saladin discusses theological questions, Biblical interpretation, and "the rapprochement of science and religious belief." Each of our approaches thus stresses that there are alternative religious choices and that one can legitimately have both scientific and religious beliefs. We each thus attempt to protect religious pluralism and so reduce a major potential disadvantage of directly addressing religiously significant questions.

Taking this argument one step further, I recently (over the last 5 years[62]) concluded that focusing solely on the scientific issues has some severe disadvantages and that these may frequently outweigh the advantages. Fundamental to my conclusion that we need to go beyond science alone is Perry's demonstration that into their senior college year (and often through it) many undergraduates retain a strong element of dualism in their general way of thinking.[63] This means that many of them will tend to assume for substantive questions that clearly correct answers exist, that proper authorities know those answers, and that the role of the student is to obtain those answers from authority. These students will typically not distinguish levels of knowing (in the sense of Gilkey, Chapter 11) nor will they usually think dialectically. In the present context, many students will assume that creation and evolution are in fact antithetical. Like the student Saladin quotes as asking "can I believe in both [creation and evolution]—somehow" (see Chapter 8), several of my students have mentioned that they have interpreted the silence of their science teachers as confirmation of the necessity of choosing either science or religion. A discussion of science or pseudoscience on an issue such as origins, where the pseudoscience attacked is clearly religious, can only increase this misapprehension. Further, a science or pseudoscience approach will tend to reinforce the students' basic presumption that knowledge is dualistic and to otherwise inhibit the development of cognitive structures that permit reasoned choice among competing opinions. In the terms used by Saladin, science-or-pseudoscience approaches, rather than developing skepticism, may only replace the certainties of blind religious faith with the certainties of blind scientific faith. This will tend to delay the students' intellectual maturation in ways that will make it difficult for them to deal effectively with science as a dynamic and changing entity and with the policy dilemmas that scientific advances will necessarily produce. Such delayed cognitive maturation is evident in the overly simple view that truth is all of one kind which Gilkey (Chapter 11) attributes both to quick creationists and to many scientists. With the intriguing circularity of human affairs, this misapprehension gives the origins controversy its vitality, and the controversy in turn provides issues of sufficient existential importance to motivate some students to transcend the cognitive structures that make the misapprehension possible.

It is in the framework of intellectual maturation and the development of skepticism (in place of blind faith) that the advantages of a decision-theory approach to controversies are most starkly evident. This approach emphasizes fundamental uncertainty, accepting scientific hypotheses whose support is less than absolutely certain (because that's the only kind of scientific hypotheses that there are), different sets of values, conflicts between advantages-if-better and consequences-if-false, and opportunity for making choices which are simultaneously logical and morally justified. Taken together, these emphases encourage the student to move from dualism and absolute answers to more complex ways of thinking and valuing.

I have implemented a decision-theory approach to origins at two levels of effort. I have given one-hour lectures addressing the key points developed in this paper and stressing the availability of multiple options for relating science and belief. I have given such presentations as public lectures, as part of a freshman western civilization course, and as the main thrust of my presentation in debates with quick creationists.[64] In my own courses, I usually include one or two lectures addressing the nature of science and its use in decision-making and several lectures addressing the questions listed in Table 9–3. These are reinforced by repeated examples throughout the course of scientific uncertainty, alternative paradigms, and tradeoffs among values both within science and in its social applications. Most students have responded well to this approach. Students starting from a perceived dichotomy between creation and evolution and a consequent necessity for choosing either science or religion, are often quite relieved to find options for combining religion with science. In their predominantly dualistic world view, such an approach by a scientific "authority" means that it is all right for them to be concerned both with belief and with science. Thus this approach encourages them "to develop a moral center from which they can make worthy decisions" (Moyer, Chapter 4) as well as a scientific center from which they can make effective decisions. When presented carefully so as not to denigrate anyone's religious views, such an approach seems to facilitate the students' understanding of how scientists choose what to accept. It now seems to me that it is much more important for students to understand why as scientists we presently think that particular theories are better than for them truly to believe those theories. Such an understanding will facilitate the students' continued understanding and application of a changing body of science in a changing world and thus will further a primary objective of science teachers.[65]

Notes

1. H.J. Muller, "One Hundred Years Without Darwinism Are Enough," *School Science and Mathematics* (April 1959): 304.

2. K. R. Popper, *Logik der Forschung* (Vienna: J. Springer, 1934); trans. *The Logic of Scientific Discovery* (London: Hutchinson, 1959).

3. F. J. Ayala, in *Evolution*, T. Dobzhansky et al. eds. (San Francisco: Freeman, 1977); see p. 471 for discussion on falsification, Ch. 17 for other issues. P. Kitcher, *Abusing Science: The Case Against Creationism* (Cambridge, Mass.: MIT Press, 1982), Ch. 2 on falsification and proof.

4. J. Bronowski, *The Origins of Knowledge and Imagination* (New Haven: Yale University Press, 1978).

5. Kitcher, *Abusing Science*, pp. 170–72. For a recent review of continental drift and its correlates see L. R. M. Cocks, ed., *The Evolving Earth* (Cambridge: British Museum and Cambridge University Press, 1981).

6. Kitcher, *Abusing Science*, p. 32.

7. W. G. Perry, Jr., *Forms of Intellectual and Ethical Development in the College Years: A Scheme* (New York: Holt, Rinehart and Winston, 1970) and W. G. Perry, Jr., "Cognitive and Ethical Growth: The Making of Meaning," in *The Modern American College* A. W. Chickering, ed. (San Francisco: Jossey-Bass, 1981), pp. 76–116.

8. L. D. Thurman, *How to Think about Evolution and Other Bible-Science Controversies*, 2d ed. (Downers Grove, Ill.: InterVarsity, 1978).

9. D. Cain, "Let There Be Light," *Eternity*, May 1982, p. 30.

10. D. Young, "Genesis—Neither More Nor Less," *Eternity*, May 1982, p. 14.

11. C. A. Holloway, *Decision-Making under Uncertainty: Models and Choices* (Englewood Cliffs, N.J.: Prentice-Hall, 1979) provides an overview of more complex decision approaches that may be useful in teaching advanced science courses. Cole and Withey's discussion of the role of risk perception in technical controversies is especially pertinent to the origins controversy ("Perspectives on Risk Perception," *Risk Analysis* 1 (1982): 143).

12. G. J. Whitrow, *The Structure and Evolution of the Universe* (New York: Harper-Torchbook, 1959).

13. T. S. Kuhn, *The Structure of Scientific Revolutions*, 2d ed. (Chicago: University of Chicago Press, 1970). Read the postscript first.

14. S. G. Brush, "Should the History of Science Be Rated X?" *Science* 183 (1974): 1164; see also Brush, Chapter 10, this volume.

15. J. G. March, "Theories of Choice in the Making of Decisions," public lecture at the annual meeting of the American Association for the Advancement of Science, Washington, D.C., 1982. (Available on tape from Mobiltape Co., Inc., 1741 Gardena Avenue, Glendale, CA 91204.)

16. Cole and Withey, "Perspectives on Risk Perception," *Risk Analysis*, p. 143.

17. My better students sometimes note that, in reality, perceptions of probability do influence the perceived value of consequences and benefits. This does not appreciably diminish the heuristic value of this approach.

18. Thurman, *How to Think About Evolution*.

19. H. M. Morris, *The Remarkable Birth of Planet Earth* (Minneapolis: Dimension Books, 1972), p. 75, See Kitcher, *Abusing Science* Ch. 7, or R. M. Price, "Creationist and Fundamentalist Apologetics: Two Branches of the Same Tree," *Creation/Evolution* 14 (1984): 19 for quotes from Morris and other authors and an analysis of this line of argumentation.

20. L. Bodat, "Countering the Creationists: The Theologian," *Academe* 68, no. 2 (1982): 17.

21. E. P. Walker et al., *Mammals of the World*, vol. 2 (Baltimore: Johns Hopkins Press, 1964), p. 1132; F. Edwords, "Those Amazing Animals: The Whales and Dolphins," *Creation/Evolution* 10 (1982): 1; E. C. Conrad, "True Vestigial Structures in Whales and Dolphins," *Creation/Evolution* 10 (1982): 8.

22. M. Landau, "Whales: Can Evolution Account for Them?," *Creation/Evolution* 10 (1982): 14. For a more general treatment see J. Cracraft, "Systematics, Comparative Biology and the Case against Creationism," in *Scientists Confront Creationism*, L. R. Godfrey, ed. (New York: Norton, 1983), pp. 163–92.

23. Ayala, *Evolution*, p. 471.

24. Kitcher, *Abusing Science*, Ch. 2 and 3.

25. There is close agreement between my list and that of Thwaites (Chapter 7, this volume). He omits my first (origin of universe) and eighth (human evolution) questions and subdivides the fifth (origin of life) and seventh (extent of change) into two each.

26. For a recent very readable and accurate summary of the scientific arguments against quick creation, I recommend Kitcher, *Abusing Science*. Chapter length treatments of the central topics are given in *Scientists Confront Creationism*. Briefer partial summaries are given by R. D. Alexander in "Evolution, Creation and Biology Teaching," *American Biology Teacher* 40 (1978): 91; C. A. Callaghan in "Evolution and Creationist Arguments," *American Biology Teacher* 42 (1980): 442; D. H. Milne in "How to Debate with Creationists—and 'Win,' " *American Biology Teacher* 43 (1981; 235; and K. Miller in "Answers to the Standard Creationist Arguments," *Creation/Evolution* 7 (1982): 1. The two most relevant journals are *The American Biology Teacher* and the new journal, *Creation/Journal* (P.O. Box 146, Amherst Branch, Buffalo, NY 14226-0146).

27. H. M. Morris, *The Scientific Case for Creation* (San Diego: Creation-Life Publishers, 1977) p. 29.

28. D. T. Gish, *Evolution: The Fossils Say No!*, 3rd ed. (San Diego: Creation-Life Publishers, 1979) pp. 33–40.

29. Chapters 3 and 4 of *Scientists Confront Creationism* deal with age. Relevant articles include: S. Freske, "Evidence Supporting a Great Age for the Universe," *Creation/Evolution* 2 (1980): 34; S. I. Dutch, "A Critique of Creationist Cosmology," *Journal of Geological Education* 30 (1982): 27; S. G. Brush, "Finding the Age of the Earth, By Physics or by Faith?," *Journal of Geological Education* 30 (1982): 34; C. G. Weber, "Answer to Creationist Attacks on Carbon-14 Dating," *Creation/Evolution* 8 (1982): 23; and S. N. Shore, "Footprints in the Dust: The Lunar Surface and Creationism," *Creation/Evolution* 14 (1984): 32. Kircher, *Abusing Science*, pp. 155–84, provides a less technical refutation of quick-creation dating.

30. E. Edelson, "Prospecting with Plate Tectonics," *Mosaid* 12 (1981): 9.

31. J. M. Edmond et al., "Chemistry of Hot Springs on the East Pacific Rise and Their Effluent Dispersal," *Nature* 297 (1982): 187.

32. Morris, *Scientific Case for Creation*, pp. 55–59.

33. D. M. Raup, "The Geological and Paleontological Arguments of Creationism," *Scientists Confront Creationism*, pp. 147–62; C. G. Weber, "The Fatal Flaws of Flood Geology," *Creation Evolution* 1 (1980): 24 and "Common Creationist Attacks on Geology," *Creation/Evolution* 2 (1980): 10; and R. J. Schadewald, "Six 'Flood' Arguments Creationists Can't Answer," *Creation/Evolution* 9 (1982): 12; and Kitcher, *Abusing Science*, pp. 127–34, 140–42. See also note 29.

34. Ibid.

35. W. W. Boardman, Jr., R. F. Koontz, and H. M. Morris, *Science and Creation* (San Diego: Creation-Science Research Center, 1973).

36. H. M. Morris, *The Remarkable Birth of the Planet Earth* (Minneapolis: Dimension Books, 1972) pp. 93–94.

37. Ibid., pp. 66–67.

38. Kitcher, *Abusing Science*, p. 46.

39. W. Thwaites and F. Awbrey, "Biological Evolution and the Second Law," *Creation/Evolution* 4 (1981): 5; S. Freske, "Creationist Misunderstanding, Misrepresentation, and Misuse of the Second Law of Thermodynamics," *Creation/Evolution* 4 (1981): 8; J. W. Patterson, "Thermodynamics and Evolution," *Scientists Confront Creationism*, pp. 99–116; and Kitcher, *Abusing Science*, pp. 89–96.

40. Ibid.

41. R. E. Dickerson, "Chemical Evolution and the Origin of Life," *Scientific American*, September 1978, p. 70; and S. Chang et al., "Prebiotic Organic Syntheses and the Origin of Life," in *Earth's Earliest Biosphere*, J. W. Schopf, ed. (Princeton, N.J., Princeton University Press, 1983) pp. 53–92.

42. Kitcher, *Abusing Science*, 108–15; J. H. Ostrom, "Archaeopteryx and the Origin of Birds," *Biological Journal of the Linnean Society*, 8 (1976): 91; and A. W. Crompton and P. Parker, "Evolution of the Mammalian Masticatory Apparatus," *American Scientists* 66 (1978): 192. R. T. Bakker gives a general overview of

the reptile to bird, dinosaur, and mammal transitions in "Dinosaur Renaissance," *Scientific American*, April 1975, p. 58. F. Edwords, in "The Dilemma of the Horned Dinosaurs," *Creation/Evolution* 9 (1982): 1, discusses dinosaur transitions. For a general review of transitions and of the ubiquity of gaps in the fossil record see E. C. Olson, "The Problem of Missing Links: Today and Yesterday," *Quarterly Review of Biology* 56 (1981): 405. L. R. Godfrey refutes some creationist uses in "Creationism and Gaps in the Fossil Record," *Scientists Confront Creationism*, pp. 193–218.

43. T. H. Jukes, "Molecular Evidence for Evolution," *Scientists Confront Creationism*, pp. 117–38; R. A. Raff and T. C. Kaufman, *Embryos, Genes, and Evolution* (New York: Macmillan, 1983), especially Ch. 3. F. T. Awbrey and W. M. Thwaites, "A Closer Look at Some Biochemical Data That 'Support' Creationism," *Creation/Evolution* 7 (1982): 14, review quick-creationist claims of biochemical support.

44. J. W. Schopf, "The Evolution of the Earliest Cells," *Scientific American*, September 1978, p. 110; *Earth's Earliest Biosphere*.

45. R. J. Gott, III, in "Unsolved Questions: Galaxy Formation and the Isotrophy of the Cosmic Microwave Background," paper presented at the annual meeting of the American Association for the Advancement of Science, Washington, D.C., 1982.

46. M. S. Turner, "Cosmology and Particle Physics," paper presented at the annual meeting of the American Association for the Advancement of Science, Washington, D.C., 1982. (Available on tape #82 AAAS/66-69 from Mobiltape Co., Inc., 1741 Gardena Ave., Glendale, CA 91204).

47. Dickerson, pp. 78–80. For one promising start on this puzzle, see M. Eigen et al., "The Origins of Genetics Information," *Scientific American*, April 1981, p. 88.

48. For example, F. Hoyle, a prominent astronomer, argues in *Lifecloud: The Origin of Life in the Universe* (New York: Harper and row, 1979) that the probability that life originated on earth is vanishingly small. Some weaknesses of improbability arguments are discussed by R. F. Doolittle, "Probability and the Origin of Life," *Scientists Confront Creationism*, pp. 85–98.

49. See note 42.

50. R. P. S. Jeffries, "Fossil Evidence Concerning the Origin of Chordates," *Symposium of the Zoological Society of London* 36 (1975): 253; but see G. M. Phillip, "Carpoids—Echiroderms or Chordates?," *Biological Reviews of the Cambridge Philosophical Society* 54 (1979): 439.

51. R. L. Numbers, "Creationism in 20th-Century America," *Science* 218 (1982): 538.

52. Young, "Genesis—Neither More Nor Less."

53. E. J. Bruce and F. J. Ayala, "Phylogenetic Relationships Between Man and the Apes: Electrophoretic Evidence" [and chromosomal evidence], *Evolution* 33 (1979): 1040; R. E. Leakey and R. Lewin, *Origins* (New York: Dutton, 1977); N. Eldredge and I. Tattersall, *The Myths of Human Evolution* (New York: Columbia University Press, 1982); D. Johanson and M. Edey, *Lucy* (New York: Simon and Schuster, 1981); and C. L. Brace, "Humans in Time and Space," *Scientists Confront Creationism*, pp. 245–82. For a discussion of some common quick-creationist misstatements on hominid fossils, see E. C. Conrad, "Are There

Human Fossils in the 'Wrong Place' for Evolution?," *Creation/Evolution* 8 (1982): 14. Ancient "footprints" are discussed by C. G. Weber, "Paluxy Man—The Creationist Piltdown," *Creation/Evolution* 6 (1981): 16; and L. R. Godfrey, "An Analysis of the Creationist Film, *Footprints in Stone*, *Creation/Evolution* 6 (1981): 23.

54. D. J. Walling in his "Letter to the Editor," *Creation/Evolution* 14 (1984): 48 cites the *Catholic Almanac* as emphasizing "the confirmation of evolution through scientific evidence while maintaining the doctrine of special creation of the human *soul*" (his emphasis).

55. J. Huxley, "The Crisis in Man's Destiny," *Playboy*, January 1966, p. 93.

56. S. J. Gould, *Ever Since Darwin* (New York: W. W. Norton, 1977), especially prologue and fifth essay.

57. Kitcher, *Abusing Science*, pp. 175–78, argues that if a two-model approach is introduced into high schools (by legal fiat), then for political reasons the critique of quick creation and the evaluative framework I suggest will often not be provided. If he is right, then considerable damage would accrue both to scientific education and to religious pluralism.

58. Morris, *The Scientific Case For Creationism*.

59. Numbers, "Creationism in 20th-Century America."

60. By emphasizing voluntary comparisons I do not mean to discount the importance of the grounds for questioning of legislative dictation as discussed, for example, by F. Edwords, "Why Creationism Should Not Be Taught as Science: Part 1, The Legal Issues," *Creation/Evolution* 1 (1980): 2; D. B. McKown, "Creationism and the First Amendment," *Creation/Evolution* 7 (1982): 24; and R. M. O'Neil, "Creationism, Curriculum, and the Constitution," *Academe* 68, no. 2 (1982): 21.

61. J. Bergman, *Teaching About the Creation/Evolution Controversy* (Bloomington, Ind.: Phi Delta Kappa Educational Foundation, 1979).

62. G. Hardin, "Hardin's Law," in *Stalking the Wild Taboo*, 2d ed. (Los Altos, Calif.: Kaufman, 1978), p. 4, says, "It takes five years for a person's mind to change."

63. In addition to the review provided by Perry (1981, cf. note 7), a bibliography and a number of relevant papers are available from L. Copes, Institute for Studies in Educational Mathematics, 10429 Barnes Way, St. Paul, MN 55075.

64. For a discussion of debates see F. Edwords, "Creation-Evolution Debates: Who's Winning Them Now?," *Creation/Evolution* 8 (1982): 30.

65. This paper has benefitted from reviews of earlier drafts by several of my colleagues. Those by P. Appleman. T. Davis, E. Pikitch, S. Pinnette, A. Ruesink, and C. Zeller were especially helpful.

CHAPTER 10

Skepticism:
Another Alternative to
Science or Belief

Stephen G. Brush
University of Maryland

In a column on the creation/evolution controversy, Boston *Globe* columnist Ellen Goodman asked "why creationism has re-emerged now, in its new scientific garb." She came to the apparently paradoxical conclusion that "current support for creationism" comes from three forces, the first of them being "a skepticism about scientific certainty" arising from popular distrust of statements by scientists.[1] One can ask why creationists want their doctrine to be considered "scientific" while at the same time exploiting a public mood of hostility to science, and this interesting question has already been answered in the preceding chapters.

Here I want to consider instead the closely related question, Why, as Ms. Goodman suggests, would creationists want to encourage *skepticism* about a scientific theory such as evolution when their own doctrine is obviously much more vulnerable to skeptical attack? For example, their claim that the universe was created less than 10,000 years ago seems to be immediately refuted by astronomical observations of galaxies more than a million light years away. The creationists answer this by postulating that God created the light en route to us in such a way as to make it *appear* that it came from galaxies in existence millions of years ago.[2] Do creationists really expect any intelligent student to accept this as a legitimate scientific explanation?

One reason for employing skepticism as a weapon is that the creationists assume that there are only two alternatives, creation and evolution, so destroying the credibility of evolution would necessarily enhance that of creationism. Such a strategy might seem illogical to anyone familiar with the recent development of scientific theories and with the wide variety of creationist and evolutionist theories that have been or might be proposed. It is not possible to establish one theory merely by criticizing another one.

The negative character of much of the creationist literature illustrates the view of the late philosopher of science Imre Lakatos, that "skepticism is an anti-intellectual movement which, with the help of the sharpest intellectual methods, discredits intellectual effort." By using pure skepticism, Lakatos argues, "we open up the door to mysticism and to irrational theology."[3]

Skepticism is a continuing tradition in the perennial contest between science and belief. It is a wild card, a weapon that can be used by either side. In recent centuries skepticism has been used to *attack* the dogmatism of religion; now we are seeing a revival of the seventeenth-century application of skepticism to *defend* divine revelation and traditional faith by undermining the certainty of other sources of knowledge. It is interesting also to look at skepticism's two younger companions, historicism and relativism. While these have been employed to question the absolute validity of religious doctrines and moral codes, more recently they have been applied by historians, sociologists, and philosophers to question the objectivity of science, its independence of cultural influences, and its ability to transcend the human failings of scientists.

There are two different kinds of skeptical criticism of science. The first challenges the validity of specific scientific propositions by pointing to logical flaws or contrary evidence; the second attempts to forbid science from even investigating certain topics by asserting that they are beyond its legitimate domain. The first kind raises objections that may ultimately strengthen science, although it may not be possible to answer such objections immediately. The second, however, implies that one can establish a permanent, rigid definition of the boundaries of science. In this latter category is the argument that evolution is not a "testable scientific theory" but only a religious belief or metaphysical axiom, and hence does not have any greater claim than creationism to preferential treatment in a science class. But before considering either kind of skeptical criticism, some background is needed.

Skepticism has a long tradition, but being a skeptic is not as easy as it might seem. Socrates declared himself to be so skeptical that he knew only one thing for sure, namely, that he knew nothing. But Pyrrho pointed out that even this position was too dogmatic to be called true skepticism; one should doubt the claim that one knows nothing, for perhaps one *does* know something—but don't be too sure about it! These views were developed by other Greek philosophers into two competing traditions of skepticism, the Academic (from Plato's Academy) and the Pyrrhonian.[4]

Most philosophers have recognized that Academic skepticism is not only logically inconsistent but futile, since it can only destroy existing knowledge-claims without providing a basis for more satisfactory ones. Skepticism is always a useful weapon against dogmatism, but if the skeptic wants to advance any positive views of his own he should adopt the Pyrrhonian attitude that allows one to believe that something may be known even if not proved rigorously. In particular, skepticism was used by French Catholics in the Counter Reformation to attack the Calvinist claims that religious knowledge can be obtained by reasoning from the Bible.[5] As an alternative they offered only *faith* in the traditional doctrines of the Church. Obviously that position had and still has a strong emotional appeal to many people, even though it runs counter to the rationalism of the dominant Western intellectual tradition.

The Scientific Revolution of the seventeenth century began by using skepticism against the Aristotelian philosophy. Francis Bacon and Pierre Gassendi argued that one should not try to find ultimate truths about the world by deduction from first principles; rather one should develop an empirical science which would be useful in correlating the observations of the senses. Bacon's emphasis on the experimental, pragmatic aspect of science was a valuable antidote to the overly abstract style and negligible utility of scholastic philosophy, and inspired much of the enthusiasm for science that characterized seventeenth century England. One could be a skeptic by maintaining that science does not seek the ultimate truth about the real world but only tries to describe the appearances. The only drawback was that skeptics did not accomplish very much in science. Although historians honor Bacon and Gassendi for promoting the cause of science in a general way, it is hard to credit them with any important discoveries.[6]

The major advances of the Scientific Revolution were made by men who thought they could use their reasoning powers to find out how the world operates and who did *not* accept agreement with empirical data as the ultimate criterion for the validity of a theory. Copernicus rejected the geocentric system, not because it failed to fit the observations of planetary motions but rather because it was not sufficiently absolute and pleasing to the mind.[7] Kepler showed how accurate observational data (furnished by Tycho Brahe) could guide the search for mathematical harmony in the world, while allowing free play to the imagination of the theorist.[8] Galileo used experiments to uncover the simple principles that govern motion in an ideal world from which friction and air resistance have been removed, and skillfully presented arguments to show that the earth really moves despite the evidence from our senses.[9]

Yet the arguments that persuaded scientists to accept the heliocentric system before 1686 were quite vulnerable to criticism—not so much from supporters of the geocentric cosmology but from skeptics who denied that astronomers could *prove* the motion of the earth and insisted that such questions are beyond the proper domain of science. The skeptical position is that since science cannot establish either the heliocentric or the geocentric postulate, everyone should be free to choose either postulate on the basis of philosophical, theological, or any other reasons and that Galileo should have respected traditional religious beliefs instead of undermining them by his exaggerated claims for the validity of scientific knowledge.[10]

If skepticism is hostile to science, perhaps scientists should attack it directly rather than claiming to be skeptics themselves. That is what Descartes did. He argued that one might start by doubting everything but then realize that a person cannot doubt, or think at all, unless he exists. *Cogito ergo sum* is the first step toward constructing a scientific philosophy by deduction from self-evident principles.[11]

Descartes was successful in discovering a metaphysical foundation for science that survived not only the attacks of the skeptics but the failure of Descartes himself to explain most of the natural phenomena to which he applied his principles. According to Descartes, there is an almost-complete separation between the world of mind and spirit (*res cogitans*) and the physical world of matter and motion (*res extensa*). Physical science should be able to explain all phenomena in terms of the motions and collisions of pieces of matter without attributing to them any properties other than size and shape and without invoking any kind of force except repulsion on impact. The later success of Newton's theory of gravity did not lead scientists to abandon the search for such mechanistic explanations, for as Newton himself said, action at a distance is a ridiculous idea; ever since Newton, physicists have tried to explain gravity in terms of a more intuitively plausible hypothesis or mechanism.[12] Similarly, biologists have always found "vital forces" and teleology to be not quite respectable as scientific explanations and keep coming back to physico-chemical mechanisms.[13]

Let us consider the year 1666. It was 123 years after the publication of Copernicus's book *On the Revolutions of the Heavenly Spheres*. Most of the scientific community had accepted the idea that the earth moves around the sun, despite the efforts of the Catholic Church to suppress it; yet astronomers did not understand in detail *how* the earth moves. There was no satisfactory mechanism aside from Descartes' qualitative vortex theory. The most basic quantitative parameters, the absolute sizes of the planetary orbits, had not yet been determined, although their relative sizes were estimated fairly accurately. One of the most direct predictions of the heliocentric theory, stellar parallax, had not been observed, a failure which was explained away by the ad hoc postulate that the stars were all so far away that their parallax was too small to detect. Surely the time was ripe for someone to propose "equal time" for the old geocentric system, on the grounds that the motion of the earth could be neither proved nor disproved, hence it was not science, and that it was offensive to some people's religious beliefs.

As you may have guessed, I chose to look at the year 1666 not only because this symposium was being held 123 years after 1859 when Darwin's *Origin of Species* was published, but also because in the year 1666 the young Isaac Newton worked out a method for explaining gravitational motion. Newton accomplished for Copernicus the same kind of spectacular vindication and elaboration that biologists are still expecting someone to accomplish for Darwin.

Although Newton himself thought his discoveries could be used to support religion, their historic impact was to replace religion by science as the source of reliable knowledge. At the same time that Newton was developing his theories, skeptics such as Isaac La Peyrere and Baruch de Spinoza were assailing the accuracy of the Bible. Pierre Bayle launched the eighteenth-century Age of Reason with his *Historical and Critical Dictionary*; like David Hume's later in the century, his skeptical arguments could be used against the reliability of any kind of knowledge, scientific or religious, but Newton's success in astronomy and physics served to suppress at least temporarily any doubts about the value of science.[14]

It was in 1734, when religion was very much on the defensive, that Bishop Berkeley published a brilliant counterattack against science. The title of his essay reveals its purpose: *The Analyst, or A Discourse addressed to an Infidel Mathematician, Wherein it is examined whether the Objects, Principles, and Inferences of the modern Analysis are more distinctly conceived, or more evidently deduced, than Religious Mysteries and Points of Faith.*[15] The "infidel mathematician" was Newton's disciple Edmund Halley, and the "modern analysis" was the differential calculus of Newton and Leibniz. Although Berkeley was trying to combat skepticism in this and other works, *The Analyst* has generally been considered one of the most successful works in the skeptical genre—in part because its effect was not purely destructive but served to publicize the need for a reformation which actually occurred a century later.

Berkeley begins by criticizing the concept of a second derivative, that is, the rate of change of a rate of change, as a "fugitive idea" which "exceeds all human understanding." He ridicules the "infinitesimal," a quantity supposedly "infinitely less than the least discernible quantity" yet infinitely greater than infinitesimals of the second degree. He professes to be indignant that mathematicians would reject religion for its reliance on mysteries that must be accepted by faith yet accept such obscurities in their own subject: "he who can digest a second or third fluxion [derivative], a second or third difference, need not, methinks, be squeamish about any point in divinity. . . ."[16]

This criticism does not impress the modern reader who knows that many mathematical concepts now considered perfectly legitimate, from negative numbers to orders of infinity, were greeted by similar cries of outrage or incomprehension when first introduced. But Berkeley was not a blustering ignoramus, denouncing every innovation whose purpose and utility was not immediately obvious to the nonexpert. In fact, he was able to pinpoint a serious logical flaw in the Newton-Leibniz calculus. In order to calculate the derivative of x^n, Newton first assumed that x increases by a nonzero quantity o. Then by the generalized binomial theorem

$$(x+o)^n = x^n + nox^{n-1} + \tfrac{1}{2}n(n-1)o^2x^{n-2} + \ldots$$

The derivative is defined as the ratio of the change in x^n to the change in x, so one must divide $nox^{n-1} + \tfrac{1}{2}n(n-1)o^2x^{n-2} + \ldots$ by o. Newton argues that the result is nx^{n-1} because the higher terms vanish when o vanishes. Berkeley objects that the calculation is valid only on the assumption that o is *not* zero, and therefore the result has been obtained by false reasoning. "All which seems a most inconsistent way of arguing, and such as would not be allowed of in Divinity." Mathematicians who argue in this way are guilty of the same crimes they attribute to religious men—submitting to authority and accepting inconceivable mysteries on faith.[17]

Berkeley could not prevent mathematicians from introducing new concepts, but he could insist that they adhere to their own standards of rigorous proof. In the nineteenth century, mathematicians did succeed in developing a satisfactory way of handling limits that avoided Berkeley's criticism, and so ultimately science was strengthened by this kind of skepticism.

There is, however, a version of skepticism which, though not explicitly presented as an attack on science in defense of religion, nevertheless has a genetic connection with the contemporary creationist assault on evolution. That version is the positivist movement, beginning with August Comte and ending, perhaps, with Karl Popper. "Positivism" is used in two rather different senses: (1) the view that only science or the scientific method can yield reliable knowledge, as opposed to philosophy, theology, and other humanistic disciplines; and (2) the view that science itself must be empirical and should not rely on theoretical concepts that cannot be directly tested by observation. In the second sense, positivism is a form of empiricism and insists that science can never discover anything about ultimate reality but must be limited to a description and prediction of appearances. Positivists in this second sense leave a clear field for religion and philosophy, unlike positivists in the first sense.

A notorious example of a positivist claim is Comte's statement that we can never expect to learn anything about the chemical composition of stars when just a few years later such knowledge was in fact obtained through spectroscopy.[18] A similar fate is probably in store for other negative predictions—that we will never invent machines that think, or rockets that go faster than the speed of light, and so on. We are reminded of the Academic skeptics who were too certain of their knowledge that they knew nothing.

A more plausible and therefore more dangerous form of positivism was the Pyrrhonic skepticism about the existence of atoms at the end of the nineteenth century. Ernst Mach did not assert that matter is not composed of atoms, but rather that the whole question is beyond the realm of science since we have never seen an atom. By fostering an atmosphere of skepticism, Mach and other positivists probably discouraged research in atomic physics and chemistry in the decades before 1910. By that time there was so much evidence for the atomic structure of matter that Mach lost his influence, even though he refused to change his own views before his death in 1916.[19]

Mach's skeptical philosophy bore no fruits, as Max Planck pointed out.[20] Although his critique of absolute time and space may have helped to prepare the way for the acceptance of relativity theory, Mach's doctrine did not hold the allegiance of Albert Einstein very long.[21] But the Vienna Circle revived it in a more sophisticated form under the name "logical positivism," later changed to "logical empiricism." Here we have no longer a skeptical attack on science but an attempt by philosophers to justify and reformulate what they think scientists actually do. One might also say that modern physics, or at least the dominant "Copenhagen interpretation" of quantum mechanics, incorporates a formal principle of skepticism about the existence of unobserved entities. Yet this principle does not restrain speculation and elaborate theorizing about such entities, for example, the "quark," which is generally regarded as a fundamental constituent of matter even though it may be intrinsically unobservable. For the physicist of the 1980s, logical positivism is dead (if, indeed, he has ever heard of it), and skepticism is sterile.

Recent attempts to test some of the more bizarre predictions of quantum mechanics, such as the "Einstein-Podolsky-Rosen effect" (so-called because those authors thought its nonexistence would demonstrate the incompleteness of quantum mechanics), give a curious twist to Bishop Berkeley's views. In his *Three Dialogues between Hylas and Philonous, in opposition to Sceptics and Atheists*, Berkeley proved that material substance does not exist outside the mind of an observer. This result led to the obvious question, Do objects continue to exist during intervals of time when no human observer happens to be perceiving them? Berkeley tried to extricate himself from this dilemma by postulating that an "omnipresent, external Mind" (i.e., God) must take over the function of observing and thus preserving the reality of objects when humans fail to discharge this duty.[22] Berkeley's argument probably failed to persuade anyone of the existence of God, since the prior conclusion that the world owes its existence to being observed seemed so implausible at the time. This conclusion is now supported to some extent by quantum mechanics. But we recognize that humans can observe events at distant times and places, and it is conceivable, at least to some physicists, that the reality of the early history of the universe may depend on the subsequent evolution of intelligent life capable of observing it. As a consequence of the "Anthropic Principle," this dependence may account for the apparently arbitrary values of fundamental physical constants.[23] Thus "secular humanism" rather than religion appears to profit by Berkeley's skeptical argument.

Earlier, I mentioned two other versions of skepticism, historicism and relativism. The first is, like positivism, a term that has at least two different meanings: (1) the thesis that events are determined or influenced by some principle of development or long-term trend; (2) the thesis that the present is to be explained by the past.[24] I will consider the term in the second sense, in particular the claim that a scientific or religious doctrine is accepted not so much because it represents an objectively discovered or divinely revealed truth but rather because it grew out of a contingent set of historical circumstances. In this sense historicism merges with relativism, the claim that scientific theories and religious beliefs may differ from one society to another, with none being able to claim more validity than another.

The Judeo-Christian tradition suffered the onslaught of historicism in the nineteenth century, in the form of Biblical criticism. Scholars no longer accepted the Bible as the revealed word of God but came to see it as a historical document shaped by men living in specific circumstances. *The Life of Jesus*, by D. F. Strauss, is credited with undermining the religious faith of many influential thinkers in Europe and America, no so much by offering historical proof that the Biblical account was wrong, as by showing how flimsy was the evidence for this or any other account.[25] If one's religious faith depends on the accuracy of a body of material that has been transmitted from one writer to another through several generations, with questionable additions, reinterpretations, erroneous translations, and resulting inconsistencies, then that faith must seem insecurely grounded. Many modern theologians have argued that the Fundamentalist insistence on the literal truth of a particular translation of the Bible, without taking account of the various paths by which this version reached us, is simply unacceptable as a basis for sound religious belief. The creationists, especially those who claim Biblical support for their postulate that the universe was created less than 10,000 years ago, refuse to admit that the Bible itself has a history.

Whereas historicism is associated with the evolutionary view of nature and society, cultural relativism arose in the early twentieth century as a reaction against dogmatic cultural evolutionism. Franz Boas and other anthropologists rejected the thesis that modern European society is necessarily superior to more "primitive" cultures because it has progressed further along a universal path of evolution.[26] Instead, they argued that each society should be studied with sympathy for its own religious beliefs, moral values, and customs, without assuming that they are inferior or less advanced than ours. This approach has shocked many Americans who believe that their own moral values are absolute and should be observed everywhere. The furor over the federal funding of the MACOS ("Man, A Course of Study") curriculum project reflects this rejection of cultural relativism.[27] More recently the campaign of the Moral Majority against abortion and tolerance of homosexuality shows that some religious people feel strongly threatened by relativism, even or especially when the alternative values and customs are as firmly rooted in American society as their own.

Since the scientist assumes that progress brings us closer to truth, he has nothing to fear from the kind of historicism that describes the gradual exposure and elimination of past errors. This is what we now call the "Whig interpretation of the history of science," taking over Herbert Butterfield's label, "the Whig interpretation of history," which referred to the tendency to interpret past events in terms of progress toward liberal democracy.[28] The assumption is that scientific research is cumulative and that new theories replace old ones because they are objectively better.

In the last two decades, the Whig interpretation has been challenged by some historians and philosophers of science who urge that scientific work be evaluated in light of the knowledge and attitudes of its own time, rather than judged by whether it represented progress toward our present theories. Moreover, T. S. Kuhn and others have argued that in a scientific revolution not only theories but also the criteria for judging theories may change. If one adopts a new world view or "paradigm" which is incommensurable with the old one, then it is no longer obvious that cumulative progress is taking place—the new theories may not even try to answer some questions that were important to the old paradigm. Thus, for example, the adoption of a theory like Newton's heliocentric celestial dynamics or Darwin's evolution by natural selection may effectively satisfy the demand for mechanistic explanation (on a macroscopic level) but fail to answer questions about ultimate purpose and meaning, as Aristotelian or creationist theories did.

In the absence of objective proof that the new paradigm is superior, the decision of scientists to adopt it may look somewhat like religious conversion experiences influenced by social pressures, and the problem of preserving the rationality of science has made some scientists and philosophers reluctant to accept the conclusions of the new history of science.[29] On the other hand, sociologists have gone even further in arguing that scientific theories, like religious beliefs, are never independent of social circumstances; they want to start from an axiom of complete relativism. No theory, indeed no "fact," should be immune from the analysis of its "social construction."[30]

It seems clear that philosophical, historical, and sociological treatments of science can provide much ammunition for anyone who wants to undermine the privileged position of a theory such as evolution, and indeed, this has already happened. Creationists have used Karl Popper's statement that Darwinism is not a falsifiable hypothesis or scientific law, but rather a "metaphysical research programme," to support their attack on the scientific status of evolution.[31] Popper himself has recanted his statement and has declared that Darwin's natural selection is indeed a legitimate scientific hypothesis, but the damage has been done.[32] One can only point out that a skeptic who interprets Popper's "falsifiability" criterion so strictly as to exclude evolution would also have to exclude most theories in geology and astronomy. Are we willing to say that phenomena in the past or at great distances from us, which cannot be brought into the laboratory for controlled experiments, can never be studied scientifically?

The philosopher Paul Feyerabend, who is perhaps the most articulate contemporary spokesman for radical skepticism, has refused to go along with Popper's defense of orthodox science. He writes, "Three cheers to the fundamentalists in California who succeeded in having a dogmatic formulation of the theory of evolution removed from the text books and an account of Genesis included." Creationists should recognize, however, that they have no true ally here, for Feyerabend continues, "But I know that they would became as chauvinistic and totalitarian as scientists are today when given the chance to run society all by themselves. Ideologies are marvelous when used in the companies of other ideologies. They become boring and doctrinaire as soon as their merits lead to the removal of their opponents."[33]

My interpretation of Kuhn's view is that, unlike Feyerabend, he applauds the tendency of the scientific community to settle on a single paradigm and push it as far as possible, rather than continually rehashing fundamental issues. It is only by enthusiastically accepting a theory and working out all its consequences (not an easy task for most modern theories) that one can discover where it breaks down and what changes are really essential.[34] The progress of science, and certainly the education of scientists, would be impaired by giving equal time to all conceivable alternatives to the accepted theory, even though that theory has not been and cannot be proved to be the ultimate truth. Thus, the reason for giving preferences to evolution over other theories is not that evolution has been completely established (which would make it a rather unattractive field for further research), but that it offers the most plausible explanation at present for a large number of observations and generates fruitful suggestions and special hypotheses to stimulate new investigations. If the theory of evolution is overthrown, it will not be by political action that forces teachers to pretend that creationism is a legitimate alternative, but rather by research inspired by evolutionary theory itself. Obviously, the creationists do not have faith that the *free* development of science will validate their theory, or they would not try to impose it by force.

This brief survey suggests to me that in the long run science has nothing to fear from honest skepticism. Skeptical attacks that challenge scientific dogmatism on its own territory, like Berkeley's critique of calculus and the Mach-Einstein rejection of absolute space and time, may point the way to important advances in sciences. Attacks that try to forbid science from dealing with certain topics, such as Comte's skepticism about stellar astronomy,

Mach's critique of atomic theory, and the creationist assault on evolution, are probably doomed to failure.

Since many of us are concerned about the lack of public understanding of science, it is encouraging that one widely read columnist does appreciate the point of this chapter. To quote again the words of Ellen Goodman:

> Is learning a matter of quest and questioning, where doubts are valued along with answers? Or is it elaborate justification created to support a single religious text?
>
> Science begins with questions and pursues answers—testing, proving, disproving. It is this process of reasoning that underpins all of modern science. Creationism begins with answers and pursues doubts only to erase them. It is fundamentally hostile to science.
>
> If creationists win their equal time, it will not be an easily shared custody. There is a deep and irreconcilable difference between the idea that learning is open-ended and the belief that knowledge is a closed book.[35]

Notes

1. Ellen Goodman, "Is It Science That's On Trial?" *The Washington Post*, 12 December 1981, A15.

2. Henry M. Morris, *The Remarkable Birth of Planet Earth* (Minneapolis: Dimension Books, 1972), pp. 61–62. I have discussed this and other aspects of the time-scale problem in "Finding the Age of the Earth: By Physics or by Faith?" *Journal of Geological Education* 30 (January 1982): 34–58

3. W. Yourgrau and A. D. Breck, eds., *Physics, Logic, and History* (New York: Plenum Press, 1970), p. 220.

4. Richard H. Popkin, *The History of Skepticism from Erasmus to Spinoza* (Berkeley: University of California Press, 1979). I have adopted the preferred U.S. spelling with a "k" rather than a "c".

5. Ibid. Ch. 4.

6. Ibid., Ch. 4 and 5; see also "Scepticism, Theology, and the Scientific Revolution in the Seventeenth Century," in *Problems in the Philosophy of Science*, I. Lakatos and A. Musgrave eds. (Amsterdam: North-Holland, 1968), pp. 1–28.

7. Nicholas Copernicus, *On the Revolutions*, trans. E. Rosen, J. Dobrzycki, ed. (Baltimore: Johns Hopkins University Press, 1978). Owen Gingerich, "Crisis versus Aesthetic in the Copernican Revolution," in *Copernicus Yesterday and Today*, vol. 17 of *Vistas in Astronomy*, A. Beer and K. A. Strand, eds. (New York: Pergamon Press, 1975), pp. 85–93.

8. Johannes Kepler, "Epitome of Copernican Astronomy," Books IV and IV (trans. from the Latin ed., 1618–1621), and "The Harmony of the World," Book V (trans. from the Latin ed., 1619), in *Great Books of the Western World*, vol. 16, R. M. Hutchins, ed. (Chicago: Encyclopedia Britannica, 1952), pp. 843–1004, 1005–85.

9. Galileo Galilei, *Dialogue Concerning the Two Chief World Systems—Ptolemaic and Copernican*, 2d ed., trans. Stillman Drake from *Dialogo . . .*, 1632 (Berkeley: University of California Press, 1967).

10. Andreas Osiander, "Foreword," in Copernicus, *On the Revolutions*, p. xvi. For Francis Bacon's rejection of the Copernican hypothesis, see Mary Hesse, "Bacon, Francis," *Dictionary of Scientific Biography* 1 (1970): 373. Pierre Duhem, *To Save the Phenomena* (trans. Fr. ed., 1908), (Chicago: University of Chicago Press, 1969). Arthur Koestler, *The Sleepwalkers* (New York: Macmillan, 1959). Paul Feyerabend, "In Defense of Classical Physics," *Studies in History and Philosophy of Science*, 1 (1970): 59–85.

11. Rene Descartes, *Discourse on Method, Optics, Geometry, and Meteorology* (trans. Fr. ed., 1637), (Indianapolis: Bobbs-Merrill, 1965).

12. Isaac Newton, *Mathematical Principles of Natural Philosophy*, F. Cajori's rev. of A. Motte's trans. of 3rd Latin ed., 1729 (Berkeley: University of California Press, 1934); for his rejection of action at a distance, see his letter of 25 February 1693 to Richard Bentley, reprinted in *Newton's Philosophy of Nature*, H. S. Thayer, ed. (New York: Hafner, 1953), p. 54. References to proposals of a "kinetic theory of gravity" are given in S. G. Brush, *The Kind of Motion We Call Heat* (Amsterdam: North-Holland, 1976), p. 22, note. 11.

13. Hilde Hein, "The Endurance of the Mechanism-Vitalism Controversy," *Journal of the History of Biology* 5 (1972): 159–88; Garland Allen, *Life Science in the Twentieth Century* (New York: Wiley, 1975).

14. Popkin, *History*, Chs. 11 and 12; "Skepticism in Modern Thought," in *Dictionary of the History of Ideas*, vol. 4, P. P. Wiener, ed. (New York: Scribner, 1973), pp. 240–51.

15. *The Works of George Berkeley, Bishop of Cloyne*, vol. 4, A. A. Luce and T. E. Jessup, eds. (London: Nelson, 1951), pp. 65–102.

16. Ibid., pp. 68–69.

17. Ibid., p. 73.

18. Auguste Comte, *Cours de Philosophie Positive*, vol. 2 (Paris: Bachelier, 1835), p. 2. W. Huggins and W. A. Miller, "Notes on the Lines in the Spectra of Some of the Fixed Stars," *Proceedings of the Royal Society of London* 12 (1862–1863): 444–45; "On the Spectra of Some Fixed Stars," *Philosophical Transactions of the Royal Society of London* 154 (1864): 413–36.

19. Brush, *The Kind of Motion*, Ch. 8. G. Buchdahl, "Sources of Scepticism in Atomic Theory," *British Journal for the Philosophy of Science* 10 (1959): 120–34. Mach and others presented the skeptical view so well that they even persuaded some recent philosophers of science that the atomistic research program was objectively "degenerating" between 1870 and 1905; see, for example, Peter Clark, "Atomism versus Thermodynamics," in *Method and Appraisal in the Physical Sciences*, C. Howson, ed. (New York: Cambridge University Press, 1976), pp. 41–105. For detailed refutation of Clark, see John Nyhof, "Instrumentalism and Beyond" (Ph.d. thesis, University of Otag Dunedin, New Zealand, 1981).

20. See the 1909–1910 papers of Planck and Mach, trans. in *Physical Reality*, Stephen Toulmin, ed. (New York: Harper and Row, 1970), pp. 1–52.

21. Gerald Holton, "Mach, Einstein, and the Search for Reality," *Daedalus* 97 (1968): 636–673.

22. *The Empiricists* (Garden City, N.Y.: Doubleday/Dolphin, n.d.), p. 274.

23. John Wheeler, "Genesis and Observership," in *Proceedings of the Fifth International Congress of Logic, Methodology, and Philosophy of Science*, Part 2, R. E. Butts and J. Hintikka, eds. (Boston: Reidel, 1977), pp. 3–33; George Gale, "The Anthropic Principle," *Scientific American*, December 1981, p. 154.

24. For other definitions see Friedrich Meinecke, *Historism* (London: Routledge, 1921); Wilhelm Dilthey, *Pattern and Meaning in History* (New York: Harper and Row, 1962); Joseph V. Femia, "An Historicist Critique of 'Revisionist' Methods for Studying the History of Ideas," *History and Theory* 20 (1981): 113–134.

25. Owen Chadwick, *The Secularization of the European in the Nineteenth Century* (New York: Cambridge University Press, 1975), pp. 70, 215, 224.

26. Franz Boas, *Race, Language, and Culture* (New York: Free Press, 1966). George W. Stocking, "Franz Boas and the Culture Concept in Historical Perspective," in *Race, Culture, and Evolution* (New York: Free Press, 1968), pp. 195–233.

27. Dorothy Nelkin, *Science Textbook Controversies and the Politics of Equal Time* (Cambridge, Mass.: MIT Press, 1977), Ch. 7.

28. Herbert Butterfield, *The Whig Interpretation of History* (London: Bell, 1931).

29. Stephen G. Brush, "Should the History of Science Be Rated X?" *Science* 183 (1974): 1164–72.

30. David Bloor, *Knowledge and Social Imagery* (London: Routledge and Kegan Paul, 1976). H. M. Collins, "Stages in the Empirical Programme of Relativism," *Social Studies of Science* 11 (1981): 3–10. Bruno Latour and Steve Woolgar, *Laboratory Life: The Social Construction of Scientific Facts* (Beverly Hills: Sage, 1979). Peter Janich, "Physics—Natural Science or Technology," in *The Dynamics of Science and Technology*, W. Krohn et al., eds. (Boston: Reidel, 1978), pp. 3–27.

31. Karl Popper, *Unended Quest* (La Salle, Ill.: Open Court, 1976) pp. 167–80. William J. Broad, "Creationists Limit Scope of Evolution Case," *Science* 211 (1981): 1331–32.

32. Karl Popper, "Natural Selection and the Emergence of Mind," *Dialectica* 32 (1978): 339–55; "Evolution," *New Scientist* 87 (1980): 611. R. E. Kofahl and H. Zeisel, "Popper on Darwinism," *Science* 212 (1981): 873.

33. Paul Feyerabend, "How to Defend Society Against Science," *Radical Philosophy* 11 (1975): 3–8; reprinted in *Introductory Readings in the Philosophy of Science*, E. D. Klemke, R. Hollinger, and H. D. Kline, eds. (Buffalo: Prometheus, 1980), p. 62. I thank Philip Ehrlich for sending me this quotation. See also Feyerabend, *Against Method* (London: Verso, 1978), pp. 31, 307. John G. McEvoy, "A 'Revolutionary' Philosophy of Science: Feyerabend and the Degeneration of Critical Rationalism into Sceptical Fallibilism," *Philosophy of Science* 42 (1975): 49–66.

34. Thomas S. Kuhn, "The Essential Tension: Tradition and Innovation in Scientific Research," *The Essential Tension* (Chicago: University of Chicago Press,

1977), pp. 225–39. According to a leading theoretical physicist, Steven Weinberg, "... I do not believe that scientific progress is always best advanced by keeping an altogether open mind ... the great thing is not to be free of theoretical prejudices, but to have the right theoretical prejudices!" *The First Three Minutes* (New York: Basic Books, 1977), p. 119.

35. Ellen Goodman, "What Is vs. What's Right," *The Washington Post* 19 December 1981, A21. For another formulation of this view, see Judge William Overton's decision overturning the Arkansas creationism law (Appendix B, this volume).

CHAPTER 11

The Creationism Issue:
A Theologian's View

Langdon Gilkey
University of Chicago

The 1982 court trials in Arkansas and Louisiana concerning "creation science" and evolution raised surprising and important issues for both the scientific and the religious communities of America. They force us again to think about the meaning of the traditional separation of church and state in modern life and about the vast complexity of the relation of science to religion in advanced technological culture. Most people in the scientific community and the media picture this controversy as simply the latest act in the age-old and continuing drama entitled, "The Warfare of Science and Religion." I shall try to show in this chapter that this is a serious misreading of the controversy. There is, as there was in the nineteenth century, a good deal of "science" and a good deal of "religion" on *both* sides of the case. Therefore, the controversy can best be seen as representing a contest between *two different sorts* of interrelations or of unions of science and religion.

Creation-Science: An Unexpected Hybrid of Science and Religion

Let us begin by stating the definition of "creation science" and of "evolution science" as the creationist movement views them and as they were expressed in Act 590 in Arkansas (Appendix A). "Creation science" represents the following points:

1. Sudden creation of all things (universe, life, man) from nothing
2. Permanent species or "kinds of things," going back to the very beginning
3. Separate ancestry of apes and of man
4. The explanation of geological formations and changes by means of "catastrophes," for example, the flood of Noah
5. Recent creation of all things (namely, within the last 10,000 to 25,000 years)

The similarity of these points to those in the Genesis account (taken literally) is, of course, immediately evident. As "creation-science" documents admit, such a model requires a Creator to be intelligible. Contrasted with this model is the other model, named "evolution science." As defined by those in the creationist movement, it specifies that the origin of the universe, of earth, of life, and of man lay in natural forces alone. Since origins cannot in either case be "observed," according to creationist arguments, "evolution science" is no more scientific than "creation science." Thus if "creation science" represents Biblical religion (the belief in creation by God), then evolution represents an atheistic and humanistic "religion" (the belief that everything arises out of blind matter). As a consequence of this reasoning, these two opposing models are presented as "equally scientific" and "equally religious." Hence, if one is taught, it is only fair that the other also be taught, and it is precisely this balanced treatment that the laws required.

The laws seeking to establish the teaching of "creation science" along with "evolution science" in the public schools have understandably enjoyed a good deal of wide public approval and support. To those quite uninterested in or even opposed to creationism as a belief they seem eminently fair. They state the proposition that these are both equally scientific models of origins. They ask further that, since these are *the only two* explanations of origins— and who, in the general public, knows this to be false?—should they not as the two available alternatives be given equal time or balanced treatment? I will seek to show here that these two claims are false.

First, "creation science" is *not* a scientific model, and therefore it is not at all a direct alternative to the scientific theory of evolution. On the contrary, it represents a religious or theological model of the explanation of origins which neither conflicts with nor excludes scientific theories of origins. By stating in legislation, as the Arkansas and Louisiana laws did, that these are alternative models categorically opposed to one another, the state officially sows a double confusion and promulgates a serious error: namely, confusion about what science is and about what religious explanation is, and additionally, the error that religious and scientific views of origins are unalterably opposed to one another, so that no one can be a Christian believer and still accept evolution. Here the state set itself explicitly *against* the forms of belief characteristic of most of the nation's churches and synagogues, not to mention those with other religious orientations.

Second, "creation science" and evolution do *not* represent the "only two explanations of origins," contrary to the statements of every "creation-science" volume and each of the two laws. These are only two of many. Among the numerous views of origins in the history of religions, "creation science" represents one rather minor interpretation or variant of the Christian view, an interpretation not shared even by most present-day Christian groups or churches and certainly not shared by the Jews, Moslems, Hindus, Buddhists, Sikhs, and American Indians who are also American citizens. For the state to require the teaching of "creation science" is, therefore, to legislate not only that a *religious* doctrine be taught as science, but even more, that a *particular* religious doctrine, which excludes vast numbers of other religious believers as well as nonbelievers, be taught to the exclusion of other religious views.

In contrast to the modern "creation-science" movement, earlier anti-evolutionary movements were explicitly antiscientific; they argued in public forums and in the courts against science and for "Biblical Christianity." In the last decades of the twentieth century, however, much has changed; the culture has become scientific and technological from top to bottom. Now we find anti-evolutionary groups claiming to represent "science" and not religion; consequently, they attack evolution not as science, but as "bad science," and they defend their views of origins as "good science" and thus as quite independent of any religious sources. Just as Fundamentalist groups have recently adopted much local television technology, commercial enterprises, and a number of brand-new "universities," so Fundamentalist intellectuals have recently entered the realm of science, become thoroughly trained there, absorbed much of its content and know-how, and now seek to shape its inquiry and teaching in their own doctrinal directions. As we have noted, they represent not so much the antagonism of religion against science as a new sort of *union* of religion (Fundamentalist religion) both with technological expertise and with theoretical science at the doctoral level.

How is it that these "scientists" can present what is clearly a literalistic account of the creation story in Genesis as a legitimate "scientific model"? First of all, they define science in terms of "scientific facts" or "scientific evidences": they say that the scientific facts that a theory explains are what make any theory scientific. This makes sense to those who think of scientific discovery as the discovery of facts, of science as an accumulation of facts and a scientific theory as the reasonable explanation of such facts. A scientific culture tends to become a culture that worships facts as embodying all truth, and gradually it loses its awareness of the importance of *theory*.

It sinks from a scientific culture to a technological one, a shift characteristic of our time.

There are three "facts" to which Fundamentalist intellectuals generally point in their arguments: (1) evidences of design, order, and purpose in nature that argue for an intelligent and purposive Creator; (2) arguments against prevailing geological and biological theories or hypotheses (and astronomical ones, when the age or the expansion of the universe is at issue) developed by other scientists; and (3) various attempts to show that the creation hypothesis "predicts" certain (carefully chosen) "facts of science" better than do evolutionary theories.

The only "good" arguments in this list are the first, those for a Creator-God from the evident design of the world. From Greek and Roman times to our own, these have seemed to many to be very convincing arguments, and as a result they have constituted most of the traditional arguments of "natural theology," that is, philosophical arguments for God's existence based not on religious authority, religious sources, or religious experiences, but on reason and experience alone. The only trouble here is that these are not— and never have been considered to be—*scientific* arguments. To some commentators they are at best speculative philosophical arguments; to other less enthusiastic interpreters, they are only pale rationalizations of religious faith. By none until the present (when science became the main model of truth) were they ever thought to be scientific. The "creation scientists" have erroneously advanced these arguments as being scientific and as "scientific evidences for creation and scientific inferences therefrom," and so it is on this ground that the traditional (literalistic) doctrine of creation is now presented as a scientific model.

The central error involved here stems from the initial misunderstanding of science. Science is not located in its facts nor in its explanations of scientific facts; science is located in its *theories*. It is the *theoretical structure*, the coherent system of theories created by scientific inquiry, that constitutes science—not the facts associated with those theories. A theory must conform to the methods and canons of science to be science, an aspect of science well known since at least the seventeenth century but obscured in a technological culture, where science is established and therefore not much thought about.

Basic to these canons of scientific procedure are three requirements. If a theory defies any of these, it cannot be said to be scientific.

1. No supernatural agent or force can be appealed to in the explanation; on the contrary, explanations must be in terms of forces or factors that are *finite* and in that sense "natural" (forces of nature, trends in history, human actions, etc.)
2. Explanations must be in terms of natural laws, that is, *invariable*

and *necessary* forces or factors. A scientific explanation must be necessary and universal; hence natural science does not explain in terms of *unique* actions, or *purposive* actions or intentions (e.g., God created out of love).

3. Scientific theories must *grow out* of experimental evidence (what they refer to must be locatable within it) and *be tested* by further experiment (shareable and public evidence).

Clearly, a theory or model that refers to the action of a transcendent Creator establishing in one unique act at the beginning of time the entire realm of nature, and thus the system of natural laws itself, defies each of these canons. Such a theory appeals to a transcendent divine power far beyond the system of finite causes; it explains in terms of the power and purpose of that Creator, not in terms of natural laws (these are established at the time of creation and so are "not yet" in effect). Being a unique, unrepeatable act, it cannot be tested in the present, since there are no similar processes available in present experience.

Whatever facts it may point to, the model of creation cannot represent a scientific theory, since it directly contravenes all the requirements that make any theory scientific. Nevertheless, even though "creation by a divine being" may not represent a scientific hypothesis or theory, it does not follow that it is not *true*, unless scientific theories are regarded as exhausting all relevant truth. It does mean, however, that it represents some other mode of cognition or of truth.

The plaintiffs' case in the Arkansas trial hung on the point that the affirmation of the creation of the universe by God, common to the Christian and Jewish religions, represents at base a "religious" type of truth, and consequently, the model of "creation science" (as a literalistic variant of that tradition) represents a religious type of explanation (see Appendix B). To show that this model was in fact a religious theory represented the center of the plaintiffs' case. Whatever it was claimed to be, and whether or not it appealed to Scripture, church authority, or church doctrine, the model could not, by the very nature of its conceptuality, avoid being an example of religious speech, an expression of religious belief. The theory of creation out of nothing, traditional to Christianity and asserted by the creationists, represents the quintessence of religious speech or of a religious concept. For here all other forces and factors are absent. Since every other agent appears *because of* and so *after* this act, in referring to this act we refer *only* to God: "God created all else out of nothing." This means that creation represents the epitome of religious speech. Even more, it means that without God, the transcendent Creator, there can be no creative act, for no other creative force is present. Without God as agent, therefore, there is no theory or model here at all. Yet with God, the model becomes essentially and inevitably a religious theory. Thus if it *is* a theory, and is internally coherent and meaningful, it is a religious theory; if it abstracts God out, and thus seeks to avoid being religious, it represents no concept at all, for it is void and meaningless. The "creation-science" model is either religious or it is nothing at all.

Returning to our analysis of "creation science," it is evident that its proponents oppose "evolution science" on two interrelated but distinguishable grounds. The first could be called religious; they see in evolutionary theory a religious perspective—which they call "secular humanism"—antithetical to Christian faith and its reverence for the Bible. Thus they see "evolution science" as a "religion," a materialistic, godless, amoral faith, the source of most of the present evils of our present history: communism, nihilism, relativism, liberalism, homosexuality, the Equal Rights Amendment, the United Nations, and the National Council of Churches! To believe in evolution, so they affirm, is to adopt, perhaps unwittingly, this secular "religion" or to be an involuntary agent of religious atheism.

There can be little doubt that there is a *connection* between modern science and "naturalistic humanism." Here the creationists are right. But it is also true that there is a *distinction* between the scientific theory, or theories, of evolution and such a naturalistic, atheistic, humanistic philosophy or religion. Part of my purpose here is to make both that connection and that distinction clearer than the creationists have made it.

Part of the struggle represented in the Arkansas trial was a contest between what creationists termed two "religions," that is, two religious perspectives on all of existence, and so on the character, responsibilities, and destiny of human existence. One of these perspectives is Biblical and Christian and centers itself on God the Creator and Redeemer: the other ("evolutionary science") is seen a naturalistic, atheistic, and humanistic, one which centers its hopes on the human being, its powers, its intelligence, and its goodness. The scientific community, or much of it, denies this "religious aura" associated with much of modern science; it sees itself as purely objective and scientific and freed from all taint of religion, as expressed in the writings of Julian Huxley, George Gaylord Simpson, Jacob Bronowski, and Carl Sagan. Nevertheless, these well-known scientists and their followers assume an *identity* between "evolutionary science" as they understand it and the naturalistic humanism they also profess, and they argue this identity in every volume they write or address they deliver. The creationists have achieved much of their credibility by pointing this out, although creationist antipathy to evolution has other bases than this "religious" one.

Creationists are opposed on religious grounds not only to modern evolutionary science as "religion" they also oppose its scientific content, that is, to the most pervasive, important, and general substantive theorem of contemporary science (of modern science as *science*). This, I would suggest, is the proposition that the natural universe we inhabit is eons old, has undergone innumerable basic changes in its process of development (for example, the stars have changed in many significant ways, a point they deny), and that new forms of stellar and galactic entities, of the earth itself, and new species of marine, plant, animal, and human life have developed in this long process. To deny this is to deny the central *content* of most of our sciences and the theorem on which our most important inquiries are based. To deny this is also to reject the theoretical foundation of our present technology and industry, as well as much of our academic culture. Creationist religious doctrines include authoritative ("revealed") statements about the age of the earth, whether the stars have changed or not, how the earth developed, how the different kinds of living things arose, and so forth, issues with which the natural and historical sciences deal directly. Just as many scientists see science to be capable of generating a true religious or philosophical perspective, so the creationists believe revelation provides us with a divine astronomy, geology, biology, and botany—not to mention the physics and chemistry that underlie these other sciences.

These matters represent, however, questions concerning relations among *finite* things, an understanding of the structure, the history, the causes, and the outcomes of natural and historical events. This is *not* the area for which religion provides authoritative information. Religion concerns the activity of God in and through events, but it does not inform us in detail about the events themselves, taken merely on their own and as we can know them empirically. This is the area within which science—and history—have developed competence, and which, we now know, they are competent provisionally, if not finally, to understand and to interpret. The creationists' participation in science and in its technological results clearly manifests that they *also* assent to and accept this "competence." Here they are utterly inconsistent: the scientific knowledge of which their writings are full and the technology they so cheerfully use both depend on that competence, on the scientific method that enacts that competence, and so on, to the very conclusions of scientific inquiry that they deny.

Here is perhaps the fundamental point at issue: though the creationists are quite right about the predominantly secularistic and even atheistic character of most of our contemporary intellectual life, they are—so most religious groups feel—quite wrong to deny and refute in the name of religion the entire scientific understanding of nature and of its history on which rests much of the civilization they also enjoy.

There is a deeper source of the error involved in this confusion of religion with science, of the religious truths about God and His Creation, which creationists treasure, with the scientific "truths" about the history of nature, which they reject. I believe it lies in the assumption that there is only *one* kind of truth; that truth exists, so to speak, all on one level. This one relevant sort of truth is material, physical, and historical, "factual truth," even a quantitative truth: the age of things, when they came to be, how they came to be, what causes brought them about, and so on. A literalist technological culture believes this is the sort of information that science tells us; literalistic religion believes this sort of information God—or revelation—

also tells us. If God created us, He must have acted as does any other physical cause, and thus in acting, *replaced* all other physical causes. Because these truths (scientific and religious) are of the same sort, when each of them tells a different story, they therefore contradict and so exclude one another. Thus does a religious theory of origins conflict with a scientific theory of origins, for they both deal with reality, or the origins of reality, in the same way and on the same level. It is this view of truth as all of one kind, as material, historical, and factual truth—that leads to the deepest error of "creation science" and its continuing antipathy to liberal religion and to scientific education.

It is also clear that this same error is not confined to the Christian Fundamentalist community. It is shared by many in the academic and the scientific communities—by all those who view religion as merely "prescientific" theories about the earth and its origins and so view scientific knowledge as replacing so-called religious knowledge; all those who say, "we scientists now know there is no God." It is because of this error that many scientists, sure that traditional religious faith in God has been dissolved by scientific inquiry, assume that with the developments of science, a naturalistic philosophical or religious perspective must replace a traditional Christian or Jewish one. Ironically, the same error, typical of a scientific and technological culture, pervades both sides of this controversy—the creationists, on the one hand, and many of their scientific opponents, on the other. Truly this controversy has been bred by the character of *both* the science and the religion in a scientific and technological culture.

Religion and Science in a Technological Culture

As both sides of the creationist controversy have illustrated, the relations of science to the religious in a technological age are complex indeed. Since there is a surprising amount of science as well as Fundamentalist religion on the side of "creation science" and more than a little of the "religious" on the side of the established scientific community, this is no simple warfare between advancing forces of scientific light and retreating forces of religious darkness. It is now time, therefore, to look more closely at the complicated relations of science and the religious in an advanced culture. Are there possibilities of a more creative sort of union between science and the religious than is offered to us in "creation science"?

Proximate Origins versus Ultimate Origins

The first area of this complex situation that needs clarification is what may be termed the "methodological nontheism" of scientific inquiry. As we have noted, scientific explanations refer to or use only natural, finite, or "earthly" causes to explain the processes and changes of nature. When science explains a process of change, or of growth and development (or of decay and disintegration), it explains it by preceding causes which are themselves part of the same stream of experience. It asks how did A arise out of B and C, B and C perforce being in principle as experienceable by the senses as is A. Two basic presuppositions are latent in this fundamental rule of scientific method.

First, as a condition of its inquiry, science presupposes a preceding "situation" and its causes out of which the events or processes of change it investigates arose. For example, it presupposes the existence of mothers and fathers when it inquires into the birth of a child (as Aristotle stated in this basic rule, "Nothing can come from nothing"). Science cannot, therefore, inquire into or know about an "absolute" beginning, an origin of the *entire* system of finite, natural causes.

Second, science is *confined to* the system of finite causes; it cannot search for or recognize—and so refer to—a trans-natural or supernatural cause that has intervened into the sequence of natural events (a miracle). As David Hume rightly argued, the commitment of the scientist is to find the natural cause.[1] Even, for example, if he or she believes that the "hand of God" was at work in a cure (or a disease), nevertheless, the medical researcher is obligated as a scientist to search for and locate the preceding *natural* cause of either one; for only then are medical knowledge and medical ability enlarged. Miracles, as well as absolute beginnings, may well be there, but scientific inquiry, because of its methodological commitments, cannot know of them. It is confined to the sequence of natural or finite causes, to the factors within the stream of ordinary experience.

As a consequence of these two presuppositions, science can and does inquire into how something arose out of *something else*, what can be called the question of *proximate origins*; it cannot seek or question beyond the powers and factors discoverable to sensory, and so to common, investigation. It cannot and does not inquire into *ultimate origins*. It does not ask the questions, Where did the entire system of finite causes come from? What is its ultimate source or ground? Or as the Scholastics put this, science deals with *secondary* causes alone (creaturely causes); it cannot deal with the primary causality of God which brought all secondary causes into existence, maintains them there, and works through them. If then God be that ultimate source and ground, the primary cause transcendent to the system of finite causes because God is their origin, then God, so conceived, *cannot* be part of a scientific hypothesis. Science is *methodologically* nontheological or nontheistic; it *cannot* raise the question of God, no matter how "religious" the scientist in question is or how firmly he or she believes the presence of the divine power and wisdom to be there.

This point is very important in this controversy. The creationists have stated that since evolutionary science explains "origins" without reference to God, *therefore* it is naturalistic, atheistic, and humanistic. Clearly this is an error, a serious misunderstanding of the character and the limits of scientific inquiry. To say that a scientific theory of origins makes no mention of God is merely to say that it is scientific; there is nothing at all intrinsically atheistic about a scientific hypothesis—unless the scientist wishes to go *beyond* science to state a naturalistic philosophical and/or religious view of the universe as a whole. But, like its stepsister "creation science," that naturalistic "extension beyond science" is not scientific.

Lest natural science seem by this account to be suspiciously secular in character, let us recall that in modern culture historical inquiry (history as study) and the law alike reflect the same restriction to finite, "earthly" causes. If I write an *historical* account of the origins of World War II and hope to have it received as an historical interpretation by the community of historians, I must confine my discussion to such causes as economic factors, historical trends, political relations, the intentions and acts of statesmen, and so on. I cannot appeal to "the judgment of God on the empires of England and of Europe" as an explanation, any more than I can explain Constantine's defeat of his brother in terms of the host of angels at the famous bridge. However, as a theologian giving a *theological* interpretation of history, I can speak— and have spoken—intelligibly and persuasively about the work of God in history.[2] Similarly, as a lawyer defending a client from the charge of murder, I cannot in a modern court advance a theory of the crime that makes God, and not my client, responsible for the death. And this does not mean that lawyer, client, or judge and jury are atheistic or that the state is atheistic. It simply means that our present law, like our historical inquiry and our natural science, proceeds as a secular discipline, confined by its own methodological presuppositions to natural and historical (secondary or finite) causes, and it can in its procedures only use such causes in the construction of its theories.

This inherent limitiation on scientific inquiry—that it can only deal with preceding finite (natural and historical) secondary causes discoverable by empirical inquiry (discoverable to sense)—separates or distinguishes scientific inquiry in itself from any general view of the whole of things, any total or global interpretation of reality as a whole—and so from any religious questions of "ultimate origins" (or of primary causality). Scientific theories are thus significantly different from metaphysical and/or theological views of all of reality or of reality as a whole. When, therefore, science offers *its* explanation of origins, it presents a limited explanation of reality viewed from a distinct and restricted perspective. Its theories, therefore, propose no view at all about the ultimate origin, ground, or source of the cosmos, of life, or of humankind, any more than a biological, zoological, physiological, or medical explanation of *my* origin in my parents and grandparents excludes a metaphysical or religious explanation of my origin and destiny in God. Evolutionary theories, like scientific, are not in themselves atheistic. By the same token, astronomical, geological, and biological theories of origins do not at

all exclude a *theistic* explanation or theory of the ultimate origin and ground
of the physical processes examined by these special sciences—processes through
which God is believed to have worked. It is the task of theology, especially
of philosophical theology, to explore how a theistic interpretation of reality
as a whole—and so of human, as well as nature's, origins and destiny—can
be developed which accords with and supports, rather than contradicts, the
scientific view of the natural world and the historical view of our common
history which the "scientific" culture that the theologian inhabits assumes
in some sense to be valid.

Such theological syntheses of modern science with the Christian and
the Jewish belief in God are not only theoretically possible, as the above
analysis shows, they have also been actual. Any number of them have appeared since modern natural science began in the seventeenth and eighteenth
centuries, and even more since the advent of evolutionary theories in the
nineteenth century. While some of these, to be sure, are more profound,
coherent, and persuasive than others, still it is evident that a theistic interpretation of evolution—or, better, an evolutionary interpretation of
theism—is perfectly coherent and, so I believe, a good deal more persuasive,
rationally as well as religiously, than is its naturalistic philosophical counter-
part. These theological syntheses, as well as a critical and symbolic interpretation of the Book of Genesis, have been central staples in the education
of theologians, ministers, and rabbis (and now, latterly, of priests) for over
one hundred years. That so many persons in our present culture, those inside as well as outside the major churches and synagogues, should be unaware
of this accord between modern scientific theories of development and faith
in God as Creator is thus a large responsibility of the churches, and especially
of their leadership. Known well by every clergyman and accepted by most,
this accord with science is still perhaps the best-kept secret in current
American religion. Thus have the churches unwittingly helped the creationist
cause, for much of the public accepts as valid the creationist claim that "if
you believe in evolution, you must have already abandoned a Christian (or
Jewish) belief in Creation."

The Myths of a Scientific Culture

Although scientific inquiry in itself leads to no particular philosophical or
religious world view, it is clearly possible for science—as an attitude, a method,
and a body of conclusions—to expand itself into a view of the whole of reality, into a naturalistic philosophy and so a humanistic religion. A scientific
culture produces its own "myths" just as a fishing culture does; and it is quite
natural that as the myths of a fishing culture have a base in fishing, so in
a scientific culture these myths have a scientific basis. This expansion into
a philosophical and religious viewpoint—or myth—of the whole has several

logical stages: (1) it begins with the understandable conviction (or faith) that science has no cognitive limits; (2) it proceeds to the more dubious and yet (in a scientific culture) plausible assertion that science represents the *only* cognitive touch with reality, that what science knows, and *only* what it knows, "is the case" (for example, instrumentalism, naturalism, and positivism); and (3) it concludes with the metaphysical/theological proposition that what is ultimately real, and is therefore the source and origin of all else, is matter in motion, the blind physical processes of nature, which natural science has uncovered in its own limited inquiries. Thus by a movement from a methodological (heuristic) principle of inquiry into a metaphysical, substantive assertion about ultimate reality, we arrive at the philosophy, that "atheistic and humanistic religious perspective" of which science as such is accused by creationists. There can be little doubt that many in the scientific community have in fact participated in, witnessed to, and proclaimed as science this "expansion" into a religious perspective. All too many distinguished scientists have stated that "science now knows" that "the religious theories of the past are outmoded myths" and "the origins of all things lie in the material nature we find around us."[3] In thus equating science with their own naturalistic humanism, these "experts" are not acting at all as objective scientific minds; rather, they are expressing, quite without logical ground or empirical testing, the folk wisdom or popular pieties abounding among the academic circles of an advanced scientific culture.

Although this identification of science with a nontheistic perspective and of both with "modern civilization" are by no means shared by all scientists or teachers of science, nevertheless the assumption that religion represents early myths now outmoded by scientific developments pervades much of the writing and teaching of science. It should, moreover, be recognized that this widespread identification of religion with primitive myth, and of modernity and science with naturalistic humanism, has been one of the "breeders" of the creationist reaction. All too often when a student in a high school comes home and says to his or her parents, "Well, we learned today in science class that Genesis is wrong," two new converts to creationism are created.

In graduate programs in science, complex questions of the relation of science and its truths to other aspects of culture—to politics, economics, morals, art, philosophy, and religion—have been blithely ignored. The history and philosophy of science—which *do* deal with these relations—are absent from most scientific programs, located as they are in the history and philosophy departments across the campus. Many scientists and teachers of science are quite unaware of modern, postcritical and postscientific interpretations of religious traditions and beliefs, for example, of the Book of Genesis. Thus, most of them are utterly unequipped to deal, however briefly, with the tricky interface of religious and scientific explanations of origins when questions concerning these relations arise, as they must in the teaching of science. The result is that all too often science is naively and perhaps innocently taught

as replacing religion, rather than as supplementing, purifying, and inform-
ing it. Both the religious and the scientific communities bear real responsibility for the crisis represented by the "creation-science" movement.

Faith in an Age of Science

Modern scientific culture has taken many unexpected turns. Perhaps most
surprising of all has been the reappearance of the religious in power and in
pervasiveness in the midst of that culture. In the nineteenth and early twentieth centuries, it was widely assumed that religion and the religious were
on the wane, made unnecessary by the growing power and influence of science,
liberalism, and democracy; an age of scientific rationalism was replacing
earlier ages dominated by religion. By the last decades of the twentieth century, this vision of a totally secular world, cleansed of the religious, seems
an illusory fantasy indeed. The forms of the religious that have reappeared,
moreover, do not represent so much the traditional religions of the West as
new political or social religions (ideologies) on the one hand and non-Western
traditions on the other. The public life of advanced cultures such as Germany
and Italy, including their science and technology, have each found themselves
dominated and directed by a fanatical and destructive faith; Russia, much
of Eastern Europe, and China have been gripped, transformed, and tightly
controlled by another "social religion" or ideology. America itself, for all its
boasted pragmatism, teeters now and again on the edge of dangerous
ideological domination by the Right Wing. In the private lives of many
modern Western people, via many traditional non-Western religions (Hindu,
Buddhist, and Sikh) and some newly appearing sects, the religious has been
equally pervasive, clearly filling some deep-felt need, or needs, unsatisfied
by scientific, technological, and industrial developments. And finally, among
other social groups, fundamentalist and charismatic forms of traditional
religions have appeared in new strength, forming, as we have noted, the
religious background for the creationist movement.

    It is clear that the religious is a permanent, pervasive, and always cen-
tral aspect of corporate and individual life, generated out of fundamental
human capacities and needs. Not only is there the ever-present necessity for
a unified set of symbols giving a pattern to all of experience and to nature,
history, the community, and the self in a coherent and meaningful vision;
without this, the self and its community have no identity, standards, tasks,
or destiny, and little cultural or personal life is possible. Even more, at certain periods of social tension or breakdown, when assumed structures of social
and personal security are badly shaken, deep anxieties arise, confidence lags
or disappears, and the need for both a renewed certainty and a persistent
courage waxes strong. To its own surprise, a technological age has found itself
generating precisely such an especially religious period. The anxieties, frustra-

tions, and dilemmas of an advanced technological age are sharper, the menace of its social future more ominous,and so the sense of the continuing tragedy and estrangement of human existence is deeper than at other times. Thus has the religious reappeared as ideology, as sect, and as dogmatism, not *despite* science and technology but precisely *because* of them. Here lies the deepest root of that "union of science and the religious" spoken of earlier as the central quality of this controversy. In a scientific age, every form of religion becomes, as we noted, "scientific"; even more in a technological age, many of those persons in scientific professions and out of them, who live amidst the terrors as well as the benefits of technology, are impelled into religion in one of its many forms. And as history continually illustrates, the religious (as do science and technology) appears in demonic, uncreative, as well as in creative, forms.

The Dangers of Ignorance

If, then, the evidence indicates that the religious is a permanent aspect both of human society and of personal existence, even in a scientific and technological culture, then immediately the issues involved with the relation of science to religion become of major significance to the social health of any community. These two aspects of culture *will* be related to one another in any case; possibly in the destructive form of the ideological domination by an irrational faith of the scientific and technological communities, as in Germany, in Russia, and in right-wing America. Such a union is infinitely dangerous to both science and religion, as well as to the world at large. And we should note that in each of the cases mentioned above, this destructive union has been welcomed and supported as much, if not more, by the scientific community as a whole as by the religious communities involved. A religious community that allows its own dogmatic intolerance and its irresponsibility to the world to expand only aids in such false union. A scientific community that ignores the relation of its truth and its life to law, to morals, and to fundamental religious symbols only makes itself and its culture vulnerable to ideological capitulation. Ignorance of the religious in both its demonic and its creative forms can be even more fatal for a scientific culture than ignorance of new scientific and technological developments. The implications of this controversy for our educational programs in the humanities, as well as in the sciences, are immense.

The questions of what religious symbols are for in this interpretation and how they may be related to the models, formulae, and theories of science (as of history and of philosophy) are too complex an issue for this brief discussion. Suffice it here to suggest that religious symbols concern the ultimate *horizon* of experience: its source and origin, its principles of fundamental reality and structure, the career of good and evil within it, its goal and destiny— in a word, its limits, its ground, and its sources of ultimate hope. The two contemporary examples of most importance are (1) the notion of progress, or of evolutionary progress, that has dominated both society and the intellectual elite of the West since 1750, and (2) the symbol of the dialetical materialism that has dominated Communist countries. Both are systems of religious symbols; both rose in explicit antagonism to rival systems (Christianity and Judaism); and both are on the wane.

Every culture and every person must live within such a coherent, all-encompassing structure. Religious symbols provide the *content* of this structure; religious speech is the way we talk about it. Both are crucial for the life of society. For from that structure derive the fundamental aims and norms of social life; on it rest life's most essential dependence, courage, and confidence. This ultimate horizon of religious symbols (be they Christian, Jewish, Marxist, or Progressivist) must be related to, as well as distinguished from, inquiry into the *foreground* of existence; into nature, history, society, and the self—in a word, the "sciences." As we noted, such a union of the "religious" and the scientific, of the ultimate base and the immediate character of life, will be there in any case. It is well that it is both rational and sane, on the one hand, and responsible and humane, on the other.

Notes

1. David Hume, "An Essay on Miracles," *An Enquiry Concerning Human Understanding* (New York: Oxford University Press, 1975).
2. See Langdon Gilkey, *Reaping the Whirlwind: A Christian Interpretation of History* (New York: Seabury Press, 1976).
3. See the recent volume edited by C. Leon Harris, *Evolution: Genesis and Revelations: Readings from Empedocles to Wilson* (Albany, N.Y.: State University System of New York Press, 1981), especially the first section, "Pre-Scientific Concepts of the Origins of Species: Genesis:" and the third section, "The Infanticide of Science: Rome and the Middle Ages—Augustine and the Dark Ages."

The Arkansas Creation Science Statute
Act 590 of 1981

State of Arkansas
73rd General Assembly
Regular Session, 1981

"AN ACT TO REQUIRE BALANCED TREATMENT OF CREATION-SCIENCE AND EVOLUTION-SCIENCE IN PUBLIC SCHOOLS; TO PROTECT ACADEMIC FREEDOM BY PROVIDING STUDENT CHOICE; TO ENSURE FREEDOM OF RELIGIOUS EXERCISE; TO GUARANTEE FREEDOM OF BELIEF AND SPEECH; TO PREVENT ESTABLISHMENT OF RELIGION; TO PROHIBIT RELIGIOUS INSTRUCTION CONCERNING ORIGINS; TO BAR DISCRIMINATION ON THE BASIS OF CREATIONISTS OR EVOLUTIONIST BELIEF; TO PROVIDE DEFINITIONS AND CLARIFICATIONS; TO DECLARE THE LEGISLATIVE PURPOSE AND LEGISLATIVE FINDINGS OF FACT; TO PROVIDE FOR SEVERABILITY OF PROVISIONS; TO PROVIDE FOR REPEAL OF CONTRARY LAWS; AND TO SET FORTH AN EFFECTIVE DATE."

BE IT ENACTED BY THE GENERAL ASSEMBLY OF THE STATE OF ARKANSAS:

SECTION 1. Requirement for Balanced Treatment. Public schools within this State shall give balanced treatment to creation-science and to evolution-science. Balanced treatment to these two models shall be given in classroom lectures taken as a whole for each course, in textbook materials taken as a whole for each course, in library materials taken as a whole for the sciences and taken as a whole for the humanities, and in other educational programs in public schools, to the extent that such lectures, textbooks, library materials, or educational programs deal in any way with the subject of the origin of man, life, the earth, or the universe.

SECTION 2. Prohibition against Religious Instruction. Treatment of either evolution-science or creation-science shall be limited to scientific evidences for each model and inferences from those scientific evidences, and must not include any religious instruction or references to religious writings.

SECTION 3. Requirement for Nondiscrimination. Public schools within this State, or their personnel, shall not discriminate, by reducing a grade of a student or by singling out and making public criticism, against any student who demonstrates a satisfactory understanding of both evolution-science and creation-science and who accepts or rejects either model in whole or part.

SECTION 4. Definitions. As used in this Act:

(a) "Creation-science" means the scientific evidences for creation and inferences from those scientific evidences. Creation-science includes the scientific evidences and related inferences that indicate: (1) Sudden creation of the universe, energy, and life from nothing; (2) The insufficiency of mutation and natural selection in bringing about development of all living kinds from a single organism; (3) Changes only within fixed limits of originally created kinds of plants and animals; (4) Separate ancestry for man and apes; (5) Explanation of the earth's geology by catastrophism, including the occurrence of a worldwide flood; and (6) A relatively recent inception of the earth and living kinds.

(b) "Evolution-science" means the scientific evidences for evolution and inferences from those scientific evidences. Evolution-science includes the scientific evidences and related inferences that indicate: (1) Emergence by naturalistic processes of the universe from disordered matter and emergence of life from nonlife; (2) The sufficiency of mutation and natural selection in bringing about development of present living kinds from simple earlier kinds; (3) Emergence by mutation and natural selection of present living kinds from simple earlier kinds; (4) Emergence of man from a common ancestor with apes; (5) Explanation of the earth's geology and the evolutionary sequence by uniformitarianism; and (6) An inception several billion years ago of the earth and somewhat later life.

(c) "Public schools" means public secondary and elementary schools.

SECTION 5. Clarifications. This Act does not require or permit instruction in any religious doctrine or materials. This Act does not require any instruction in the subject of origins, but simply requires instruction in both scientific models (of evolution-science and creation-science) if public schools choose to teach either. This Act does not require each individual textbook or library book to give balanced treatment to the models of evolution-science and creation-science; it does not require any school books to be discarded. This Act does not require each individual classroom lecture in a course to give such balanced treatment, but simply requires the lectures as a whole to give balanced treatment; it permits some lectures to present evolution-science and other lectures to present creation-science.

SECTION 6. Legislative Declaration of Purpose. This Legislature enacts this Act for public schools with the purpose of protecting academic freedom for students' differing values and beliefs; ensuring neutrality toward students' diverse religious convictions; ensuring freedom of religious exercise for students and their parents; guaranteeing freedom of belief and speech for students; preventing establishment of Theologically Liberal, Humanist, Nontheist, or Atheist religions; preventing discrimination against students on the basis of their personal beliefs concerning creation and evolution; and assisting students in their search for truth. This Legislature does not have the purpose of causing instruction in religious concepts or making an establishment of religion.

SECTION 7. Legislative Findings of Fact. This Legislature finds that:

(a) The subject of the origin of the universe, earth, life, and man is treated within many public school courses, such as biology, life science, anthropology, sociology, and often also in physics, chemistry, world history, philosophy, and social studies.

(b) Only evolution-science is presented to students in virtually all of those courses that discuss the subject of origins. Public schools generally censor creation-science and evidence contrary to evolution.

(c) Evolution-science is not an unquestionable fact of science, because evolution cannot be experimentally observed, fully verified, or logically falsified, and because evolution-science is not accepted by some scientists.

(d) Evolution-science is contrary to the religious convictions or moral values or philosophical beliefs of many students and parents, including individuals of many different religious faiths and with diverse moral values and philosophical beliefs.

(e) Public school presentation of only evolution-science without any alternative model of origins abridges the United States Constitution's protections of freedom of religious exercise and of freedom of belief and speech for students and parents, because it undermines their religious convictions and moral or philosophical values, compels their unconscionable professions of belief, and hinders religious training and moral training by parents.

(f) Public school presentation of only evolution-science furthermore abridges the Constitution's prohibition against establishment of religion, because it produces hostility toward many Theistic religions and brings preference to Theological Liberalism, Humanism, Nontheistic religions, and Atheism, in that these religious faiths general include a religious belief in evolution.

(g) Public school instruction in only evolution-science also violates the principle of academic freedom, because it denies students a choice between scientific models and instead indoctrinates them in evolution-science alone.

(h) Presentation of only one model rather than alternative scientific models of origins is not required by any compelling interest of the State, and exemption of such students from a course or class presenting only evolution-science does not provide an adequate remedy because of teacher influence and student pressure to remain in that course or class.

(i) Attendance of those students who are at public schools is compelled by law, and school taxes from their parents and other citizens are mandated by Law.

(j) Creation-science is an alternative scientific model of origins and can be presented from a strictly scientific standpoint without any religious doctrine just as evolution-science can, because there are scientists who conclude that scientific data best support creation-science and because scientific evidence and inferences have been presented for creation-science.

(k) Public school presentation of both evolution-science and creation-science would not violate the Constitution's prohibition against establishment of religion, because it would involve presentation of the scientific evidence and related inferences for each model rather than any religious instruction.

(l) Most citizens, whatever their religious beliefs about origins, favor balanced treatment in public schools of alternative scientific models of origins for better guiding students in their search for knowledge, and they favor a neutral approach toward subjects affecting the religious and moral and philosophical convictions of students.

SECTION 8. Short Title. This Act shall be known as the "Balanced Treatment for Creation-Science and Evolution-Science Act."

SECTION 9. Severability of Provisions. If any provision of this Act is held invalid, that invalidity shall not affect other provisions that can be applied in the absence of the invalidated provisions, and the provisions of this Act are declared to be severable.

SECTION 10. Repeal of Contrary Laws. All State laws or parts of State laws in conflict with this Act are hereby repealed.

SECTION 11. Effective Date. The requirements of the Act shall be met by and may be met before the beginning of the next school year if that is more than six months from the date of enactment, or otherwise one year after the beginning of the next school year, and in all subsequent school years.

Creationism in Schools:
The Decision in McLean versus the Arkansas Board of Education

On 5 January 1982 U.S. District Court Judge William R. Overton enjoined the Arkansas Board of Education from implementing the "Balanced Treatment for Creation-Science and Evolution-Science Act" of the state legislature. This is the complete text of his judgment, injunction, and opinion in the case.

Judgment

Pursuant to the Court's Memorandum Opinion filed this date, judgment is hereby entered in favor of the plaintiffs and against the defendants. The relief prayed for is granted.
Dated this January 5, 1982.

Injunction

Pursuant to the Court's Memorandum Opinion filed this date, the defendants and each of them and all their servants and employees are hereby permanently enjoined from implementing in any manner Act 590 of the Acts of Arkansas of 1981.
It is so ordered this January 5, 1982.

Memorandum Opinion

Introduction

On March 19, 1981, the Governor of Arkansas signed into law Act 590 of 1981, entitled the "Balanced Treatment for Creation-Science and Evolution-Science Act." The Act is codified as Ark. Stat. Ann. §80-1663, *et. seq.*, (1981 Supp). Its essential mandate is stated in its first sentence: "Public schools within this State shall give balanced treatment to creation-science and to evolution-science." On May 27, 1981, this suit was filed *(1)* challenging the constitutional validity of Act 590 on three distinct grounds.

First, it is contended that Act 590 constitutes an establishment of religion prohibited by the First Amendment to the Constitution, which is made applicable to the states by the Fourteenth Amendment. Second, the plaintiffs argue the Act violates a right to academic freedom which they say is guaranteed to students and teachers by the Free Speech Clause of the First Amendment. Third, plaintiffs allege the Act is impermissibly vague and thereby violates the Due Process Clause of the Fourteenth Amendment.

The individual plaintiffs include the resident Arkansas Bishops of the United Methodist, Episcopal, Roman Catholic and African Methodist Episcopal Churches, the principal official of the Presbyterian Churches in Arkansas, other United Methodist, Southern Baptist and Presbyterian clergy, as well as several persons who sue as parents and next friends of minor children attending Arkansas public schools. One plaintiff is a high school biology teacher. All are also Arkansas taxpayers. Among the organizational plaintiffs are the American Jewish Congress, the Union of American Hebrew Congregations, the American Jewish Committee, the Arkansas Education Association, the National Association of Biology Teachers and the National Coalition for Public Education and Religious Liberty, all of which sue on behalf of members living in Arkansas *(2)*.

The defendants include the Arkansas Board of Education and its members, the Director of the Department of Education, and the State Textbooks and Instructional Materials Selecting Committee *(3)*. The Pulaski County Special School District and its Directors and Superintendent were voluntarily dismissed by the plaintiffs at the pretrial conference held October 1, 1981.

The trial commenced December 7, 1981, and continued through December 17, 1981. This Memorandum Opinion constitutes the Court's findings of fact and conclusions of law. Further orders and judgment will be in conformity with this opinion.

I

There is no controversy over the legal standards under which the Establishment Clause portion of this case must be judged. The Supreme Court has on a number of occasions expounded on the meaning of the clause, and the pronouncements are clear. Often the issue has arisen in the context of public education, as it has here. In *Everson v. Board of Education*, 330 U.S. 1, 15–16 (1947), Justice Black stated:

> The "establishment of religion" clause of the First Amendment means at least this: Neither a state nor the Federal Government can set up a church. Neither can pass laws which aid

one religion, aid all religions, or prefer one religion over another. Neither can force nor influence a person to go to or to remain away from church against his will or force him to profess a belief or disbelief in any religion. No person can be punished for entertaining or professing religious beliefs or disbeliefs, for church-attendance or non-attendance. No tax, large or small, can be levied to support any religious activities or institutions, whatever they may be called, or whatever form they may adopt to teach or practice religion. Neither a state nor the Federal Government can, openly or secretly, participate in the affairs of any religious organizations or groups and *vice versa*). In the words of Jefferson, the clause . . . was intended to erect "a wall of separation between church and State."

The Establishment Clause thus enshrines two central values; voluntarism and pluralism. And it is in the area of the public schools that these values must be guarded most vigilantly.

> Designed to serve as perhaps the most powerful agency for promoting cohesion among a heterogeneous democratic people, the public school must keep scrupulously free from entanglement in the strife of sects. The preservation of the community from divisive conflicts, of Government from irreconcilable pressures by religious groups, of religion from censorship and coercion however subtly exercised, requires strict confinement of the State to instruction other than religious, leaving to the individual's church and home, indoctrination in the faith of his choice. [*McCollum v. Board of Education*, 333 U.S. 203, 216–217 (1948), (Opinion of Frankfurter, J., joined by Jackson, Burton and Rutledge, J.J.)]

The specific formulation of the establishment prohibition has been refined over the years, but its meaning has not varied from the principles articulated by Justice Black in *Everson*. In *Abbington School District v. Schempp*, 374 U.S. 203, 222 (1963), Justice Clark stated that "to withstand the strictures of the Establishment Clause there must be a secular legislative purpose and a primary effect that neither advances nor inhibits religion." The Court found it quite clear that the First Amendment does not permit a state to require the daily reading of the Bible in public schools, for "[s]urely the place of the Bible as an instrument of religion cannot be gainsaid." *Id.* at 224. Similarly, in *Engel v. Vitale*, 370 U.S. 421 (1962), the Court held that the First Amendment prohibited the New York Board of Regents from requiring the daily recitation of a certain prayer in the schools. With characteristic succinctness, Justice Black wrote, "Under [the First] Amendment's prohibition against governmental establishment of religion, as reinforced by the provisions of the Fourteenth Amendment, government in this country, be it state or federal, is without power to prescribe by law any particular form of prayer which is to be used as an official prayer in carrying on any program of governmentally sponsored religious activity." *Id.* at 430. Black also identified the objective at which the Establishment Clause was aimed: "Its first and most immediate purpose rested on the belief that a union of government and religion tends to destroy government and to degrade religion." *Id.* at 431.

Most recently, the Supreme Court has held that the clause prohibits a state from requiring the posting of the Ten Commandments in public school classrooms for the same reasons that officially imposed daily Bible reading is prohibited. *Stone v. Graham*, 449 U.S. 39 (1980). The opinion in *Stone* relies on the most recent formulation of the Establishment Cause test, that of *Lemon v. Kurtzman*, 403 U.S. 602, 612–613 (1971):

> First, the statute must have a secular legislative purpose; second, its principal or primary effect must be one that neither advances nor inhibits religion . . .; finally, the statute must not foster "an excessive government entanglement with religion." [*Stone v. Graham*, 449 U.S. at 40]

It is under this three part test that the evidence in this case must be judged. Failure on any of these grounds is fatal to the enactment.

II

The religious movement known as Fundamentalism began in nineteenth century America as a part of evangelical Protestantism's response to social changes, new religious thought and Darwinism. Fundamentalists viewed these developments as attacks on the Bible and as responsible for a decline in traditional values.

The various manifestations of Fundamentalism have had a number of common characteristics (4), but a central premise has always been a literal interpretation of the Bible and a belief in the inerrancy of the Scriptures. Following World War I, there was again a perceived decline in traditional morality, and Fundamentalism focused on evolution as responsible for the decline. One aspect of their efforts, particularly in the South, was the promotion of statutes prohibiting the teaching of evolution in public schools. In Arkansas, this resulted in the adoption of Initiated Act 1 of 1929 (5).

Between the 1920's and early 1960's, anti-evolutionary sentiment had a subtle but pervasive influence on the teaching of biology in public schools. Generally, textbooks avoided the topic of evolution and did not mention the name of Darwin. Following the launch of the Sputnik satellite by the Soviet Union in 1957, the National Science Foundation funded several programs designed to modernize the teaching of science in the nation's schools. The Biological Sciences Curriculum Study (BSCS), a nonprofit organization, was among those receiving grants for curriculum study and revision. Working with scientists and teachers, BSCS developed a series of biology texts which, although emphasizing different aspects of biology, incorporated the theory of evolution as a major theme. The success of the BSCS effort is shown by the fact that fifty percent of American school children currently use BSCS books directly and the curriculum is incorporated indirectly in virtually all biology texts. (Testimony of Mayer; Nelkin, Px 1) (6).

In the early 1960's, there was again a resurgence of concern among Fundamentalists about the loss of traditional values and a fear of growing secularism in society. The Fundamentalist movement became more active and has steadily grown in numbers and political influence. There is an emphasis among current Fundamentalists on the literal interpretation of the Bible and the Book of Genesis as the sole source of knowledge about origins.

The term "scientific creationism" first gained currency around 1965 following publication of *The Genesis Flood* in 1961 by Whitcomb and Morris. There is undoubtedly some connection between the appearance of the BSCS texts emphasizing evolutionary thought and efforts by Fundamentalists to attack the theory. (Mayer)

In the 1960's and early 1970's, several Fundamentalist organizations were formed to promote the idea that the Book of Genesis was supported by scientific data. The terms "creation science" and "scientific creationism" have been adopted by these Fundamentalists as descriptive of their study of creation and the origins of man. Perhaps the leading creationist organization is the Institute for Creation Research (ICR), which is affiliated with the Christian Heritage College and supported by the Scott Memorial Baptist Church in San Diego, California. The ICR, through the Creation-Life Publishing Company, is the leading publisher of creation science material. Other creation science organizations include the Creation Science Research Center (CSRC) of San Diego and the Bible Science Association of Minneapolis, Minnesota. In 1963, the Creation Research Society (CRS) was formed from a schism in the American Scientific Affiliation (ASA). It is an organization of literal Fundamentalists (7) who have the equivalent of a master's degree in some recognized area of science. A purpose of the organization is "to reach all people with the vital message of the scientific and historic truth about creation." Nelkin, *The Science Textbook Controversies and the Politics of Equal Time*, 66. Similarly, the CSRC was formed in 1970 from a split in the CRS. Its aim has been "to reach the 63 million children of the United States with the scientific teaching of Biblical creationism." *Id.* at 69.

Among creationist writers who are recognized as authorities in the field by other creationists are Henry M. Morris, Duane Gish, G. E. Parker, Harold S. Slusher, Richard B. Bliss, John W. Moore, Martin E. Clark, W. L. Wysong, Robert E. Kofahl and Kelly L. Segraves. Morris is Director of ICR, Gish is Associate Director and Segrave is associated with CSRC.

Creationists view evolution as a source of society's ills, and the writing of Morris and Clark are typical expressions of that view.

> Evolution is thus not only anti-Biblical and anti-Christian, but it is utterly unscientific and impossible as well. But it has served effectively as the pseudo-scientific basis of atheism, agnosticism, socialism, fascism, and numerous other false and dangerous philosophies over the past century. [Morris and Clark, *The Bible Has The Answer*, (Px 31 and Pretrial Px 89) (8)]

Creationists have adopted the view of Fundamentalists generally that there are only two positions with respect to the origins of the earth and life: belief in the inerrancy of the Genesis story of creation and of a worldwide flood as fact, or belief in what they call evolution.

Henry Morris has stated, "It is impossible to devise a legitimate means of harmonizing the Bible with evolution." Morris, "Evolution and the Bible," *ICR Impact Series* Number 5 (undated, unpaged), quoted in Mayer, Px 8, at 3. This dualistic approach to the subject of origins permeates the creationist literature.

The creationist organizations consider the introduction of creation science into the public schools part of their ministry. The ICR has published at least two pamphlets (9) containing suggested methods for convincing school boards, administrators and teachers that creationism should be taught in public schools. The ICR has urged its proponents to encourage school officials to voluntarily add creationism to the curriculum (10).

Citizens For Fairness In Education is an organization based in Anderson, South Carolina, formed by Paul Ellwanger, a respiratory therapist who is trained in neither law nor science. Mr. Ellwanger is of the opinion that evolution is the forerunner of many social ills, including Nazism, racism and abortion. (Ellwanger Depo. at 32–34). About 1977, Ellwanger collected several proposed legislative acts with the idea of preparing a model state act requiring the teaching of creationism as science in opposition to evolution. One of the proposals he collected was prepared by Wendell Bird, who is now a staff attorney for ICR (11). From these various proposals, Ellwanger prepared a "model act" which calls for "balanced treatment" of "scientific creationism" and "evolution" in public schools. He circulated the proposed act to various people and organizations around the country.

Mr. Ellwanger's views on the nature of creation science are entitled to some weight since he personally drafted the model act which became Act 590. His evidentiary deposition with exhibits and unnumbered attachments (produced in response to a subpoena *duces tecum*) speaks to both the intent of the Act and the scientific merits of creation science. Mr. Ellwanger does not believe creation science is a science. In a letter to Pastor Robert E. Hays he states, "While neither evolution nor creation can qualify as a scientific theory, and since it is virtually impossible at this point to educate the whole world that evolution is not a true scientific theory, we have freely used these terms—the evolution theory and the theory of scientific creationism—in the bill's text." (Unnumbered attachment to Ellwanger Depo., at 2.) He further states in a letter to Mr. Tom Bethell, "As we examine evolution (remember, we're not making any scientific claims for creation, but we are challenging evolution's claim to be scientific) . . . " (Unnumbered attachment to Ellwanger Depo. at 1.)

Ellwanger's correspondence on the subject shows an awareness that Act 590 is a religious crusade, coupled with a desire to conceal this fact. In a letter to State Senator Bill Keith of Louisiana, he says, "I view this whole battle as one between God and anti-God forces, though I know there are a large number of evolutionists who believe in God." And further, ". . . it behooves Satan to do all he can to thwart our efforts and confuse the issue at every turn." Yet Ellwanger suggests to Senator Keith, "If you have a clear choice between having grassroots leaders of this statewide bill promotion effort to be ministerial or non-ministerial, be sure to opt for the non-ministerial. It does the bill no good to have ministers out there in the public forum and the adversary will surely pick at this point. . . . Ministerial persons can accomplish a tremendous amount of work from behind the scenes, encouraging their congregations to take the organizational and P.R. initiatives. And they can lead their churches in storming Heaven with prayers for help against so tenacious an adversary." (Unnumbered attachment to Ellwanger Depo. at 1.)

Ellwanger shows a remarkable degree of political candor, if not finesse, in a letter to State Senator Joseph Carlucci of Florida:

> 2. It would be very wise, if not actually essential, that all of us who are engaged in this legislative effort be careful not to present our position and our work in a religious framework. For example, in written communications that might somehow be shared with those other persons whom we may be trying to convince, it would be well to exclude our own personal testimony and/or witness for Christ, but rather, if we are so moved, to give that testimony on a separate attached note. (Unnumbered attachment to Ellwanger Depo. at 1.)

The same tenor is reflected in a letter by Ellwanger to Mary Ann Miller, a member of FLAG (Family, Life, America under God) who lobbied the Arkansas Legislature in favor of Act 590:

> . . . we'd like to suggest that you and your co-workers be very cautious about mixing creation-science with creation-religion . . . Please urge your co-workers not to allow themselves to get sucked into the "religion" trap of mixing the two together, for such mixing does incalculable harm to the legislative thrust. It could even bring public opinion to bear adversely upon the higher courts that will eventually have to pass judgment on the constitutionality of this new law. (Ex. 1 to Miller Depo.)

Perhaps most interesting, however, is Mr. Ellwanger's testimony in his deposition as to his strategy for having the model act implemented:

Q. You're trying to play on other people's religious motives.

A. I'm trying to play on their emotions, love, hate, their likes, dislikes, because I don't know any other way to involve, to get humans to become involved in human endeavors. I see emotions as being a healthy and legitimate means of getting people's feelings into action, and . . . I believe that the predominance of population in America that represents the greatest potential for taking some kind of action in this area is a Christian community. I see the Jewish community as far less potential in taking action . . . but I've seen a lot of interest among Christians and I feel, why not exploit that to get the bill going if that's what it takes. (Ellwanger Depo. at 146–147.)

Mr. Ellwanger's ultimate purpose is revealed in the closing of his letter to Mr. Tom Bethell: "Perhaps all this is old hat to you, Tom, and if so, I'd appreciate your telling me so and perhaps where you've heard it before—the idea of killing evolution instead of playing these debating games that we've been playing for nigh over a decade already." (Unnumbered attachment to Ellwanger Depo. at 3.)

It was out of this milieu that Act 590 emerged. The Reverend W. A. Blount, a Biblical literalist who is pastor of a church in the Little Rock area and was, in February, 1981, chairman of the Greater Little Rock Evangelical Fellowship, was among those who received a copy of the model act from Ellwanger (12).

At Reverend Blount's request, the Evangelical Fellowship unanimously adopted a resolution to seek introduction of Ellwanger's act in the Arkansas Legislature. A committee composed of two ministers, Curtis Thomas and W. A. Young, was appointed to implement the resolution. Thomas obtained from Ellwanger a revised copy of the model act which he transmitted to Carl Hunt, a business associate of Senator James L. Holsted, with the request that Hunt prevail upon Holsted to introduce the act.

Holsted, a self-described "born again" Christian Fundamentalist, introduced the act in the Arkansas Senate. He did not consult the State Department of Education, scientists, science educators or the Arkansas Attorney General (13). The Act was not referred to any Senate committee for hearing and was passed after only a few minutes' discussion on the Senate floor. In the House of Representatives, the bill was referred to the Education Committee which conducted a perfunctory fifteen minute hearing. No scientist testified at the hearing, nor was any representative from the State Department of Education called to testify.

Ellwanger's model act was enacted into law in Arkansas as Act 590 without amendment or modification other than minor typographical changes. The legislative "findings of fact" in Ellwanger's act and Act 590 are identical, although no meaningful fact-finding process was employed by the General Assembly.

Ellwanger's efforts in preparation of the model act and campaign for its adoption in the states were motivated by his opposition to the theory of evolution and his desire to see the Biblical version of creation taught in the public schools. There is no evidence that the pastors, Blount, Thomas, Young or The Greater Little Rock Evangelical Fellowship were motivated by anything other than their religious convictions when proposing its adoption or during their lobbying efforts in its behalf. Senator Holsted's sponsorship and lobbying efforts in behalf of the Act were motivated solely by his religious beliefs and desire to see the Biblical version of creation taught in the public schools (*14*).

The State of Arkansas, like a number of states whose citizens have relatively homogeneous religious beliefs, has a long history of official opposition to evolution which is motivated by adherence to Fundamentalist beliefs in the inerrancy of the Book of Genesis. This history is documented in Justice Fortas' opinion in *Epperson v. Arkansas*, 393 U.S. 97 (1968), which struck down Initiated Act 1 of 1929, Ark. Stat. Ann. §§80-1627–1628, prohibiting the teaching of the theory of evolution. To this same tradition may be attributed Initiated Act 1 of 1930, Ark. Stat. Ann. §80-1606 (Repl. 1980), requiring "the reverent daily reading of a portion of the English Bible" in every public school classroom in the State (*15*).

It is true, as defendants argue, that courts should look to legislative statements of a statute's purpose in Establishment Clause cases and accord such pronouncements great deference. See, e.g., *Committee for Public Education & Religious Liberty v. Nyquist*, 413 U.S. 756, 773 (1973) and *McGowan v. Maryland*, 366 U.S. 420, 445 (1961). Defendants also correctly state the principle that remarks by the sponsor or author of a bill are not considered controlling in analyzing legislative intent. See, e.g., *United States v. Emmons*, 410 U.S. 396 (1973) and *Chrysler Corp. v. Brown*, 441 U.S. 281 (1979).

Courts are not bound, however, by legislative statements of purpose or legislative disclaimers, *Stone v. Graham*, 449 U.S. 39 (1980); *Abbington School Dist. v. Schempp*, 374 U.S. 203 (1963). In determining the legislative purpose of a statute, courts may consider evidence of the historical context of the Act, *Epperson v. Arkansas*, 393 U.S. 97 (1968), the specific sequence of events leading up to passage of the Act, departures from normal procedural sequences, substantive departures from the normal, *Village of Arlington Heights v. Metropolitan Housing Corp.*, 429 U.S. 252 (1977), and contemporaneous statements of the legislative sponsor, *Fed. Energy Admin. v. Algonquin SNG, Inc.*, 426 U.S. 548, 564 (1976).

The unusual circumstances surrounding the passage of Act 590, as well as the substantive law of the First Amendment, warrant an inquiry into the stated legislative purposes. The author of the Act had publicly proclaimed the sectarian purpose of the proposal. The Arkansas residents who sought legislative sponsorship of the bill did so for purely sectarian purpose. These circumstances alone may not be particularly persuasive, but when considered with the publicly announced motives of the legislative sponsor made contemporaneously with the legislative process; the lack of any legislative investigation, debate or consultation with any educators or scientists; the unprecedented intrusion in school curriculum (*16*); and official history of the State of Arkansas on the subject, it is obvious that the statement of purposes has little, if any, support in fact. The State failed to produce any evidence which would warrant an inference or conclusion that at any point in the process anyone considered the legitimate educational value of the Act. It was simply and purely an effort to introduce the Biblical version of creation into the public school curricula. The only inference which can be drawn from these circumstances is that the Act was passed with the specific purpose by the General Assembly of advancing religion. The Act therefore fails the first prong of the three-pronged test, that of secular legislative purpose, as articulated in *Lemon v. Kurtzman, supra,* and *Stone v. Graham, supra.*

III

If the defendants are correct and the Court is limited to an examination of the language of the Act, the evidence is overwhelming that both the purpose and effect of Act 590 is the advancement of religion in the public schools.

Section 4 of the Act provides:

Definitions, as used in this Act:

(a) "Creation-science" means the scientific evidence for creation and inferences from those scientific evidences. Creation-science includes the scientific evidences and related inferences that indicate: (1) Sudden creation of the universe, energy, and life from nothing; (2) The insufficiency of mutation and natural selection in bringing about development of all living kinds from a single organism; (3) Changes only within fixed limits of originally created kinds of plants and animals; (4) Separate ancestry for man and apes; (5) Explanation of the earth's geology by catastrophism, including the occurrence of a worldwide flood; and (6) A relatively recent inception of the earth and living kinds.

(b) "Evolution-science" means the scientific evidences for evolution and inferences from those scientific evidences. Evolution-science includes the scientific evidences and related inferences that indicate: (1) Emergence by naturalistic processes of the universe from disordered matter and emergence of life from nonlife; (2) The sufficiency of mutation and natural selection in bringing about development of present living kinds from simple earlier kinds; (3) Emergence by mutation and natural selection of present living kinds from simple earlier kinds; (4) Emergence of man from a common ancestor with apes; (5) Explanation of the earth's geology and the evolutionary sequence by uniformitarianism; and (6) An inception several billion years ago of earth and somewhat later life.

(c) "Public schools" mean public secondary and elementary schools.

The evidence establishes that the definition of "creation science" contained in 4(a) has as its unmentioned reference the first 11 chapters of the Book of Genesis. Among the many creation epics in human history, the account of sudden creation from nothing, or *creatio ex nihilo*, and subsequent destruction of the world by flood is unique to Genesis. The concepts of 4(a) are the literal Fundamentalists' view of Genesis. Section 4(a) is unquestionably a statement of religion, with the exception of 4(a)(2) which is a negative thrust aimed at what the creationists understand to be the theory of evolution (*17*).

Both the concepts and wording of Section 4(a) convey an inescapable religiosity. Section 4(a)(1) describes "sudden creation of the universe, energy and life from nothing." Every theologian who testified, including defense witnesses, expressed the opinion that the statement referred to a supernatural creation which was performed by God.

Defendants argue that: (1) the fact that 4(a) conveys ideas similar to the literal interpretation of Genesis does not make it conclusively a statement of religion; (2) that reference to a creation from nothing is not necessarily a religious concept since the Act only suggests a creator who has power, intelligence and a sense of design and not necessarily the attributes of love, compassion and justice (*18*); and (3) that simply teaching about the concept of a creator is not a religious exercise unless the student is required to make a commitment to the concept of a creator.

The evidence fully answers these arguments. The ideas of 4(a)(1) are not merely similar to the literal interpretation of Genesis; they are identical and parallel to no other story of creation (*19*).

The argument that creation from nothing in 4(a)(1) does not involve a supernatural deity has no evidentiary or rational support. To the contrary, "creation out of nothing" is a concept unique to Western religions. In traditional Western religious thought, the conception of a creator of the world is a conception of God. Indeed, creation of the world "out of nothing" is the ultimate religious statement because God is the only actor. As Dr. Langdon Gilkey noted, the Act refers to one who has the power to bring all the universe into existence from nothing. The only "one" who has this power is God (20).

The leading creationist writers, Morris and Gish, acknowledge that the idea of creation described in 4(a)(1) is the concept of creation by God and make no pretense to the contrary (21). The idea of sudden creation from nothing, or *creatio ex nihilo*, is an inherently religious concept. (Vawter, Gilkey, Geisler, Ayala, Blount, Hicks.)

The argument advanced by defendants' witness, Dr. Norman Geisler, that teaching the existence of God is not religious unless the teaching seeks a commitment, is contrary to common understanding and contradicts settled case law. *Stone v. Graham*, 449 U.S. 39 (1980); *Abbington School District v. Schempp*, 374 U.S. 203 (1963).

The facts that creation science is inspired by the Book of Genesis and that Section 4(a) is consistent with a literal interpretation of Genesis leave no doubt that a major effect of the Act is the advancement of particular religious beliefs. The legal impact of this conclusion will be discussed further at the conclusion of the Court's evaluation of the scientific merit of creation science.

IV(A)

The approach to teaching "creation science" and "evolution science" found in Act 590 is identical to the two-model approach espoused by the Institute for Creation Research and is taken almost verbatim from ICR writings. It is an extension of Fundamentalists' view that one must either accept the literal interpretation of Genesis or else believe in the godless system of evolution.

The two model approach of the creationists is simply a contrived dualism (22) which has no scientific factual basis or legitimate educational purpose. It assumes only two explanations for the origins of life and existence of man, plants and animals: It was either the work of a creator or it was not. Application of these two models, according to creationists, and the defendants, dictates that all scientific evidence which fails to support the theory of evolution is necessarily scientific evidence in support of creationism and is, therefore, creation science "evidence" in support of Section 4(a).

IV(B)

The emphasis on origins as an aspect of the theory of evolution is peculiar to creationist literature. Although the subject of origins of life is within the province of biology, the scientific community does not consider origins of life a part of evolutionary theory. The theory of evolution assumes the existence of life and is directed to an explanation of *how* life evolved. Evolution does not presuppose the absence of a creator or God and the plain inference conveyed by Section 4 is erroneous (23).

As a statement of the theory of evolution, Section 4(b) is simply a hodgepodge of limited assertions, many of which are factually inaccurate.

For example, although 4(b)(2) asserts, as a tenet of evolutionary theory, "the sufficiency of mutation and natural selection in bringing about the existence of present living kinds from simple earlier kinds," Drs. Ayala and Gould both stated that biologists know that these two processes do not account for all significant evolutionary change. They testified to such phenomena as recombination, the founder effect, genetic drift and the theory of punctuated equilibrium, which are believed to play important evolutionary roles. Section 4(b) omits any reference to these. Moreover, 4(b) utilizes the term "kinds" which all scientists said is not a word of science and has no fixed meaning. Additionally, the Act presents both evolution and creation science as "package deals." Thus, evidence critical of some aspect of what the creationists define as evolution is taken as support for a theory which includes a worldwide flood and a relatively young earth (24).

IV(C)

In addition to the fallacious pedagogy of the two model approach, Section 4(a) lacks legitimate educational value because "creation science" as defined in that section is simply not science. Several witnesses suggested definitions of science. A descriptive definition was said to be that science is what is "accepted by the scientific community" and is "what scientists do." The obvious implication of this description is that, in a free society, knowledge does not require the imprimatur of legislation in order to become science.

More precisely, the essential characteristics of science are:
(1) It is guided by natural law;
(2) It has to be explanatory by reference to natural law;
(3) It is testable against the empirical world;
(4) Its conclusions are tentative, i.e., are not necessarily the final word; and
(5) It is falsifiable. (Ruse and other science witnesses).

Creation science as described in Section 4(a) fails to meet these essential characteristics. First, the section revolves around 4(a)(1) which asserts a sudden creation "from nothing." Such a concept is not science because it depends upon a supernatural intervention which is not guided by natural law. It is not explanatory by reference to natural law, is not testable and is not falsifiable (25).

If the unifying idea of supernatural creation by God is removed from Section 4, the remaining parts of the section explain nothing and are meaningless assertions.

Section 4(a)(2), relating to the "insufficiency of mutation and natural selection in bringing about development of all living kinds from a single organism," is an incomplete negative generalization directed at the theory of evolution.

Section 4(a)(3) which describes "changes only within fixed limits of originally created kinds of plants and animals" fails to conform to the essential characteristics of science for several reasons. First, there is no scientific definition of "kinds" and none of the witnesses was able to point to any scientific authority which recognized the term or knew how many "kinds" existed. One defense witness suggested there may be 100 to 10,000 different "kinds." Another believes there were "about 10,000, give or take a few thousand." Second, the assertion appears to be an effort to establish outer limits of changes within species. There is no scientific explanation for these limits which is guided by natural law and the limitations, whatever they are, cannot be explained by natural law.

The statement in 4(a)(4) of "separate ancestry of man and apes" is a bald assertion. It explains nothing and refers to no scientific fact or theory (26)

The statement in 4(a)(4) refers to "explanation of earth's geology by catastrophism, including the occurrence of a worldwide flood." This assertion completely fails as science. The Act is referring to the Noachian flood described in the Book of Genesis (27). The creationist writers concede that *any* kind of Genesis Flood depends upon supernatural intervention. A worldwide flood as an explanation of the world's geology is not the product of natural law, nor can its occurrence be explained by natural law.

Section 4(a)(6) equally fails to meet the standards of science. "Relatively recent inception" has no scientific meaning. It can only be given meaning by reference to creationist writings which place the age at between 6,000 and 20,000 years because of the geneaology of the Old Testament. See, e.g., Px 78, Gish (6,000 to 10,000); Px 87, Segraves (6,000 to 20,000). Such a reasoning process in not the product of natural law; not explainable by natural law; nor is it tentative.

Creation science, as defined in Section 4(a), not only fails to follow the canons defining scientific theory, it also fails to fit the more general descriptions of "what scientists think" and "what scientists do." The scientific community consists of individuals and groups, nationally and internationally, who work independently in such varied fields as biology, paleontology, geology and astronomy. Their work is published and subject to review and testing by their peers. The journals for publication are both numerous and varied. There is, however, not one recognized scientific journal which has published an article espousing the creation science theory described in Section 4(a). Some of the State's witnesses suggested that the scientific community was "close-minded" on the subject of creationism and that explained the lack of acceptance of the creation science arguments. Yet no witness produced a scientific article for which publication had been refused. Perhaps some members of the scientific community are resistant to new ideas. It is, however, inconceivable that such a loose knit group of independent thinkers in all the varied fields of science could, or would, so effectively censor new scientific thought.

The creationists have difficulty maintaining among their ranks consistency in the claim that creationism is science. The author of Act 590, Ellwanger, said that neither evolution nor creationism was science. He thinks both are religion. Duane Gish recently responded to an article in *Discover* critical of creationism by saying:

> Stephen Jay Gould states that creationists claim creation is a scientific theory. This is a false accusation. Creationists have repeatedly stated that neither creation nor evolution is a scientific theory (and each is equally religious). (Gish, letter to editor of *Discover*, July, 1981, App. 30 to Plaintiffs' Pretrial Brief)

The methodology employed by creationists is another factor which is indicative that their work is not science. A scientific theory must be tentative and always subject to revision or abandonment in light of facts that are inconsistent with, or falsify, the theory. A theory that is by its own terms dogmatic, absolutist and never subject to revision is not a scientific theory.

The creationists' methods do not take data, weigh it against the opposing scientific data, and thereafter reach the conclusions stated in Section 4(a). Instead, they take the literal wording of the Book of Genesis and attempt to find scientific support for it. The method is best explained in the language of Morris in his book (Px31) *Studies in The Bible and Science* at page 114:

> . . . it is . . . quite impossible to determine anything about Creation through a study of present processes, because present processes are not creative in character. If man wishes to know anything about Creation (the time of Creation, the duration of Creation, the order of Creation, the methods of Creation, or anything else) his sole source of true information is that of divine revelation. God was there when it happened. We were not there. . . . Therefore, we are completely limited to what God has seen fit to tell us, and this information is in His written Word. This is our textbook on the science of Creation!

The Creation Research Society employs the same unscientific approach to the issue of creationism. Its applicants for membership must subscribe to the belief that the Book of Genesis is "historically and scientifically true in all of the original autographs" (28). The Court would never criticize or discredit any person's testimony based on his or her religious beliefs. While anybody is free to approach a scientific inquiry in any fashion they choose, they cannot properly describe the methodology used as scientific, if they start with a conclusion and refuse to change it regardless of the evidence developed during the course of the investigation.

IV(D)

In efforts to establish "evidence" in support of creation science, the defendants relied upon the same false premise as the two model approach contained in Section 4, i.e., all evidence which criticized evolutionary theory was proof in support of creation science. For example, the defendants established that the mathematical probability of a chance chemical combination resulting in life from non-life is so remote that such an occurrence is almost beyond imagination. Those mathematical facts, the defendants argue, are scientific evidences that life was the product of a creator. While the statistical figures may be impressive evidence against the theory of chance chemical combinations as an explanation of origins, it requires a leap of faith to interpret those figures so as to support a complex doctrine which includes a sudden creation from nothing, a worldwide flood, separate ancestry of man and apes, and a young earth.

The defendants' argument would be more persuasive if, in fact, there were only two theories or ideas about the origins of life and the world. That there are a number of theories was acknowledged by the State's witnesses, Dr. Wickramasinghe and Dr. Geisler. Dr. Wickramasinghe testified at length in support of a theory that life on earth was "seeded" by comets which delivered genetic material and perhaps organisms to the earth's surface from interstellar dust far outside the solar system. The "seeding" theory further hypothesizes that the earth remains under the continuing influence of genetic material from space which continues to affect life. While Wickramasinghe's theory (29) about the origins of life on earth has not received general acceptance within the scientific community, he has, at least, used scientific methodology to produce a theory of origins which meets the essential characteristics of science.

The Court is at a loss to understand why Dr. Wickramasinghe was called in behalf of the defendants. Perhaps it was because he was generally critical of the theory of evolution and the scientific community, a tactic consistent with the strategy of the defense. Unfortunately for the defense, he demonstrated that the simplistic approach of the two model analysis of the origins of life is false. Furthermore, he corroborated the plaintiffs' witnesses by concluding that "no rational scientist" would believe the earth's geology could be explained by reference to a worldwide flood or that the earth was less than one million years old.

The proof in support of creation science consisted almost entirely of efforts to discredit the theory of evolution through a rehash of data and theories which have been before the scientific community for decades. The arguments asserted by creationists are not based upon new scientific evidence or laboratory data which has been ignored by the scientific community.

Robert Gentry's discovery of radioactive polonium haloes in granite and coalified woods is, perhaps, the most recent scientific work which the creationists use as argument for a "relatively recent inception" of the earth and a "worldwide flood." The existence of polonium haloes in granite and coalified wood is thought to be inconsistent with radiometric dating methods based upon constant radioactive decay rates. Mr. Gentry's findings were published almost ten years ago and have been the subject of some discussion in the scientific community. The discoveries have not, however, led to the formulation of any scientific hypothesis or theory which would explain a relatively recent inception of the earth or a worldwide flood. Gentry's discovery has been treated as a minor mystery which will eventually be explained. It may deserve further investigation, but the National Science Foundation has not deemed it to be of sufficient import to support further funding.

The testimony of Marianne Wilson was persuasive evidence that creation science is not science. Ms. Wilson is in charge of the science curriculum for Pulaski County Special School District, the largest school district in the State of Arkansas. Prior to the passage of Act 590, Larry Fisher, a science teacher in the District, using materials from the ICR, convinced the School Board that it should voluntarily adopt creation science as part of its science curriculum. The District Superintendent assigned Ms. Wilson the job of producing a creation science curriculum guide. Ms. Wilson's testimony about the project was particularly convincing because she obviously approached the assignment with an open mind and no preconceived notions about the subject. She had not heard of creation science until about a year ago and did not know its meaning before she began her research.

Ms. Wilson worked with a committee of science teachers appointed from the District. They reviewed practically all of the creationist literature. Ms. Wilson and the committee members reached the unanimous conclusion that creationism is not science; it is religion. They so reported to the Board. The Board ignored the recommendation and insisted that a curriculum guide be prepared.

In researching the subject, Ms. Wilson sought the assistance of Mr. Fisher who initiated the Board action and asked professors in the science departments of the University of Arkansas at Little Rock and the University of Central Arkansas (30) for reference material and assistance, and attended a workshop conducted at Central Baptist College by Dr. Richard Bliss of the ICR staff. Act 590 became law during the course of her work so she used Section 4(a) as a format for her curriculum guide.

Ms. Wilson found all available creationists' materials unacceptable because they were permeated with religious references and reliance upon religious beliefs.

It is easy to understand why Ms. Wilson and other educators find the creationists' textbook material and teaching guides unacceptable. The materials misstate the theory of evolution in the same fashion as Section 4(b) of the Act, with emphasis on the alternative mutually exclusive nature of creationism and evolution. Students are constantly encouraged to compare and make a choice between the two models, and the material is not presented in an accurate manner.

A typical example is *Origins* (Px 76) by Richard B. Bliss, Director of Curriculum Development of the ICR. The presentation begins with a chart describing "preconceived ideas about origins" which suggests that some people believe that evolution is atheistic. Concepts of evolution, such as "adaptive radiation" are erroneously presented. At page 11, figure 1.6., of the text, a chart purports to illustrate this "very important" part of the evolution model. The chart conveys the idea that such diverse mammals as a whale, bear, bat and monkey all evolved from a shrew through the process of adaptive radiation. Such a suggestion is, of course, a totally erroneous and misleading application of the theory. Even more objectionable, especially when viewed in light of the emphasis on asking the student to elect one of the models, is the chart presentation at page 17, figure 1.6. That chart purports to illustrate the evolutionists' belief that man evolved from bacteria to fish to reptile to mammals and, thereafter, into man. The illustration indicates, however, that the mammal from which man evolved was *a rat*.

Biology, A Search For Order in Complexity (31) is a high school biology text typical of creationists' materials. The following quotations are illustrative:

> Flowers and roots do not have a mind to have purpose of their own; therefore, this planning must have been done for them by the Creator. (at page 12)

> The exquisite beauty of color and shape in flowers exceeds the skill of poet, artist, and king. Jesus said (from Matthew's gospel), "Consider the lilies of the field, how they grow; they toil not, neither do they spin . . ." (Px 129 at page 363)

The "public school edition" texts written by creationists simply omit Biblical references but the content and message remain the same. For example, *Evolution— The Fossils Say No!* (32) contains the following:

> Creation. By creation we mean the bringing into being by a supernatural Creator of the basic kinds of plants and animals by the process of sudden, or fiat, creation.
>
> We do not know how the Creator created, what processes He used, *for He used processes which are not now operating anywhere in the natural universe.* This is why we refer to creation as Special Creation. We cannot discover by scientific investigation anything about the creative processes used by the Creator. (page 40)

Gish's book also portrays the large majority of evolutionists as "materialistic atheists or agnostics."

Scientific Creationism (Public School Edition) by Morris, is another text reviewed by Ms. Wilson's committee and rejected as unacceptable. The following quotes illustrate the purpose and theme of the text:

Foreword

Parents and youth leaders today, and even many scientists and educators, have become concerned about the prevalence and influence of evolutionary philosophy in modern curriculum. Not only is this system inimical to orthodox Christianity and Judaism, but also, as many are convinced, to a healthy society and true science as well. (at page iii)

The rationalist of course finds the concept of special creation insufferably naive, even "incredible." Such a judgment, however, is warranted only if one categorically dismisses the existence of an omnipotent God. (at page 17)

Without using creationist literature, Ms. Wilson was unable to locate one genuinely scientific article or work which supported Section 4(a). In order to comply with the mandate of the Board she used such materials as an article from *Readers Digest* about "atomic clocks" which inferentially suggested that the earth was less than 4½ billion years old. She was unable to locate any substantive teaching material for some parts of Section 4 such as the worldwide flood. The curriculum guide which she prepared cannot be taught and has no educational value as science. The defendants did not produce any text or writing in response to this evidence which they claimed was usable in the public school classroom. (33).

The conclusion that creation science has no scientific merit or education value as science has legal significance in light of the Court's previous conclusion that creation science has, as one major effect, the advancement of religion. The second part of the three-pronged test for establishment reaches only those statutes having as their *primary* effect the advancement of religion. Secondary effects which advance religion are not constitutionally fatal. Since creation science is not science, the conclusion is inescapable that the *only* real effect of Act 590 is the advancement of religion. The Act therefore fails both the first and second portions of the test in *Lemon v. Kurtzman*, 403 U.S. 602 (1971).

IV(E)

Act 590 mandates "balanced treatment" for creation science and evolution science. The Act prohibits instruction in any religious doctrine or references to religious writings. The Act is self-contradictory and compliance is impossible unless the public schools elect to forego significant portions of subjects such as biology, world history, geology, zoology, botany, psychology, anthropology, sociology, philosophy, physics and chemistry. Presently, the concepts of evolutionary theory as described in 4(b) permeate the public school textbooks. There is no way teachers can teach the Genesis account of creation in a secular manner.

The State Department of Education, through its textbook selection committee, school boards and school administrators will be required to constantly monitor materials to avoid using religious references. The school boards, administrators and teachers face an impossible task. How is the teacher to respond to questions about a creation suddenly and out of nothing? How will a teacher explain the occurrence of a worldwide flood? How will a teacher explain the concept of a relatively recent age of the earth? The answer is obvious because the only source of this information is ultimately contained in the Book of Genesis.

References to the pervasive nature of religious concepts in creation science texts amply demonstrate why State entanglement with religion is inevitable under Act

590. Involvement of the State in screening texts for impermissible religious references will require State officials to make delicate religious judgments. The need to monitor classroom discussion in order to uphold the Act's prohibition against religious instruction will necessarily involve administrators in questions concerning religion. These continuing involvements of State officials in questions and issues of religion create an excessive and prohibited entanglement with religion. *Brandon v. Board of Education*, 487 F.Supp 1219, 1230 (N.D.N.Y.), *aff'd.*, 635 F.2d 971 (2nd Cir. 1980).

V

These conclusions are dispositive of the case and there is no need to reach legal conclusions with respect to the remaining issues. The plaintiffs raised two other issues questioning the constitutionality of the Act and, insofar as the factual findings relevant to these issues are not covered in the preceding discussion, the Court will address these issues. Additionally, the defendants raised two other issues which warrant discussion.

V(A)

First, plantiff teachers argue the Act is unconstitutionally vague to the extent that they cannot comply with its mandate of "balanced" treatment without jeopardizing their employment. The argument centers around the lack of a precise definition in the Act for the word "balanced." Several witnesses expressed opinions that the word has such meanings as equal time, equal weight, or equal legitimacy. Although the Act could have been more explicit, "balanced" is a word subject to ordinary understanding. The proof is not convincing that a teacher using a reasonably acceptable understanding of the word and making a good faith effort to comply with the Act will be in jeopardy of termination. Other portions of the Act are arguably vague, such as the "relatively recent" inception of the earth and life. The evidence establishes, however, that relatively recent means from 6,000 to 20,000 years, as commonly understood in creation science literature. The meaning of this phrase, like Section 4(a) generally, is, for purposes of the Establishment Clause, all too clear.

V(B)

The plaintiffs' other argument revolves around the alleged infringement by the defendants upon the academic freedom of teachers and students. It is contended this unprecedented intrusion in the curriculum by the State prohibits teachers from teaching what they believe should be taught or requires them to teach that which they do not believe is proper. The evidence reflects that traditionally the State Department of Education, local school boards and administration officials exercise little, if any, influence upon the subject matter taught by classroom teachers. Teachers have been given freedom to teach and emphasize those portions of subjects the individual teacher considered important. The limits to this discretion have generally been derived from the approval of textbooks by the State Department and preparation of curriculum guides by the school districts.

Several witnesses testified that academic freedom for the teacher means, in substance, that the individual teacher should be permitted unlimited discretion subject only to the bounds of professional ethics. The Court is not prepared to adopt such a broad view of academic freedom in the public schools.

In any event, if Act 590 is implemented, many teachers will be required to teach material in support of creation science which they do not consider academically sound. Many teachers will simply forego teaching subjects which might trigger the "balanced treatment" aspects of Act 590 even though they think the subjects are important to a proper presentation of a course.

Implementation of Act 590 will have serious and untoward consequences for students, particularly those planning to attend college. Evolution is the cornerstone of modern biology, and many courses in public schools contain subject matter relating to such varied topics as the age of the earth, geology and relationships among living things. Any student who is deprived of instruction as to the prevailing scientific thought on these topics will be denied a significant part of science education. Such a deprivation through the high school level would undoubtedly have an impact upon the quality of education in the State's colleges and universities, especially including the pre-professional and professional programs in the health sciences.

V(C)

The defendants argue in their brief that evolution is, in effect, a religion, and that by teaching a religion which is contrary to some students' religious views, the State is infringing upon the student's free exercise rights under the First Amendment. Mr. Ellwanger's legislative findings, which were adopted as a finding of fact by the Arkansas Legislature in Act 590, provides:

> Evolution-science is contrary to the religious convictions or moral values or philosophical beliefs of many students and parents, including individuals of many different religious faiths and with diverse moral and philosophical beliefs. Act 590, §7(d).

The defendants argue that the teaching of evolution alone presents both a free exercise problem and an establishment problem which can only be redressed by giving balanced treatment to creation science, which is admittedly consistent with some religious beliefs. This argument appears to have its genesis in a student note written by Mr. Wendell Bird, "Freedom of Religion and Science Instruction in Public Schools," 87 Yale L.J. 515 (1978). The argument has no legal merit.

If creation science is, in fact, science and not religion, as the defendants claim, it is difficult to see how the teaching of such a science could "neutralize" the religious nature of evolution.

Assuming for the purposes of argument, however, that evolution is a religion or religious tenet, the remedy is to stop the teaching of evolution, not establish another religion in opposition to it. Yet it is clearly established in the case law, and perhaps also in common sense, that evolution is not a religion and that teaching evolution does not violate the Establishment Clause, *Epperson v. Arkansas, supra, Willoughby v. Stever*, No. 15574-75 (D.D.C. May 18, 1973); *aff'd*. 504 F.2d 271 (D.C. Cir. 1974), *cert. denied*, 420 U.S. 924 (1975); *Wright v. Houston Indep. School Dist.*, 366 F.Supp. 1208 (S.D. Tex. 1978), *aff'd*. 486 F.2d 137 (5th Cir. 1973), *cert. denied* 417 U.S. 969 (1974).

V(D)

The defendants presented Dr. Larry Parker, a specialist in devising curricula for public schools. He testified that the public school's curriculum should reflect the subjects the public wants taught in schools. The witness said that polls indicated a significant majority of the American public thought creation science should be taught if evolution was taught. The point of this testimony was never placed in a legal context. No doubt a sizeable majority of Americans believe in the concept of a Creator or, at least, are not opposed to the concept and see nothing wrong with teaching school children about the idea.

The application and content of First Amendment principles are not determined by public opinion polls or by a majority vote. Whether the proponents of Act 590 constitute the majority or minority is quite irrelevant under a constitutional system of government. No group, no matter how large or small, may use the organs of government, of which the public schools are the most conspicuous and influential, to foist its religious beliefs on others.

The Court closes this opinion with a thought expressed eloquently by the great Justice Frankfurter:

> We renew our conviction that "we have staked the very existence of our country on the faith that complete separation between the state and religion is best for the state and best for religion." *Everson v. Board of Education*, 330 U.S. at 59. If nowhere else, in the relation between Church and State, "good fences make good neighbors." [*McCollum v. Board of Education*, 333 U.S. 203, 232 (1948)]

An injunction will be entered permanently prohibiting enforcement of Act 590. It is ordered this January 5, 1982.

—WILLIAM R. OVERTON *in the U.S. District Court, Eastern District of Arkansas, Western Division*

Notes

1. The complaint is based on 42 U.S.C. §1983, which provides a remedy against any person who, acting under color of state law, deprives another of any right, privilege or immunity guaranteed by the United States Constitution or federal law. This Court's jurisdiction arises under 28 U.S.C. §§ 1331, 1343 (3) and 1343(4). The power to issue declaratory judgments is expressed in 28 U.S.C. §§2201 and 2202.

2. The facts necessary to establish the plaintiffs' standing to sue are contained in the joint stipulation of facts, which is hereby adopted and incorporated herein by reference. There is no doubt that the case is ripe for adjudication.

3. The State of Arkansas was dismissed as a defendant because of its immunity from suit under the Eleventh Amendment. *Hans v. Louisiana*, 134 U.S. 1 (1890).

4. The authorities differ as to generalizations which may be made about Fundamentalism.

For example, Dr. Geisler testified to the widely held view that there are five beliefs characteristic of all Fundamentalist movements, in addition, of course, to the inerrancy of Scripture: (1) belief in the virgin birth of Christ, (2) belief in the deity of Christ, (3) belief in the substantial atonement of Christ, (4) belief in the second coming of Christ, and (5) belief in the physical resurrection of all departed souls. Dr. Marsden, however, testified that this generalization, which has been common in religious scholarship, is now thought to be historical error. There is no doubt, however, that all Fundamentalists take the Scriptures as inerrant and probably most take them as literally true.

5. Initiated Act 1 of 1929, Ark. Stat. Ann. §80-1627 *et seq.*, which prohibited the teaching of evolution in Arkansas schools, is discussed *infra* at text accompanying note 26.

6. Subsequent references to the testimony will be made by the last name of the witness only. References to documentary exhibits will be by the name of the author and the exhibit number.

7. Applicants for membership in the CRS must subscribe to the following statement of belief: "(1) The Bible is the written Word of God, and because we believe it to be inspired thruout (sic), all of its assertions are historically and scientifically true in all of the original autographs. To the student of nature, this means that the account of origins in Genesis is a factual presentation of simple historical truths. (2) All basic types of living things, including man, were made by direct creative acts of God during Creation Week as described in Genesis. Whatever biological changes have occurred since Creation have accomplished only changes within the original created kinds. (3) The great Flood described in Genesis, commonly referred to as the Noachian Deluge, was an historical event, worldwide in its extent and effect. (4) Finally, we are an organization of Christian men of science, who accept Jesus Christ as our Lord and Savior. The account of the special creation of Adam and Eve as one man and one woman, and their subsequent Fall into sin, is the basis for our belief in the necessity of a Savior for all mankind. Therefore, salvation can come only thru (sic) accepting Jesus Christ as our Savior." (Px 115)

8. Because of the voluminous nature of the documentary exhibits, the parties were directed by pre-trial order to submit their proposed exhibits for the Court's convenience prior to trial. The numbers assigned to the pre-trial submissions do not correspond with those assigned to the same documents at trial and, in some instances, the pre-trial submissions are more complete.

9. Px 130, Morris, *Introducing Scientific Creationism Into the Public Schools* (1975), and Bird, "Resolution for Balanced Presentation of Evolution and Scientific Creationism." *ICR Impact Series* No. 71, App. 14 to Plaintiffs' Pretrial Brief.

10. The creationists often show candor in their proselytization. Henry Morris has stated, "Even if a favorable statute or court decision is obtained, it will probably be declared unconstitutional, especially if the legislation or injunction refers to the Bible account of creation." In the same vein he notes, "The only effective way to get creationism taught properly is to have it taught by teachers who are both willing and able to do it. Since most teachers now are neither willing nor able, they must first be both persuaded and instructed themselves." Px 130, Morris, *Introducing Scientific Creationism Into the Public Schools* (1975) (unpaged).

11. Mr. Bird sought to participate in this litigation by representing a number of individuals who wanted to intervene as defendants. The application for intervention was denied by this Court. *McLean v. Arkansas,* _____ F. Supp. _____, (E.D. Ark. 1981), aff'd. *per curiam*, Slip Op. No. 81-2023 (8th Cir. Oct. 16, 1981).

12. The model act had been revised to insert "creation science" in lieu of creationism because Ellwanger had the impression people thought creationism was too religious a term. (Ellwanger Depo. at 79.)

13. The original model act had been introduced in the South Carolina Legislature, but had

died without action after the South Carolina Attorney General had opined that the act was unconstitutional.

14. Specifically, Senator Holsted testified that he holds to a literal interpretation of the Bible; that the bill was compatible with his religious beliefs; that the bill does favor the position of literalists; that his religious convictions were a factor in his sponsorship of the bill; and that he stated publicly to the *Arkansas Gazette* (although not on the floor of the Senate) contemporaneously with the legislative debate that the bill does presuppose the existence of a divine creator. There is no doubt that Senator Holsted knew he was sponsoring the teaching of a religious doctrine. His view was that the bill did not violate the First Amendment because, as he saw it, it did not favor one denomination over another.

15. This statute is, of course, clearly unconstitutional under the Supreme Court's decision in *Abbington School Dist. v Schempp*, 374 U.S. 203 (1963).

16. The joint stipulation of facts establishes that the following areas are the only *information* specifically required by statute to be taught in all Arkansas schools: (1) the effects of alcohol and narcotics on the human body. (2) conservation of national resources. (3) Bird Week. (4) Fire Prevention, and (5) Flag etiquette. Additionally, certain specific courses, such as American history and Arkansas history, must be completed by each student before graduation from high school.

17. Paul Ellwanger stated in his deposition that he did not know why Section 4(a)(2) (insufficiency of mutation and natural selection) was included as an evidence supporting creation science. He indicated that he was not a scientist, "but these are the postulates that have been laid down by creation scientists." Ellwanger Depo. at 136.

18. Although defendants must make some effort to cast the concept of creation in non-religious terms, this effort surely causes discomfort to some of the Act's more theologically sophisticated supporters. The concept of a creator God distinct from the God of love and mercy is closely similar to the Marcion and Gnostic heresies, among the deadliest to threaten the early Christian church. These heresies had much to do with development and adoption of the Apostle's Creed as the official creedal statement of the Roman Catholic Church in the West. (Gilkey.)

19. The parallels between Section 4(a) and Genesis are quite specific: (1) "sudden creation from nothing" is taken from Genesis, 1:1-10 (Vawter, Gilkey); (2) destruction of the world by a flood of divine origin is a notion peculiar to Judeo-Christian tradition and is based on Chapters 7 and 8 of Genesis (Vawter); (3) the term "kinds" has no fixed scientific meaning, but appears repeatedly in Genesis (all scientific witnesses); (4) "relatively recent inception" means an age of the earth from 6,000 to 10,000 years and is based on the genealogy of the Old Testament using the rather astronomical ages asssigned to the patriarchs (Gilkey and several of defendants' scientific witnesses); (5) Separate ancestry of man and ape focuses on the portion of the theory of evolution which Fundamentalists find most offensive, *Epperson v. Arkansas*, 393 U.S. 97 (1968).

20. "[C]oncepts concerning . . . a supreme being of some sort are manifestly religious . . . These concepts do not shed that religiosity merely because they are presented as philosophy or as a science . . . " *Malnak v. Yogi*, 440 F.Supp. 1284, 1322 (D.N.J. 1977); *aff'd per curiam*, 592 F.2d 197 (3d Cir. 1979).

21. See, e.g., Px 76, Morris, *et al.*, *Scientific Creationism*, 203 (1980) ("If creation really is a fact, this means there is a *Creator*, and the universe is His creation.") Numerous other examples of such admissions can be found in the many exhibits which represent creationist literature, but no useful purpose would be served here by a potentially endless listing.

22. Morris, the Director of ICR and one who first advocated the two model approach, insists that a true Christian cannot compromise with the theory of evolution and that the Genesis version of creation and the theory of evolution are mutually exclusive, Px 31, Morris, *Studies in the Bible & Science*, 102–103. The two model approach was the subject of Dr. Richard Bliss's doctoral dissertation. (Dx 35). It is presented in Bliss, *Origins: Two Models—*

Evolution, Creation (1978). Moreover, the two model approach merely casts in education language the dualism which appears in all creationist literature—creation (i.e. God) and evolution are presented as two alternative and mutually exclusive theories. See, e.g., Px. 75, Morris, *Scientific Creationism* (1974) (public school edition); Px 59, Fox, *Fossils: Hard Facts from the Earth*. Particularly illustrative is Px 61, Boardman, *et al.*, *Worlds Without End* (1971) a CSRC publication: "One group of scientists, known as creationists, believe that God, in a miraculous manner, created all matter and energy . . .

"Scientists who insist that the universe just grew, by accident, from a mass of hot gases without the direction or help of a Creator are known as evolutionists."

23. The idea that belief in a creator and acceptance of the scientific theory of evolution are mutually exclusive is a false premise and offensive to the religious views of many. (Hicks) Dr. Francisco Ayala, a geneticist of considerable reknown and a former Catholic priest who has the equivalent of a Ph.D. in theology, pointed out that many working scientists who subscribed to the theory of evolution are devoutly religious.

24. This is so despite the fact that some of the defense witnesses do not subscribe to the young earth or flood hypotheses. Dr. Geisler stated his belief that the earth is several billion years old. Dr. Wickramasinghe stated that no rational scientist would believe the earth is less than one million years old or that all the world's geology could be explained by a worldwide flood.

25. "We do not know how God created, what processes He used, for *God used processes which are not now operating anywhere in the natural universe*. This is why we refer to divine creation as Special Creation. We cannot discover by scientific investigation anything about the creative processes used by God." Px 78, Gish, *Evolution? The Fossils Say No!*, 42 (3d ed. 1979) (emphasis in original).

26. The evolutionary notion that man and some modern apes have a common ancestor somewhere in the distant past has consistently been distorted by anti-evolutionists to say that man descended from modern monkeys. As such, this idea has long been most offensive to Fundamentalists. See, *Epperson v. Arkansas*, 393 U.S. 97 (1968).

27. Not only was this point acknowledged by virtually all the defense witnesses, it is patent in the creationist literature. See, e.g. Px 89, Kofahl & Segraves, *The Creation Explanation*, 40: "The Flood of Noah brought about vast changes in the earth's surface, including vulcanism, mountain building, and the deposition of the major part of sedimentary strata. This principle is called "Biblical catastrophism."

28. See n. 7, *supra*, for the full text of the CRS creed.

29. The theory is detailed in Wickramasinghe's book with Sir Fred Hoyle, *Evolution From Space* (1981), which is Dx 79.

30. Ms. Wilson stated that some professors she spoke with sympathized with her plight and tried to help her find scientific materials to support Section 4(a). Others simply asked her to leave.

31. Px 129, published by Zonderman Publishing House (1974), states that it was "prepared by the Textbook Committee of the Creation Research Society," It has a disclaimer pasted inside the front cover stating that it is not suitable for use in public schools.

32. Px 77, by Duane Gish.

33. The passage of Act 590 apparently caught a number of its supporters off guard as much as it did the school district. The Act's author, Paul Ellwanger, stated in a letter to "Dick," (apparently Dr. Richard Bliss at ICR): "And finally, if you know of any textbooks at any level and for any subjects that you think are acceptable to you and also constitutionally admissible, these are things that would be of *enormous* to these bewildered folks who may be caught, as Arkansas now has been, by the sudden need to implement a whole new ball game with which they are quite unfamiliar." (sic) (Unnumbered attachment to Ellwanger depo.)

Index